Endorsements for *Step in to Study Counselling and Psychotherapy* (4th edition)

There are books that have their rightful place in the collective memories of students and qualified practitioners. *Step in to Study Counselling and Psychotherapy* is one of those – originally authored by Pete Sanders and now with the skilled addition of co-author Deborah Lee. This is an excellent text, and this fourth edition ensures it remains as contemporary and vital as it has always been. It is authoritative yet accessible, ambitious yet detailed, and academic yet practical. This book will support you to build confidence and knowledge so that you can translate theory into practice and be the best therapist you can for your clients. A highly recommended text from two great writers.
Andrew Reeves, Professor in Counselling Professions and Mental Health, University of Chester

This new edition of *Step in to Study Counselling and Psychotherapy* is comprehensive, inclusive, accessible, involving, informative and more. Deborah Lee and Pete Sanders guide the reader with grace and generosity through a range of considerations, challenges and dilemmas. Prospective, new and existing counselling and psychotherapy students will all find themselves welcomed, reassured, inspired and enlightened.
Jonathan Wyatt, Professor of Qualitative Inquiry, Counselling, Psychotherapy and Applied Social Sciences, University of Edinburgh

This book is a meticulous exploration of the world of counselling, from study into practice. The book is an invitation to explore yourself, leading to self-reflection and growth – essential preparation for working with clients and peers. If you are just starting out, the insights into the various modalities are great for recognising what sparks your interest and what is the right approach for you. The book explains how courses and academic qualifications are structured, the costs involved in training, and the current political and professional landscapes within which you will develop your counselling career. The guidance on assignments will be invaluable to new and returning students alike, with pointers on structure and marking criteria. The sections on neurodiversity and difference and the exploration of community organisations give the publication a fully inclusive feel. A wonderful companion to study.
Claire Jones, graduate certificate student progressing to the MSc in counselling & psychotherapy, Keele University

This is an excellent book for levels 1 to 8 counselling and psychotherapy students, as well as those considering training. Lee and Sanders present a clear and thorough roadmap to training in counselling/psychotherapy, covering all the key milestones. Each chapter focuses on different training aspects, such as relational dynamics, assessments and skills and techniques for effective learning. The inclusion of a wide range of personal experiences of different counsellors and trainers is a particularly valuable resource for students. This new edition also includes contemporary contextual issues and a range of useful information about student support provision. It is a challenging task to capture the shared and common aspects of the complex counselling and psychotherapy training landscapes. Lee and Sanders have done this brilliantly. Sadly, Pete passed away before the publication of this book, but his legacy and spirit are very much alive in this text.

Dr Faisal Mahmood, Head of Subject – Counselling & Psychotherapy, Newman University, Birmingham

I write with sadness and poignant recognition of Pete Sanders' legacies to our profession, foregrounded powerfully in this essential 'Step in to Study' guidance for those looking to enter into counsellor or psychotherapy training. Pete and Deborah Lee's updated text delivers an essential read in its fourth edition. Contributions from many leading counselling and psychotherapy colleagues add a rich dimension. The array of voices and breadth of content offer readers helpful tools for meaning making in the complex landscape of counselling and psychotherapy training. For 25 years, Pete Sanders has guided students seeking to step into counselling and psychotherapy. His work lives on and, with Deborah Lee now on board, can continue to offer this unique contribution to the field. The book covers key material for those considering training, from choosing a course and making sense of relationships and dynamics during training, through to the inevitable tensions and conflicts evident in the book's socio-political content. The text is relevant to trainees as well as trainers and lecturers and should be essential reading on training courses. Perfectly pitched, and a powerful legacy, Pete!

Lynne Gabriel, Professor of Counselling and Mental Health, York St John University

4TH EDITION

Step in to Study Counselling & Psychotherapy

A STUDENT'S GUIDE TO TACKLING TRAINING AND COURSE ASSIGNMENTS

DEBORAH A. LEE
AND PETE SANDERS

First edition published 1995
Second edition published 1998
Third edition published 2003
Fourth edition published 2022

PCCS Books Ltd, Wyastone Business Park, Wyastone Leys, Monmouth NP25 3SR
contact@pccs-books.co.uk
www.pccs-books.co.uk

© Deborah A. Lee, Pete Sanders, 2022

All rights reserved.
No part of this publication may be reproduced, stored in a retrieval system, transmitted or utilised in any form by any means, electronic, mechanical, photocopying or recording or otherwise, without permission in writing from the publishers.

The authors have asserted their right to be identified as the authors of this work in accordance with the Copyright, Designs and Patents Act 1988.

Step in to Study Counselling and Psychotherapy: A student's guide to tackling training and course assignments (4th edition)

British Library Cataloguing in Publication data: a catalogue record for this book is available from the British Library.

ISBNs
paperback – 978 1 915220 14 1
epub – 978 1 915220 15 8

Cover design Jason Anscomb
Typeset in-house by PCCS Books
Printed in the UK by Bell & Bain Ltd, Glasgow

Contents

	About the authors	*v*
	A tribute to Pete Sanders	*vii*
	Introduction	*1*
1	Preparing the ground for successful studying	*11*
2	Learning relationships in counselling and psychotherapy courses	*47*
3	Learning processes in counselling and psychotherapy courses	*77*
4	Skills and techniques for effective study	*103*
5	Assessment and assignments in counselling and psychotherapy courses	*123*
6	Writing essays and case studies (and doing it differently!)	*151*
7	Continuing professional development	*175*
	Appendix: References for sample essay introduction	*187*
	Name index	*191*
	Subject index	*195*

About the authors

Deborah A. Lee is a lecturer in counselling and psychotherapy at the University of Salford and a Senior Fellow of the Higher Education Academy (SFHEA). She has more than 20 years of experience in higher education, leading and teaching undergraduate and postgraduate courses and advising students on study skills. Deborah is UKCP registered, MBACP, and NCS (Accred), and has a private practice offering person-centred counselling and psychotherapy. Deborah's current teaching and writing have a focus on social justice in counselling and psychotherapy education, training and practice, drawing on heuristic research, autoethnography, creative non-fiction and arts-based presentations. She is co-editor, with Emma Palmer, of *#MeToo: Counsellors and psychotherapists speak about sexual violence and abuse* (PCCS Books, 2020), guest editor of the special issue of *Psychotherapy and Politics International* (2020) on therapists' lived experiences, and her case-study research has appeared in the *British Journal of Guidance and Counselling* (2017) and *Self & Society* (2019).

Pete Sanders worked as a volunteer at Off The Record, Newcastle-upon Tyne in 1972 before completing a degree in psychology at the university there, and then the postgraduate diploma in counselling at Aston University. He practised as a counsellor, educator and clinical supervisor for more than 30 years. He wrote, co-wrote and edited numerous books, chapters and papers on many aspects of counselling, psychotherapy and mental health, including PCCS Books' very popular 'Steps' series (to which this book belongs) for people entering and progressing through counselling training and into practice. He was co-founder of PCCS Books, which he launched with Maggie Taylor-Sanders almost 30 years ago to publish high-quality training materials and books that put the person in distress at the centre of the help offered. After he retired from practice and publishing, Pete continued to maintain an active interest in the development of person-centred theory, the politics of counselling and psychotherapy and the demedicalisation of distress, and to write and edit books on these topics. Pete died in February 2022, shortly after completing this fourth edition of *Step in to Study Counselling and Psychotherapy* with Deborah A. Lee.

A tribute to Pete Sanders

I felt so honoured when asked to pitch to work with Pete Sanders on this fourth edition of *Step in to Study Counselling and Psychotherapy*. I'd read all of Pete's work and loved it. I was a bit star struck, to be honest. The idea of my name on a book cover alongside his!

It's terribly sad now to be writing a tribute to Pete, rather than looking forward to celebrating the launch of this book alongside him, and then together watching its progress.

I loved meeting Pete. I loved the sparkle in his eyes. I loved his person-centredness. If I'd told him I was a bit star struck, I can imagine how gracefully he would have responded. He was a kind man.

With all his other projects ongoing, Pete was content to hand over to me most of the updating of this book – which means that if there's anything new here that you don't like, it's likely to be my responsibility, not his!

Pete said he trusted me to do the work, and he did. It's not something you hear very often, and when you do, it's not always honoured. Pete was a man of his word, and he was there when I needed him, offering his thoughts as questions (except when he hated my original title for the final chapter!). I enjoyed working with him.

I'm very glad Pete and I had agreed the final manuscript just before he died, and I've much appreciated having Pete's long-term colleague Catherine Jackson alongside me as we completed the final edits of the book.

Pete, with love for all you did in the world of counselling and psychotherapy, I dedicate the fourth edition of *Step in to Study Counselling and Psychotherapy* to you.

Deborah A. Lee, April 2022

Introduction

Welcome to the new, completely updated, fourth edition of *Step in to Study Counselling and Psychotherapy: A student's guide to tackling training and course assignments* – the study skills book that has accompanied so many students through their studies over the past 25 years.

The aims of the book are: 1) to introduce you to the world of counselling and psychotherapy courses and training, and 2) to help you improve your performance when tackling training and course assignments.

Even if you're already doing brilliantly, there's always more to learn, explore, reflect on and test out.

Importantly, you'll find that this book places psychotherapy and counselling courses/training and assessments in the context of the wider world and your place in it. We take the view that understanding the socio-political is increasingly vital for counsellors and psychotherapists and needs to be built in throughout your training too.

This is a book for you if you're taking anything from Level 1 introductory courses to the highest academic qualification – Level 8 PhD courses. Some of the socio-political material can be used as continuing professional development (CPD) by qualified practitioners.

The book is not rigidly organised as a progression through levels of training (with Chapter 1 about Level 1, and so on). It's more about practices that are common across most courses, trainings and assessments, and how you might prepare for them.

There will be material here that doesn't apply to what you're doing right now – either you've already covered it, or you don't need it yet. Check out the chapter titles and sections, and the index, and take what you need when you need it.

But be open to the possibility that something you thought not relevant to you or not relevant to you now may, in fact, have something significant to say to you.

The book is also very relevant to teachers, tutors, trainers and lecturers of counselling and psychotherapy. (And we feel it's important to list you all, as you all identify quite distinctly and don't easily come under a collective title.) There are activities and materials here that you're welcome to incorporate into your classes, and/or to adapt for your own purposes. We're happy to share with you, and we welcome your feedback.

To say a bit about us – Pete trained as a counsellor in 1974 and retired from active training to write books about it instead. Very sadly, he died in February 2022, just after we completed the book. Deborah qualified as a psychotherapist more recently, and has more than 20 years of experience teaching the socio-political, as well as current experience of teaching counselling and psychotherapy. (We'll say more about ourselves later on in this Introduction.) In this book, we're going to tell you about how we support and advise our own students, and say what has worked for us, too, as lifelong learners.

We've sometimes heard people decry study-skills texts as 'patronising', but as two person-centred practitioners, we take a person-centred view: we say that it would be patronising *not* to share what we know. You won't always agree with everything we say. We see that as a desirable outcome of a study-skills book. Independence of thought is an essential outcome of studying.

If this is your copy of the book and if it feels right for you to do so, why not make notes alongside the text about what *you* think and feel as you read it? We strongly encourage you to find your own way, to work out what's best for you. We see ourselves as primarily your fellow travellers, because learning counselling and psychotherapy is a rich, ongoing journey for everyone.

We are both neurotypical. In order for this book to be as inclusive and useful as possible, we've shared some of our developing work with members of the Association of Neurodiverse Therapists (ANDT) and applied what we learned to the rest of the text (you'll hear more about ANDT's work in Chapter 2, and from one of their founders/student members in Chapter 3).

Alongside our voices as co-authors, as the book progresses, you'll be hearing from an array of other people in the counselling and psychotherapy world, all of whom generously agreed to share their experiences and passions with you.

We've chosen to feature them for three reasons:

- First, so that at least some of you will find people like yourselves in these pages – in terms of gender identity, sexuality, 'race', religion, disability and neurodiversity, for instance. Counselling and psychotherapy is a very white, heterosexual, middle-class and female profession – although that is changing, slowly. It needs to be much more diverse to represent the populations it serves. And hearing from a range of different people, some of whom are people like us, can be nourishing and encouraging if you are entering a profession dominated by people who are not like you.

- Second, to give you a taste of some of the interesting individuals, networks and communities you can find in the psychotherapy and counselling world.

- Third, interrelatedly, to invite you to take your own place in this world, when you're ready, in whatever way calls to you.

Sometimes people will say that 'skills' in the therapy room matter more than 'academic' work in counselling and psychotherapy courses/training; that academic work is a chore to endure so you can work as a counsellor and psychotherapist; that reading and writing essays doesn't help you become a 'good' psychotherapist/counsellor. We strongly disagree. We see all of what is learned and assessed on counselling and psychotherapy courses as a whole, vital package. All of it is about developing ourselves so we can be of service to people coming to see us in the therapy room. We encourage you to take all of it seriously.

Taking your course seriously doesn't mean that you can't be playful, unusual and creative. In this book, we stress the importance of meeting learning outcomes and assessment criteria (you can't pass an assignment if you don't meet the learning outcomes and assessment criteria, however good your work), but once you understand how to do that, and you are doing that, you may choose to take some risks.

We feel it's high time to get beyond the belief often heard in counselling and psychotherapy training (among other places) that being successful is about finding out what the 'rules' are and following them, whether you want to or not. When that happens, opportunities for growth are missed. We also need to aim to get past the equally often-spoken comment that 'I just kept my head down and did what was necessary to get through the course and qualify'. Training should be so much more inspiring, creative and relevant than that, and especially training in counselling and psychotherapy, which demands so much from you personally and should give you so much in return.

The starting point for our journey, which we then weave through the book, is that bringing your whole unique self to engaging seriously in learning to study counselling and psychotherapy, passing your assessments and qualifying as a counsellor/psychotherapist can and should be fun. There is so much to study, explore, appreciate and challenge.

We want to convey to you our excitement about reading, writing and talking about psychotherapy and counselling, as well as doing psychotherapy and counselling.

We never underestimate, of course, the challenges of learning and being assessed, particularly if you have not studied for a while, and/or if you are entering a new and unfamiliar field of study, and juggling all sorts of other commitments alongside.

We know that very powerful feelings and emotions can arise from studying and being assessed, including fear of failure (whatever that looks like for you). We'll certainly hold that, and talk with you about it. We'd also like to say here that success in this sort of work can't just be measured by grades – some of it will be about speaking/writing your truth, however it is received by markers and tutors.

Yes, you will experience times when you aren't enjoying your studies, when you wish you'd never started, and when you think of leaving your course. In those times, which occur in any course of study, we encourage you to check in with yourself, work out what is happening and reflect with gentle curiosity on what – if anything, beyond sitting with it – you need to do in response. You're training for a demanding role, one that will challenge you every day. Sitting with uncertainty is something you will have to do daily as practising counsellors and psychotherapists. Powerful feelings and emotions can be grist for our mills.

And yes, while you'll learn lots about yourself and others – learning that will be enriching and beautiful, that you'll feel honoured to be a part of – sometimes human relationships can be deeply discomforting and even terrifying. When fear and danger arise in your training, stay close to yourself, ground yourself, and consider questioning what does not feel right. Our profession has to be robust enough to be open to your questioning, so that it – as well as you – can grow and develop.

You may also, of course, think differently about something that impacted you when you reflect back weeks, months and years later. Stay open to possibilities.

If you choose not to complete your course, for whatever reason, please do not regard this necessarily as 'failure'. It can be the right thing for you to do at that particular time. Whatever happens, you'll most likely have developed (in ways you might not always see until later). You may have found out what you really wanted to do, or be on the way to doing so.

What you'll find in this book…

The book has been written as a coherent whole, as a progression, and we've thought carefully about connections between chapters. Nevertheless, we invite you to use the book how you wish, dipping in and out if you choose. Do what's right for you; go at your own pace.

Chapters

We've arranged the book into what we hope are a series of clearly titled and readable chapters. We've chosen not to include lots of quotes and references. We want what you see on a page to be what you need to know.

We've organised the book in these ways so that you can easily find what you need, and so that you don't feel overwhelmed by too much scholarly text to read. You'll already have lots of academic books and articles to read/listen to for your course and we want this book to be as accessible and easy to take in as possible.

The content of the chapters is intended to give you a good overview of topics you're likely to be engaging with, and/or that we feel you need to know about in order to train as a psychotherapist and counsellor. As we said earlier, we look at practices that are common to most counselling and psychotherapy courses/training and assessments, rather than the specifics of what is required at particular levels of study.

The book can't be fully exhaustive, of course; it is designed to stand alongside the other materials you'll be given in your training courses.

We've been careful to stick with our book subheading: *a student's guide to tackling training and course assignments*, even though there is so much more we could have shared with you. Have a look at the other books in the PCCS Books 'Steps' counselling training series. Together they make a package that can help you in all sorts of ways.

Each chapter will start by setting out what you'll find in it.

Chapter 1: Preparing the ground for successful studying

Chapter 2: Learning relationships in counselling and psychotherapy courses

Chapter 3: Learning processes in counselling and psychotherapy courses

Chapter 4: Skills and techniques for effective study

Chapter 5: Assessment and assignments in counselling and psychotherapy courses
Chapter 6: Writing essays and case studies (and doing it differently!)
Chapter 7: Continuing professional development.

Layout

We both believe in learning by doing. We know that people easily lose focus if they're presented with a lot of text, without an invitation to engage practically with the material.

So, all chapters have a range of different material – for reading, for activity, and for reflection – as well as different voices – ours and those of other practitioners in the field.

Any activity we offer is an *invitation* for you to take up if it feels right for you to do so. Check in with yourself and choose what suits you. You might come back to some activities later.

Here are the types of material you'll find in this book, all clearly signposted:

Experiences: People – students and tutors – talking with you about their lived experiences of counselling and psychotherapy courses/training and assessments. Reflect on the material. If there are invitations to do some activities related to the experiences, respond to some of the questions/suggestions, if you would like to. We'll often invite you to do some journalling (in whatever way works for you – prose, mind-maps, drawing, speaking out loud, recording thoughts (these days it's so easy just to use your mobile phone)). As a counsellor and psychotherapist, you will be meeting clients and exploring their lived experiences every day. Take up as many opportunities as possible for deep explorations with what people are saying and writing.

Activities: A particular invitation to activity will be journalling, with some prompts that you might like to use. Discard the prompts if they don't call to you, and do what does call to you. Where there isn't an invitation and you want to respond, respond! Personal learning journals (which can be written, drawn or recorded) are often part of psychotherapy and counselling training – either formally or as a suggested activity beyond the classroom. You'll use them to reflect on your experiences during each academic year. So why not keep a personal learning journal of your process of reading and reflecting on this book? Buy some notebooks that you can write and/or draw in (unless you prefer to work digitally – if so, remember to keep a copy carefully backed up, as these journals are for reference and reflection and you will want to go back to them).

Further reading: We will sometimes make suggestions for extra readings you might do. Some of these will be selected counselling and psychotherapy books and articles, and others may be outside the field.

Sample assignment answers: The book contains two examples of work completed by students, together with a marking tutor's comments and, in one case, grading (in Chapter 6). We had mixed feelings about including this: we know that students can find it reassuring to see the work of others, so we felt it important to respond to that, but we also know that, however much we say otherwise, offering sample assignment answers can be seen as saying, 'Here is a model answer and this is the best way of doing this sort of assignment.' We implore you, please don't see what you read here as 'correct'. Sample assignment answers are not *the* answers – they are simply an invitation to explore some of the processes involved in writing and marking. Your own writing may be very different and still bring you academic rewards.

Takeaway messages: At the end of each chapter, you will find a box containing what we see as the key points from that chapter. Maybe your ideas about the key points differ – if this is your copy of the book, and it feels right to you to do so, please list your own takeaway messages, or write them in your journal.

> ### ACTIVITY
>
> **An invitation to note some reasons why you want to study your counselling and psychotherapy course**
> And here is the first activity for you to do.
>
> If you're reading this book because you're thinking about enrolling for a counselling and psychotherapy course, or you're already under way (at whatever level of study), you'll have some ideas why you might want, or do want, to do this course (rather than studying or doing something else).
>
> Spend some time creating a list of up to 10 reasons why you think you want to study the counselling and psychotherapy course you're doing/thinking of doing.
>
> Write in prose, or as a mind-map, or draw, or speak out loud to someone, or record your thoughts.
>
> Once you have up to 10 reasons, spend five minutes free-writing – free-writing means writing whatever comes to mind when you look at the reasons you've noted down. Or continue making mind-maps, drawing or speaking/recording instead.
>
> After five minutes, review what you have produced and check in with yourself. What's happening for you right now?
>
> You might have gone very deep with your responses to this invitation. If you have, take care of yourself gently; do something that feels calming. As you progress through your studies, you're going to find that there will be a lot of challenging work to do. Self-care is going to be vital.

About us

We'd like to finish off the main part of the Introduction by telling you a little about how we came to be writing this book. Bringing yourself is something asked of you in a counselling and psychotherapy course (as far as you wish to), so we want to model some of that for you here.

Deborah: After A levels, I didn't want to go to university, but I was at a sixth form that insisted on it, saying that otherwise you were a 'failure'. The French teacher had told me I wasn't capable of studying French, so I decided to prove her wrong by enrolling for a BA in French Studies. I hated it – I rarely went to classes, and when I did, I never spoke – partly because I'd never read whatever was required, and mostly because I was very anxious. Handing back my first essay, my personal tutor asked, 'You don't really expect me to mark *that*, do you?' The rest of the class were outside, waiting to hear what grade everyone had achieved. While I said nothing when I came out, I guess my expression spoke for me. I was not only humiliated; I had absolutely no idea what was wrong with the essay.

I eventually dropped out in my second year, and spent a few months as an office junior. That was more than enough to force me back to (a different) university to finish my degree. I did well in the literary subjects, but it remained the wrong degree – I never learned how to think in French. An external option in sociology in my final year (for which I achieved a First) led to postgraduate work (I talked my way in somehow, helped very much by a good reference from the sociology lecturer). And so I started my academic career as a sociologist.

After I began personal therapy, I realised that psychotherapy interested me. I took an ABC counselling concepts course (see Chapter 1 for my view of its value), and then enrolled for an MSc in person-centred and experiential psychotherapy. It was a revelation to be a student confident enough to talk in classes. I read widely. I joined associations (I was on the steering group of Psychotherapists and Counsellors for Social Responsibility (PCSR) for a while – see Chapter 2). I also joined the UK Council for Psychotherapy (UKCP) Ethics Committee. A lot of what I wrote as a student, I reworked for publication, and my MSc dissertation is part of a book I co-edited with Emma Palmer, which will also feature in Chapter 2.[1]

I became an associate editor of *Psychotherapy and Politics International*, and spend a lot of time now editing other people's work for publication. I'm external examiner for an undergraduate course. I moved to my present lectureship in counselling and psychotherapy in 2021. Learning psychotherapy and counselling and being 'good at it' (I got a Distinction) has brought me many opportunities – and, I haven't forgotten what it feels like to not know what to do, or what it feels like to fail.

Pete: I am a white, cis het man and I have spent my working life enjoying the added privilege of being in the right place at the right time. I became interested in counselling when I attended a recruitment meeting for the voluntary agency Off The Record in Newcastle-upon-Tyne in 1972. I went to the meeting to accompany my then girlfriend, without understanding why we all sat in a circle and were invited to talk about various topics. To my surprise, I was selected to take part in the training, went on to be a volunteer, and followed my degree in psychology with a full-time postgraduate diploma in counselling at the University of Aston. It was there that I became interested in study skills, since if we

---

1. Lee, D.A. & Palmer, E. (Eds.). (2020). *#MeToo: Counsellors and psychotherapists speak about sexual violence and abuse.* PCCS Books.

were going to work as counsellors in education, one of the ways for a counsellor to reach out was to offer some psychoeducational help with study problems. I then took a job split between counselling and teaching the then brand-new A level in psychology.

I discovered that I loved teaching and, if the A level results were anything to go by, I seemed to be quite good at it. I found out pretty quickly that I learned much more about psychology as I prepared to teach each class than I had ever learned during my degree. The same proved to be true when I first thought about starting training courses in counselling. I co-founded a full-time diploma in counselling in the mid-1980s, alongside part-time professional courses where we developed several self- and peer-assessment methods in which the tutors were always equal partners in assessment alongside the students. I have been lucky to work with people who wanted to put person-centred psychology into practice as a student-centred learning model. In those days, most courses were held in further and adult education colleges and many applicants had not completed formal education and/ or had few academic qualifications. They struggled with returning to study, reading and assignments, and so the idea for the first edition of *Step in to Study Counselling* was born. I was thrilled when Deborah joined me to work on a long-overdue revamp of the original book.

ACTIVITY

An invitation to introduce yourself
You've just read what we decided to say about ourselves at this point (note that there's always a decision to be made in what we say about ourselves – no one has the right to demand that we say more than we wish).

Here's an invitation to you: How would you describe yourself, in terms of your studies and work so far? Where are you planning to go with your study of counselling and psychotherapy? (Use what we wrote as a template, if you like.) You might write in prose, make a mind-map, draw, or record yourself on your phone.

TAKEAWAY MESSAGES

- This book offers you a warm welcome, an invitation to 'step in' to studying counselling and psychotherapy. In this book, we will promote learning as serious and challenging, as well as playful and creative.
- The book will offer advice, with the best of intentions – but we all need to apply judgement to any advice we're given, even from a study-skills text written by experienced lecturers/writers. Finally, it's up to us what we take to be useful.
- We're always developing as learners, however well we've done so far. Even a person getting an Exceptional First, an A+, a Distinction, 100% etc., can

- learn more and achieve more. Success in psychotherapy and counselling training isn't always about achieving the highest of grades, it's about self-development and honouring your own truths.
- 'Not doing well', 'failing' and 'dropping out' can sometimes be the right thing. Let's get beyond simplistic notions of what 'failure' means, as well as what 'success' looks like. Life happens, it's complex – counsellors and psychotherapists have to know that.
- Bringing yourself is part of learning and doing psychotherapy and counselling – but take care not to go further than you can at a particular time, even if you think it's expected of you.
- Remember, in this Introduction – as in any of the chapters of this book – your own takeaway messages may be quite different to ours. Honour your own process!

Further reading

In this chapter, you've heard something of our lived experiences as students/lecturers and you've been invited to contribute a little about yourself.

For further reading, staying with the lived experience theme, why not have a look at:
Pine E. (2019). *Notes to self*. Penguin.

The book contains many of Emilie Pine's lived experiences, and it is written very accessibly.

If you like graphic novels, and would like to learn more about counselling and psychotherapy from reading one, try:
Perry, P. (2020). *Couch fiction: A graphic tale of psychotherapy*. Penguin Life.

The next chapter...

Chapter 1 will now guide you through five key questions to ask yourself and others before you enrol and pay your fees for your counselling and psychotherapy course.

We take the view that you need as much information as possible before you decide whether you wish to 'step in' to study counselling and psychotherapy, and that acquiring such information is an integral part of 'study skills'.

1

Preparing the ground for successful studying

Introduction

In a book about 'tackling counselling training and course assignments', we could have launched straight into 'What might happen in a personal development group', 'How you might write a case study', 'What it's like to have your client work assessed by a clinical supervisor'…

That guidance is certainly coming – so don't worry.

In this first chapter, though, we're taking a step back – so that we can help you step forwards as sure-footedly as possible. We are going to start with some questions to ask yourself and others before you enrol and pay your fees for your counselling and psychotherapy course.

We're doing this because we take the view (from our own experiences of studying, and those of other people) that if you are in the wrong field of study, at the wrong level, at the wrong time for you (for a variety of reasons), then no amount of support is going to entirely change that – and you're likely to find it difficult to tackle your work and to be successful in your assessments.

Choosing the right directions for any studies requires you to make the best decisions you can with the material available to you at the time. And we don't always have enough material, or the most useful, available to us when making decisions about our studies.

We suggest that choosing wisely is even more important when considering a counselling and psychotherapy course – as we're going to see in this book. It's a field of study that can be incredibly demanding in all sorts of ways. Be as sure as you can be before you enrol and pay your fees that: a) you know what you are signing up for, and b) that it's a course of study that is likely to be right for you, as far as you know right now. Being as sure as you can be forms part of the ground for successful studying. It is a 'study skill' in itself. It has an important place in a book like this.

So this first chapter leads you through some questions you could ask yourself and others in order to decide if, and if so, how, to proceed with enrolling for study in the field of counselling and psychotherapy. The chapter is likely to prompt other questions for you, too (which we encourage you to note down and look into).

The questions we've chosen to focus on in this chapter are:

- **Question 1**: What does the study of counselling and psychotherapy involve, and what is the job I'd be studying for actually like?
- **Question 2**: If I decide I might like to study counselling and psychotherapy, at what level might I start my studies, and to where can I progress?
- **Question 3**: There are a variety of modalities (approaches) in counselling and psychotherapy. Which one/s might appeal to me?
- **Question 4**: Where might I study?
- **Question 5**: How much is my training likely to cost, and how could I fund it?

The chapter offers some answers to these questions by offering relevant information and guidance, people's personal experiences to read about and learn from, and prompts and opportunities for your own reflections. You'll be invited to write some of your responses to what you are reading in a personal journal, or draw your responses there, or speak aloud and record your words. As you saw in the Introduction, journalling/recording your experiencing is often part of psychotherapy and counselling courses/training.

The chapter is particularly aimed at the student considering counselling and psychotherapy courses from Level 1 onwards. But if you're already engaged in studying, at any level, some of the questions and material will still be interesting to explore, including when you are questioning your decision to train, or questioning particular aspects of what you are doing. (We want to take this opportunity to stress again a point we made in the Introduction: that questioning your decision to train is something that happens to everyone, and you are likely to do this many times, however carefully you've prepared for your studies; it's actually part of the process of training.)

Question 1:
What does the study of counselling and psychotherapy involve, and what is the job I'd be studying for actually like?

Let's start by meeting a qualified counsellor/psychotherapist, Katy Lees. We asked Katy to reflect on their journey from thinking about training to qualifying and setting up in private practice. We hope you'll find Katy's account a useful and interesting starting point for your own thoughts.

Experiences

Katy Lees describes their journey from thinking about taking an MSc in person-centred and experiential psychotherapy to becoming a qualified psychotherapist in private practice.

I began to train and work towards my MSc in person-centred and experiential psychotherapy in my early 20s, immediately after completing my BSc in psychology. I chose to train after a lifetime of understanding that therapy would be my vocation – I had always been an empathetic listener who was curious about people's stories and wanted to help people by understanding them, so therapy felt like a career that was made for me. I specifically decided to train as a person-centred therapist because I thoroughly believed in the egalitarian ideals of this modality: the ideal that a therapist is there to support others to be who they really are while helping to strip away unhelpful beliefs of what they 'should' be was very appealing to me as a young, queer, neurodivergent person.

My experience of this training was joyous – because I felt that I was finally doing what I was meant to be doing, alongside other trainees who felt the same way. It was also devastating, as many aspects of my training left me emotionally bruised, physically exhausted and financially struggling. The MSc course I undertook was designed to be both part time and intensive and, as I was managing a full-time job, several side-hustles and placement work, it required an ardent commitment to the training and to my own self-care. I had so little time to care well for myself that I had to learn to prioritise physical rest, my own therapy and time spent with trusted loved ones whenever I had a moment that was not reserved for work. The personal learning and practical work undertaken was as emotionally difficult as it was academically testing.

It did not help that the academic system did not always hold the best interests of all students at heart. Often, if I and other trainees were seen to be learning and passing assignments, we were deemed to be doing well, despite the obvious emotional, financial and physical strains many of us were under. Even so, I found that I was able to get through this strenuous period of training thanks to my belief in the person-centred process, the support of many people in my life, and the bone-deep knowledge that being a therapist was what I wanted to do and who I am. My excitement for learning more about myself and about person-centred psychotherapy always pushed me onwards through the seven years it took me to complete the course.

My placement work involved working for charities and organisations across the North East and the Midlands, gaining the 450 clinical hours I needed for accreditation. It was hard work for no pay, and I enjoyed meeting a huge variety of people with many different presenting issues. The service users I have worked with have included survivors of sexual assault, people who needed help managing their stress and anxiety, trans people seeking support through their transitions, and many more. The areas I lived in were not so highly populated that I had much choice about where I volunteered for my placement work, but I was lucky to work with client groups that I found myself 'clicking' with.

While working with service users in my clinical placements, it became imperative that I work on myself – a full-time job that I could not have succeeded at without the help of my clinical supervisor and a particularly patient therapist. I also believe that I would not be the therapist I am today without that intimate knowledge of what it is like to be a client. Being a client throughout my training helped me fully understand the power that the client has in the therapeutic relationship, and I was able to see for myself how much a client can grow and change because I knew that was happening to me.

Like the practice of therapy, you will find that training to be a therapist is about being alongside the other. There are lots of others that you will end up working with, for and next to as a trainee, including clients, tutors, other students and other parts of yourself that you find along the way. Part of the process of my training involved being assessed in multiple ways, by many – if not all – of these others. Graded essays, presentations, peer reviews, group processes, observed journals, recorded sessions with clients, self-reviews, tutor meetings and other such assessment processes were part of daily life throughout my training. The hardest assessments for me to deal with were the dreaded 'triads' and 'goldfish bowls', where students are observed by tutors and other students, putting their therapeutic skills to the test before being offered critiques. While I understood the need for these tests in making sure I was working ethically with my clients, it did not stop the all-consuming anxiety I experienced when I took part, whether as an observer, a client or the practising practitioner. Being alongside peers who were as nervous as I was helped a great deal; we were able to offer each other support, practical help and kindness as we faced being assessed. I think that part of what kept my passion and determination alive from the beginning to the end of my training was knowing there were peers I could turn to for help when I needed it.

Now, a few years after completing my training, I'm a registered and accredited practitioner working in a busy private practice. I absolutely love my job. Most of my clients are members of the LGBTQ+ community, and I've been lucky enough to work with people of many different genders, sexualities and romantic orientations over the last few years. I have also written and published a book with Jessica Kingsley Publishers – a guide to good mental health for trans people. I still hold fast to the ideal that therapy is about working alongside my clients to support them to become who they are, instead of who they were told they should be, and I work hard to ensure I am not another voice in anyone's life telling them how to live. It has been my experience, through training and as a trained practitioner, that it is of utmost importance to prioritise a balance of power in the therapeutic relationship. I am also lucky that many of my peers who helped me through my training are now my friends, and that we have continued to help each other grow and find joy in our therapeutic practices. I have also never lost my passion for learning more about myself and the practice of psychotherapy, so am still doing extra training, reading textbooks and engaging in my own therapy.

My advice to anyone considering training to be a therapist, or anyone who is already in training, is to prioritise yourself and your needs before and during your studies. This training is likely to be one of the best and most difficult things you will ever do, and you will need to be prepared in ways that your training provider may not make clear. Make sure you have more than enough of everything you will need – money, time, support, self-care provisions, and anything else you think might help you. Part of this preparation will mean finding a therapist that you love working with, both during your training and in general. Spend some time working out what you need in order to be at your absolute best, and check in with yourself often throughout your training course to see if you are still getting what you need to thrive.

If you are thriving, you will be much more able to support others – the peers you are training with and the clients and service users you will be working with.

Katy's book

Lees, K. (2022). *The trans guide to mental health and well-being*. Jessica Kingsley.

ACTIVITY

An invitation to explore your responses to reading about Katy's journey

You might write in prose, make mind-maps, draw or speak out loud (and perhaps record your words on your phone).

- Katy described what their training was like, and the emotions it evoked for them. Having read about their experience and what training involves, what do you think training might be like for you?
- If you are already embarked on training, how do your experiences compare with Katy's? What does it feel like to hear from someone else who is taking a course like your own?
- Katy is positive about their experiences as a client. How do you feel about being in therapy yourself while training? (Some courses require it, others do not, as we will see later in this chapter.)
- Katy advises giving a lot of attention to self-care. What self-care do you already do? What strategies and activities might you put in place ready for training?
- What does Katy's account tell you about the work of a counsellor/psychotherapist? Does what they say inspire you to become a psychotherapist/counsellor? How does Katy's account connect with your reasons for wanting to do psychotherapy and counselling training (if you did the activity offered in the Introduction)?
- What else do you feel you need to know about training and becoming a counsellor/psychotherapist? Make a list of what's coming up for you. Keep reading, as we hope many of your points will be answered in this chapter.

Further reading recommendations

Allen, R. (2021). *Grounded: How connection with nature can improve our mental and physical well-being*. Welbeck Publishing. (A self-care book with beautiful photos, to dip into – things to do as well as think about.)

Bager-Charleson, S. (2018). *Why therapists choose to become therapists: A practice-based enquiry*. Karnac. (Accounts of six therapists, working together in a group, where they did reflective writing activities.)

Iantaffi, A. & Barker, M.-J. (2021). *Hell, yeah, self-care: A trauma-informed workbook.* Jessica Kingsley. (Again, things to do, as well as to read about.)

Question 2:
If I decide I might like to study counselling and psychotherapy, at what level might I start my studies, and to where can I progress?

Introductory points

The levels of education and training mentioned in this section relate to England, Wales, and Northern Ireland. You can find a helpful explanation of qualification levels for England, Wales and Northern Ireland here: **www.gov.uk/what-different-qualification-levels-mean/list-of-qualification-levels**

In Scotland, the website to check is: **https://scqf.org.uk**

You can start studying counselling and psychotherapy a Level 1 (or higher, depending on your previous qualifications/experience), and go all the way to a PhD (Level 8).

There are also opportunities for continuing professional development (CPD) (see Chapter 7), both during and in particular after qualification.

Studying counselling and psychotherapy can be a lifelong journey; it can also be a short trip, or somewhere in between. You can also pause for a while in your journey.

For different courses there will be differences in:

- entry requirements
- mode of study – full-time or part-time, in person, online or blended (i.e. a mixture of online and in-person work)
- course length
- how you'll study
- how you'll be assessed
- what you'll need to do outside of the classroom, such as requirements for personal therapy/personal development, client work and clinical supervision.

All this depends on:

- the level of qualification for which you are studying
- where you are studying
- the modality or approach/es to counselling and psychotherapy you're studying
- if your course is accredited by a professional body – the main ones in the UK are the British Association for Counselling and Psychotherapy (BACP) (**bacp.co.uk**), the UK Council for Psychotherapy (UKCP) (**psychotherapy.org.uk**) and the National Counselling Society (NCS) (**nationalcounsellingsociety.org**).

You should note that when you apply, the course provider will want to be sure that you are academically ready for the level of study for which you are applying, and that you are personally ready for the demands of training in psychotherapy and counselling. Even someone with academic qualifications at Level 8 may not yet be ready for the particular demands of counselling and psychotherapy training. You should also note that entry to many courses is likely to be competitive, and that you should apply as early as you can for the next academic year.

When you're writing your application, remember that your previous experiences/study will be useful in training and, later, in the therapy room. Sometimes this gets forgotten; people tend to think psychotherapy and counselling are completely different from everything else you have done. In fact, everything we bring to training and therapy is important and relevant, and should be honoured and valued. Martin Fisher is a good example of this.

Experiences

Social worker, charity manager, criminal defence barrister, psychotherapist, actor…
Martin Fisher MBPsS, MBACP has an MSc in psychology and trained in applied psychology, transactional analysis and addiction psychology and counselling. Martin began his career as a social worker. He then became a charity manager, then trained in law, was called to the bar, and worked as a criminal defence barrister. Since training as a psychotherapist and alongside his practice, Martin has become a part-time actor. He's performed for the Donmar Warehouse in London, and other places. On his website, Martin lets potential clients know about these experiences, so people from the legal profession, charity management, and/or the arts can see that he 'gets' something of the contexts in which they are working. (We'll hear from Martin again in Chapter 2, as he's also a Pink Therapy mentor.)

ACTIVITY

An invitation to do some journalling in response to reading about Martin's career

- How might what you've already done in life so far connect with the course you're considering, or have embarked on, and the career it can lead to? How might you make meaningful connections if you were writing about your previous experiences on your own psychotherapy and counselling website?

As before, you can write in prose, make mind-maps, draw your thoughts, or record them on your phone.

Entry level courses at Levels 1 and 2

Regardless of the level of study you have previously completed, a short introductory course can give you an experiential taster of what it might be like *for you* to study psychotherapy and counselling. Reading about what a course might involve (such as the material in this book) is a really good starting point, but actually trying out, at an introductory level, some of the kind of work that would be required will tell you whether it appeals to you in practice.

You might take a Level 1 introduction to interpersonal skills course, and then progress to a Level 2 award in counselling. Or you could start at Level 2. Both are entry level. Local colleges/training organisations regularly offer Level 1 and Level 2 introductory courses, during the day, at weekends, or as an evening class. Check out the websites of colleges/training organisations in your area to see what's available. You can also search for online courses if you prefer, or need, to study online. This website may also be useful in your search for a course (it also lists courses at higher levels): **www.findcourses.co.uk/search/counselling-training-courses**

Experiences

I (Deborah) took a Level 2 ABC Counselling Concepts course before enrolling for an MSc. Here's why I did that, and what it provided.
I thought I wanted to become a psychotherapist and counsellor partly because personal tutoring of university students had always been an important part of my work, and I had/have strong views that the job of a university lecturer should not simply be to refer students on to the counselling service, but to be a human being alongside them. I thought I could do this sort of work, and I was starting to think about a career change – but I wasn't really sure what the training or the job of a therapist would involve, or if I'd really like it. Qualified psychotherapist and counsellor friends were telling me which modality they thought I should study (integrative), but I didn't really get the differences between them all. I noted how expensive an MSc course would be, and I didn't want to make a costly mistake – wrong modality, or wrong choice altogether. The ABC course allowed me to look at a variety of modalities, and to check out how it felt to be in the therapist's chair. I noticed that the 'not knowing' what might happen when you meet with another person in the therapy room didn't terrify me, in the way that it did some people – in fact, it really appealed. Successfully completing the course confirmed for me that I did indeed want to enrol for an MSc. To be fair, I still didn't know which modality to choose – I really needed the information about the variety of modalities that we provide in this chapter. But I strongly recommend doing a short course first. Some undergraduate and postgraduate courses require it, and some don't. Either way, it's money well spent in making a reasonably informed decision about doing a longer, expensive training in counselling and psychotherapy.

An important note about introductory courses

While we hope you'll already know this, we feel it's very important to say it, and to say it very clearly: a short course does not qualify you to work as a counsellor or psychotherapist. Nor does it mean you can register with a professional body – BACP's accreditation, for instance, starts at Level 4/5, and UKCP only accredits postgraduate courses. If you do an internet search for 'counselling training', you're likely to find all sorts of courses advertised. Some will imply that completing a short course *does* make you a qualified counsellor and launch you on a highly paid career for a minimal investment of time and money. Do not believe them. As you read through this book, you'll come to understand how much is really involved in training to work as a counsellor and psychotherapist.

Levels you might study at after introductory courses – Levels 3–8

Introductory courses do offer transferable skills that you can use in a variety of jobs and activities, so you might stop at that point, or pause and use what you've learned in your current work or in a different career (you might enrol for a course in social work or community work, for example), or use the skills in life in general.

If you want to keep going, you can progress to other counselling and psychotherapy courses. You can progress gradually through the next few levels, or you could join a course at a higher level if you already have the entry requirements.

The sorts of learning and assessments you might do from Levels 3–8 are explored in later chapters of this book.

Level 3 is 'pre-practitioner training'. You won't meet clients. You will be studying elements of theory, ethics, self-awareness, skills and what it will be like working as a counsellor. You will be involved in all sorts of academic and practical assessment.

Level 4 and 5 diplomas deepen learning, and this is the level of training at which you will meet clients. If you have a Level 5 qualification, there are courses you can join afterwards to 'top-up' to a degree qualification (see Chapter 7, where we hear from a student who did just that).

You might, if you already have the required qualifications, decide to enrol for an undergraduate degree – a BA or BSc (a Level 6 qualification). There will be entry requirements to meet – some courses require previous study in counselling and psychotherapy and some don't, so check for that, and you'll have to apply through UCAS. You can find the UCAS website here: **www.ucas.com**

BACP offers accreditation at Levels 4/5 and above. You can find a BACP-accredited course on its website, at **www.bacp.co.uk**

You can also find BACP's *Course Accreditation Scheme Eligibility Guide* on its website, at **www.bacp.co.uk** (You will need to use the search function to get hold of the latest version.)

To be accredited by BACP, courses currently have to comprise 400 hours of face-to-face training (classroom-based learning) and require students to complete 100 hours of supervised practice with clients. BACP states on its website:

> All cases must be presented for supervision. The supervision must be at least fortnightly in frequency, not fall below an overall amount of 1.5 hours per month and require at least one hour's presentation for eight hours of client work.

BACP does not ask that accredited courses require students to have personal therapy. Rather, BACP asks that:

> … students have the opportunity to benefit from a regular process of self-exploration, self-examination and reflection in a confidential setting in order to develop an understanding of themselves.

This means that course providers can make their own decisions about how much, if any, personal therapy they expect their students to have during their training. Some courses fulfil this requirement through personal development groups (see Chapter 3).

If you graduate from a BACP-accredited course and register with BACP, you can display the letters MBACP after your name.

If your course is not accredited by BACP and you want to join BACP afterwards, and you meet its requirements for study and placement, you can take the BACP Certificate of Proficiency (CoP). The CoP is an online two-hour test of your knowledge of counselling in practice (rather than your recall of information about particular theory, philosophy etc.). This then establishes that you meet BACP's accreditation standards and can use MBACP after your name.

The National Counselling Society also accredits courses from Level 4 onwards. You can find their *Standards of Training and Education for Accredited Courses* on the NCS website (as with BACP above, you will need to use the search function to find the latest version): **nationalcounsellingsociety.org**

As with the BACP accreditation standards, 100 supervised client hours are required and there is no formal requirement from NCS for students to be in personal therapy. Instead NCS states that:

> The programme must contain opportunities for experiential learning about self and others. This should support trainees in managing and making use of their own experience within the therapeutic relationship.

A registered member of NCS can use MNCS (Accred) after their name.

You may be ready to do a postgraduate degree – an MA or MSc (a Level 7 qualification). There will be entry requirements to meet, and you'll need to apply directly to the university/training institute of your choice. You can search for these courses at **www.findamasters.com**

You can filter your search on this website – for instance, by whether the course is part time or full time, and/or whether it is available online. Note that to apply for an MA/MSc, your undergraduate degree does not need to be in psychotherapy/counselling, or in a field related to psychotherapy/counselling (like psychology).

It is possible to leave an MA/MSc course before completing it and still be a qualified counsellor and psychotherapist. You could do a postgraduate diploma (the level you reach in a postgraduate course if you do not do a dissertation). You might choose this route if you already have postgraduate qualifications at MA/MSc level and/or above and are training to change career, rather than needing an MA/MSc with a view to applying for a PhD course.

UKCP only accredits postgraduate courses. You can find a list of UKCP-accredited courses on its website here: www.psychotherapy.org.uk/psychotherapy-training. You can find information about the UKCP standards for course accreditation on its website here: www.psychotherapy.org.uk/ukcp-members/standards-guidance-and-policies

UKCP comprises several individual 'colleges', representing different specialisms and branches of psychotherapy, and each has its own requirements. As explained on the UKCP website, to become a UKCP-registered psychotherapist or psychotherapeutic counsellor, you need to complete training that typically takes between three and six years, part time. You also need to complete approximately 450 hours of practice, theory and skills, and have therapy and supervision yourself throughout. The amount of personal therapy varies, again depending on which field (or 'college') you wish to train in. For example, for psychotherapeutic counselling with adults it is 105 hours, but in other fields it is 110. It is normally undertaken concurrently with your training, and with a qualified registered UKCP psychotherapeutic counsellor or psychotherapist. Full clinical registration allows you to put 'UKCP Reg' after your name.

Level 8 is a PhD, which you will do if you want to research a particular topic. There are also opportunities for Professional Doctorates, which involve some taught work as well as a research dissertation.

If you're starting at Level 1 now, a PhD (Level 8) will, of course, look a long way off, but it is there on the horizon if you would like to progress towards it, either immediately after completing an MA/MSc or later on. You might think the idea of doing 'research' is a bit daunting, or beyond you. We think you should regard it as an exciting opportunity to pursue further knowledge and contribute to the development of the profession.

We asked Dr Peter Blundell, who you'll meet a few times in this book, to give you an overview of his doctoral journey, as it began right from his early experiences of studying counselling and psychotherapy. Peter is an experienced person-centred/experiential therapist who has worked in a variety of counselling agencies, and is now in private practice. He is the founder and co-lead of #TherapistsConnect, an international, not-for-profit platform for connecting therapists. The platform includes a community of, and projects for, students of counselling and psychotherapy, called #TraineeTalk, details of which can be found here: **www.Therapists-Connect.com**

In addition to his work as a therapist, Peter is a senior lecturer at Liverpool John Moores University on the MA programme in counselling/psychotherapy, and a sessional lecturer at the Metanoia Institute, in London, on the MSc in Contemporary Person-Centred Psychotherapy and Applications. He also runs a hybrid publishing company, called Open Voices, which seeks to address social inequality by providing a platform for different identities (**www.open-voices.com**).

Experiences

Dr Peter Blundell describes his journey towards starting and completing a doctorate.

I first had the idea of researching boundaries in counselling and psychotherapy during my early counselling training. As a student counsellor, I was taught about the importance of boundaries to my practice, but became frustrated and confused at how difficult it was to pin down and clearly define what boundaries are. The breadth of interpretation by tutors, fellow students and other counsellors of what are acceptable boundaries in counselling practice has both surprised and intrigued me! I began to read about boundaries and noticed a gap in the literature, and so began to feel very passionate about exploring this topic. I was very lucky to know two lecturers from my undergraduate studies who could supervise my project, one of whom was also a counsellor and supervisor. I found completing my thesis very hard work, and I would advise anyone who is interested in completing a PhD to find the right supervisors. They will be your main guides and sources of support during your studies, so a good relationship with them is really important. It took me eight years to complete my thesis, which I completed part-time, while also working full time, so it took up all my spare time. It was really hard work, but it was also a great experience and also improved my counselling practice, as I began to have a better understanding of boundaries. In 2019, after presenting my research at the BACP Research Conference in Belfast, I won the CPCAB Counselling Research Award, which helps disseminate research that is important for counselling or counselling training. I now supervise other PhD students, which I absolutely love, and enjoy using my experiences to help guide other students through study at this level.

Peter's article

Blundell, P., Oakley, L. & Kinmond K. (2022) Who are we protecting? Exploring counsellors' understanding and experience of boundaries. *European Journal of Qualitative Research in Psychotherapy*, *12*, 13–28, https://ejqrp.org/index.php/ejqrp/issue/view/12

Question 3:

There are many modalities (different approaches, different schools of thought, with particular theories, philosophies, histories and ways of working) in counselling and psychotherapy. Which one/s might appeal to me?

Counselling and psychotherapy come in a wide variety of flavours. The many different approaches to counselling and psychotherapy have different histories, theories, philosophies and ways of working.

The main modalities include cognitive behavioural therapy, person-centred and experiential counselling, psychodynamic psychotherapy and integrative psychotherapy or counselling. These all come under the broad heading of 'humanistic therapies'.

The particular approach to psychotherapy and counselling that you are studying will determine, to some extent, what your studies will be like, how you'll complete your assessments, and what you're going to be doing if you work as a counsellor and psychotherapist after qualification (unless you then do more study and qualify in a new area, as Matthew Horrocks did, see below).

You may see courses referred to as 'counselling' and/or 'psychotherapy', rather than branded in their title as being training in a particular approach, but all courses will involve studying one or more approaches, so look closely at the course details before you sign up. You should be sure that the approach is in sympathy with your own beliefs about human development.

As Katy Lees explained earlier on in this chapter, you have to consider which approach feels right for you right now. You can only do that meaningfully when you have some idea what the differences between the approaches might be. We invited four experienced counsellors/psychotherapists representing four approaches regularly taught in universities/training institutes (integrative, person-centred, psychodynamic and cognitive behavioural) to briefly introduce them to you and to suggest some further reading that you might do if you wanted to explore any of them further.

Even if you think you already know which approach to counselling and psychotherapy you'd like to study, we suggest you read about the other approaches, so you can be even more sure of your choice (you might even change direction). Deborah initially applied to a course in integrative therapy, started reading a book about it and couldn't finish it – which suggested that something was amiss.

Knowing about the variety of approaches will be useful to you whatever modality you train in, as sometimes clients will need or want something that you can't offer, and if you know what might be useful to them, you'll be better equipped to refer them on.

Experiences

Nicola Blunden is Director of Studies for the BSc Person-Centred Pluralistic Counselling at the Metanoia Institute. She writes here about integrative training.

Training in counselling and psychotherapy has its trends, just as all movements have phases and fashions. In the past, integrative trainings were widely popular, because they seemed to offer a valuable 'added extra' of versing students in multiple schools of therapy. But integrative trainings sit alongside single-modality or 'core trainings', which train students in one model at depth, such as in person-centred counselling, Gestalt psychotherapy and transactional analysis. In this section, I aim to give you a thorough understanding of what constitutes a good integrative training and its relative benefits and limitations as compared with a single-modality training, and an opportunity to consider whether it would suit you personally, as well as suit your future career as a therapist. I also offer you three books to read, so that you can find out more about integrative approaches.

Within the counselling world, there is a vast variety of practice. There is equally great disagreement, too, as to what constitutes a good model (or, more likely, the *best* model) of practice, and large bodies of theory and research underpinning all these approaches. At the same time, progress and growth in one school or modality cannot help but influence, and sometimes radically change, the methods or character of other therapeutic approaches, resulting in the intertwining of many ideas and techniques. It is no wonder that students, clients, and therapists themselves often feel confused.

A good integrative course draws from two or more different models of therapy and teaches you how to integrate or combine these into a standard way of working with clients. The challenge of an integrative training is to balance *depth* and *variety* of approaches. This is made more complex by the fact that not all schools of therapy dovetail neatly together, and sometimes they conflict. Take, for instance, the apparently simple question of how to support a client to decide on their goals for therapy. Let's explore this question with regard to three main approaches: person-centred, psychodynamic and cognitive behavioural.

A person-centred practitioner may argue that clients are the best authority about themselves and that all of us have the tendency to grow and protect ourselves. Consequently, they might carefully and respectfully follow the client's lead in the moment, unconditionally accepting their expressed wishes and desires. They would be careful not to introduce their own goals or preferences into the client's decision-making. The client might spend some time weighing up what they really want from the therapy, perhaps feeling for their own sense of what is right for them, while the therapist carefully and patiently follows the client's lead.

A psychodynamic practitioner might see this question more in terms of the client's relationship style and history. They might argue that the client's unconscious wishes and habitual patterns might influence and cloud their chosen goal in therapy, and perhaps even sabotage its success. Perhaps, on the surface, the client wants to explore their difficult relationships at work, but the therapist suspects that deeper relationship issues, perhaps in the client's family of origin, are at play. Given the impact of those unspoken elements, this practitioner might not expect the true purpose of therapy to emerge for some time.

A cognitive behavioural practitioner might reason that the goals and methods of therapy should be informed by the therapist's knowledge of the presenting issue of the client, as well as by the client's stated goals. They might explicitly label the client's presenting issue (for example, anxiety or depression), take the lead in identifying a set of specific outcomes of therapy that can be achieved within a set timescale, and educate and coach the client towards them.

These differences result from the very different philosophical foundations underpinning each modality of therapy. In each case, the approach towards client goal setting might rest on fundamentally different assumptions about the reliability of a client's face-value account of herself. Nevertheless, in practice, despite these foundational differences, most practitioners working in these modalities would invite the client to talk about the reasons behind them coming to therapy, and how they would like the therapy to help. All the practitioners would aim to create a productive and connected relationship with the client, and would seek to promote the client's autonomy, which is the ethical principle that describes the client's right to make their own decisions and live in the way that seems most suitable to them. This might result in quite similar discussions with clients about their wishes for the therapy. So, in practice, while there are significant fundamental variances in approaches, there is also as much that unites therapists from different modalities as separates us. In fact, research has shown that the personal qualities of the therapist, as well as those of the client, are the strongest influence on outcomes, regardless of the therapeutic modality being practised.

Because of these differences and similarities, an integrative training asks you to hold in mind the possibility that the values and theories underpinning therapy sometimes conflict and contradict each other, and sometimes complement each other too. You will need to hold theories 'lightly', which is to say that you will be expected to understand them as metaphors or hypotheses, and as equally valuable and different ways of seeing the world, rather than regarding them as facts.

Despite this inner openness and flexibility towards theory, you will still need to be able to explain what you do as a therapist, and why you do it, more or less consistently and coherently. This is what characterises integration. It is not a jumble of ideas, but a digested whole, even if that process of digestion is always in a state of becoming, rather than an achieved state. Each training course should be able to articulate how this integration occurs for its students. When considering an integrative training, do not be afraid to ask how this integration is understood and taught and how the course supports students to have a coherent understanding of theory and practice. Where the course team is not able to explain this, you might end up with a training that confuses you, or, worse, encourages you to practice in incoherent, and therefore unhelpful, ways.

Is an integrative training for me? Questions to ponder

One school, versus many schools:

- Do I already have a special relationship to one form of therapy, perhaps as a client or because I have read the work of a particular founder of the approach (such as Carl Rogers or Irvin Yalom)?
- When I learn something new, do I aim for a specialised skill or a broad range of skills?
- In my future career, do I see myself being more engaged by depth of practice or variety of practice?

Philosophical differences:

- How comfortable am I looking at the world and at human development through multiple lenses?
- How easy or challenging would I find it to hold in mind many perspectives on a problem?
- How much do I value the internal consistency of my world view?
- When I imagine myself working with clients in the future, do I see myself offering one way of understanding their experience or multiple ways?

Further reading recommendations from Nicola

To help you further with your decision, here are three examples of integrative frameworks, which you can read to understand integration in more depth.

Faris, A. & van Ooijen, E. (2013). *Integrative counselling and psychotherapy.* **Sage.**

This model emphasises the dynamic integration process that happens between the client, the therapist, and the models of therapy. The approach takes a postmodernist attitude towards theory, seeing knowledge as contextual and co-constructed and limited in its attempts to make sense of the world and its phenomena. The integration of theory and practice that happens within the therapist is applied to the unique situation and history of the client, in the service of a therapeutic and transformative relationship.

Cooper, M. & McLeod, J. (2011). *Pluralistic counselling and psychotherapy.* **Sage.**
This model originated within the person-centred approach and offers a critique of the 'schoolism' inherent to single-modality therapy approaches ('my approach is better than your approach'). Resting on an ethic of care and a valuing of diversity, pluralistic approaches centre the needs and desires of the client, who explicitly chooses the direction that therapy will take, as well as the tasks and methods used in that therapy. Cooper and McLeod differentiate it from a traditional integrative approach, in that the therapist does not formally develop an integrated model that they use consistently with all clients, but coproduces a new approach with each client, in response to the idiosyncratic preferences of each client and drawing on the range of abilities of each counsellor.

Lapworth, P. & Sills, C. (2010). *Integration in counselling and psychotherapy.* **Sage.**
This approach begins by acknowledging the core generic elements that can be found across a range of therapeutic modalities. It then offers a dual integrative strategy that is both a framework (what we understand) and a process (what we do), drawing on a selection of particular 'integratable' theories and methods of counselling. This multidimensional model centres the client's meaning-making, situated in time (past, present and future), in their relationships, and in their sensory inner world. The eventual model of integration is developed by the student, in response to their own questions about the nature of human suffering and striving.

Experiences

Dr Matthew Horrocks is Assistant Professor of Mental Health and Psychological Therapies at the University of Nottingham. He introduces cognitive behavioural therapy (CBT) training.

You might not know this, but cognitive behavioural therapy (CBT) is not just one approach to counselling and psychotherapy – it is, in fact, an umbrella term covering a range of related but different approaches, which are all based on psychological theory and research and the idea that our thoughts, feelings, behaviours, and how our bodies respond, are all connected (for a helpful explanation, see **www.babcp.com/What-is-CBT**).

Examples of approaches under the umbrella of CBT include cognitive therapy, which focuses on how someone thinks; behavioural therapy, which focuses on how someone behaves in relation to certain trigger factors, and newer forms of CBT, such as acceptance and commitment therapy or schema-focused therapy, which focus on how a person responds in relation to their thoughts, feelings, behaviours and the contexts they live, experience and exist within.

In addition to being based on psychological theory and research and the connections between thoughts, feelings, behaviours and bodily responses, all CBT approaches are collaborative. That means that the counsellor and client work together in a spirit of team working and joint problem-solving. All CBT approaches also encourage clients and counsellors to collect data to see if the changes in thinking and behaviour tested out in CBT do make a difference.

CBT approaches were developed in healthcare settings, which means that, in its development, CBT was focused on helping clients reduce distress associated with psychological problems such as depression, anxiety, anger, and interpersonal difficulties. The newest forms of CBT focus on empowering clients to identify and work towards personally meaningful hopes and aspirations and to take part in personally meaningful activities. However, most CBT is probably still aimed at reducing clients' experiences of distress.

This focus on reducing distress is intended to be pragmatic, which many people in distress find useful. CBT is probably well suited to clients who want to work out how some of the things they do, or the ways in which they think, can make them feel more unwell or more upset, and to those who can identify what they value and want to work towards. It is well suited too to counsellors who want to collaborate with clients taking this journey.

CBT work is usually time-limited and brief, typically between six and 20 sessions. Sessions are highly focused on predetermined topics, following an 'agenda' agreed at the start of each meeting. The agenda can include an update on the client's wellbeing, key points for the session – such as practising a new coping skill – and jointly working out ways in which the client can test out ideas covered during the session. A similar agenda is used for each subsequent session. Clients are often asked to conduct 'homework tasks', to test ideas discussed during CBT sessions or to practise new coping skills, and to report back at the next session. There is a distinct purpose to homework: practice and repetition are important aspects of all CBT approaches, derived from underlying behavioural psychology theory that sees repetition as important to develop new ways of thinking and reacting. CBT also involves a very strong commitment to trying to measure the relative success of any new coping skill and the client's subjective level of distress. A range of generic and bespoke psychological measures is used to record the client's experience before, during and at the end of therapy. Sometimes clients' scores on these measures may be compared with population norms for reference.

Over the last 30 years, CBT has established itself as the type of counselling recommended by healthcare services in many countries. In England, a national government scheme to increase the availability of psychological therapy in NHS primary care was launched in 2008. The Improving Access to Psychological Therapies programme (IAPT) has radically increased the number of CBT therapists in the NHS and access to talking therapies in primary care, making CBT the main counselling approach available in NHS settings today.

CBT training involves learning about theories that are thought to explain psychological distress, and techniques to help clients gain increased understanding of their own experience and change how they think or respond. You don't need a psychology degree to learn CBT, as these ideas are covered in the training, but many people interested in CBT are also interested in the wider field of psychology.

During training, you'll be asked to take part in role-plays in which you'll be the counsellor helping clients to learn CBT techniques. Your skills will be evaluated in relation to how well you can use the specific techniques and your ability to teach clients how to use them. This might involve role-playing a session with a member of the course team, a professional actor or another student.

Once you can demonstrate appropriate levels of skill within the in-course assessments, you will have the opportunity to start seeing clients in supervised therapy placements. The availability of student placements depends on where you are training. Some parts of the country (e.g. urban areas) have more organisations able to support student placements than do others (eg. rural areas with smaller populations). The type of course you are enrolled on might also have a bearing. For example, if you are studying on a designated IAPT course, you would be offered a placement within the NHS. If your course is independent, you will probably need to find your own placement, with support from your institute.

During the training placement, you will be required to record parts of or whole sessions with clients so you can show your placement supervisors your developing skills and abilities. Recorded client work and role-plays within the course are observed and assessed against competency frameworks that reflect the standards required of qualified CBT therapists.

In addition, you will be asked to complete academic essays, coursework, presentations, reflective diaries, logs of therapeutic practice and case studies of your work with individual clients.

When I looked into what CBT training involved, I was surprised to discover personal therapy is not usually required, although self-application of CBT techniques (such as examining your own thoughts and behaviours) and personal reflection (for example by writing a reflective diary) are encouraged.

Many excellent counselling courses now incorporate CBT, such as integrative counselling courses at Levels 2–4, and there are also now Level 5 diplomas in CBT offered by an increasing number of counselling training providers. There are also specialist CBT psychotherapist training courses.

Funded training positions are frequently available within the IAPT programme. You can be employed as a trainee therapist and the NHS pays your salary and training fees and provides clinical supervision and ready access to clients for you to work with.

Other such paid trainee positions may be available. For example, at the time of writing, the NHS is also looking to fund training places for related roles that use some aspects of CBT in a focused way. These include psychological wellbeing practitioners, educational mental health practitioners and children's wellbeing practitioners.

If you search on **www.jobs.nhs.uk**, and put in the keyword search term 'IAPT', it should bring up all currently advertised trainee or qualified roles. The job description and person specifications will tell you more about what you need to be able to demonstrate to obtain an IAPT trainee role. The different roles will ask for you to show different levels of experience, and some roles might need you to demonstrate the ability to study at postgraduate level. For some roles, life experience can be taken into account as equivalent to a degree qualification.

All IAPT trainee roles are likely to be highly competitive and attract a lot of interest, so I think it pays dividends to look at the type of experiences that the NHS looks for in applicants for the different funded training places. You can find information about the different roles online here: **www.ppn.nhs.uk/resources/careers-map**

I initially trained as a person-centred counsellor, but then later trained as a CBT therapist through a funded IAPT trainee role. I saw the scheme as a tremendous opportunity to gain marketable skills and a professional qualification while earning a decent wage, leading to secure, well-paid employment. I studied a full-time CBT course at postgraduate level, and I needed to complete 200 hours of CBT practice within one academic year. I also had to pass a range of academic assessments, showing understanding of CBT theories, techniques and concepts, while working with clients, some of whom had long-term and complex problems. I experienced the course as a short, sharp learning experience, where I developed a level of CBT skill and ability. After passing the course, I was employed within the NHS on a band 7 salary.

I have continued learning every year since qualifying, and it took me quite a few years to gain a sense of actually knowing the theory and concepts reasonably well enough. In the years since qualifying, I have worked in IAPT services, developed specialist services within the NHS for people with anxiety or depression and long-term physical health problems and gained experience teaching on counselling and CBT training courses. So, for me, CBT training has been a rich, rewarding and valuable experience, and continues to provide ongoing learning and development.

Is CBT training for you? Some points to consider

The underpinning perspectives on which CBT is based create a therapy where there is a strong 'scientific flavour' that often incorporates ideas and language from medicine (such as understanding deep despair as depression and intense fear as anxiety) and psychological theory.

If you are not comfortable with an approach that uses ideas from psychology and the medical model of psychological distress, such as 'assessing' a client's 'problem', 'applying' a previously tested 'treatment' approach and 'evaluating' the treatment outcome, you might find CBT is not for you. If you are someone who, on the whole, prefers to privilege individuals' experience over theory, you might also find CBT difficult to get on with.

It seems to me that people who resonate with CBT are those who can, at least partially, accept the notion of counselling as a type of scientific endeavour, exploring clients' experiences through the lens of theory, and using data to see if the CBT approaches are helping. In my opinion, CBT training suits people are who intellectually curious, who like solving problems by drawing on psychological theory and research, who like a degree of structure and routine, and who are able to create a warm professional relationship with a very wide range of people – remember that CBT involves collaborating with clients, teamworking and problem-solving. If this sounds like you, CBT could be for you. In my view, it is a rich, dynamic, and thriving area of counselling practice, which I think will only become stronger and more established in the years ahead.

I hope these thoughts have been of some help to you and I wish you all the best on your counselling journey.

Further reading recommendations from Matthew

Here are some books on CBT that I think are really helpful:

Branch, R., Paget J. & Dryden, W. (2021). *The cognitive behaviour therapy primer* **(2nd ed.). PCCS Books.**

This book provides a concise introduction to CBT by three of its leading proponents, and is written in a clear and accessible way. It offers an overview of the theory and a good sense of what CBT looks like in practice.

Kennerley, H., Kirk, J. & Westbrook, D. (2016). *An introduction to cognitive behaviour therapy skills and applications* (3rd ed.). Sage.

This book is a brilliant resource, which guides you through a really good overview of CBT basic theory, skills and applications. It does a great job of conveying complex information in a fairly accessible way. It also features some very good reflective learning exercises to encourage you to think more about CBT and your own experiences.

Lowenthal, D. & Proctor, G. (Eds.). (2018). *Why not CBT? Against and for CBT revisited* (2nd ed.). PCCS Books.

This is an excellent, more academic book, which provides theoretically based arguments for and against CBT in relation to other counselling approaches. It explores the strengths and limitations of CBT, and where it fits within contemporary society as a healthcare intervention and as a form of counselling. You may find many of the chapters challenging to read, but the book is highly thought provoking and a rich source of different viewpoints about CBT.

Experiences

Myira Khan is a BACP accredited counsellor, supervisor, counselling tutor and founder of the Muslim Counsellor and Psychotherapist Network (www.mcapn.co.uk). She introduces psychodynamic counselling training.

Training in psychodynamic counselling and psychotherapy is all about you and your own emotional and psychological development, which is an unfolding and emergent process towards becoming a robust, resilient, self-aware and psychologically minded person who can build, maintain and engage in therapeutic relationships. The process speaks to your ability to 'be' rather than 'do'. It is this ability to 'be' in relationship with your client that is core to the training and the process of becoming a counsellor/therapist.

This process can often provoke anxieties, challenges, difficulties and defences in students, as you each need to look at yourself throughout the training process (and beyond) to gain greater self-awareness and the ability to be reflective, sit with, feel and process a full range of emotions and feelings and to be in relationship with another person.

Essentially, the training will provoke and engage your anxieties and defences because it will shine a spotlight on your own lived experiences and conscious and unconscious relationships. This reflects the psychodynamic modality itself. You will have to consciously start to identify and explore your own use of defence mechanisms and the anxieties you are defending yourself against.

This is a parallel process and mirrors what you then do in your work with your clients to help them identify and explore their own experiences and the anxieties they are defending themselves against and how, which leads to greater self-awareness for the client.

It's important to choose the modality that suits you. The 'right' choice will be a modality that sits comfortably with your way of understanding and viewing emotional and psychological development and how you want to approach working with clients. I would highly recommend that you first experience psychodynamic counselling yourself, to get a feel for the modality, how you experience being the client and if it sits comfortably with you. Very often your own experience of counselling will be a very close indicator of the type or modality of counselling that will suit you as a counsellor.

The premise or 'philosophy' of psychodynamic counselling is that our childhood experiences and relationships create an unconscious internal blueprint for how we conduct all our relationships (known as an internal world of object relations), which becomes the template or blueprint for future relationships in adulthood. When working with clients, we are supporting them to understand their present-day relationships and experiences while trying to reveal their underlying relationship blueprint, and how it was created by childhood experiences and replicated in the adult relationships and experiences they are exploring in counselling. We are addressing both present-day and childhood experiences in order to reveal the pattern and replication of their relationship blueprint. A cornerstone of psychodynamic counselling is the belief in the existence and influence of a person's unconscious self, where the internal world resides, and how this is played out in our relationships.

This 'philosophy' is what drew me to psychodynamic counselling and why I continue to work in it. It offers me a framework for understanding my own relationship blueprint, how it manifests in my relationships and particularly in my therapeutic relationships, how I can understand my own experiences and the countertransference and empathy with my clients, and how I can support clients to understand their own relationship blueprint and experiences and how they will play out their blueprint in the therapeutic relationship with me.

Psychodynamic counselling can be long or short term. It can be quite usual in long-term counselling that clients work with their counsellor for up to two years, attending weekly sessions. In some cases, the client will be offered an 'ongoing' contract where there is no end date decided in advance and the ending is negotiated when the client feels ready.

As the counselling process is focused on exploring and understanding the client's experiences through talking with the therapist, there are no homework tasks and the client leads the process in deciding what they want to explore each session. The belief is that the client is able to find understanding, meaning and answers to their concerns, so the counsellor doesn't offer any advice or answers. The counsellor holds and contains what the clients brings.

It's important, then, that the client is offered a consistent frame of weekly sessions at the same time and on the same day, so the counselling process and relationship between client and counsellor are clearly boundaried. This frame offers the client an example and experience of being in a consistent, boundaried and reliable relationship, which they may not have experienced before.

Studying psychodynamic counselling includes being assessed on your progress through role-plays of counselling sessions, case studies of client work, essays, presentations and submitting a personal learning journal that records your own understanding and experience of the course and how you are making meaning and sense of the teaching. As the emphasis in the psychodynamic modality is on our conscious experience of relationships and our unconscious relationship blueprint, students are asked to include and reflect on their own experiences of empathy, countertransference (how we feel towards the other person or client, how we experience the other person or client, or any feeling when in relationship with another person or client) and the relationship dynamics between you, or how you understand the blueprints being played out. For example, a case study will ask you to reflect on the client's material and how you worked with the client to explore their material. However, as the work includes working with the 'in here' therapeutic relationship, you will also be expected to record your experience of the therapeutic relationship, transference and countertransference 'in here', and how this helps you to make sense of the client's blueprint and how it is being played out with you in the therapy room.

Are you ready? The key question to ask yourself

Given the emphasis in psychodynamic counselling on relationship blueprints and the creation of our blueprints through our childhood and family experiences and the impact of these experiences on our adulthood experiences and sense of self, it's important to ask yourself 'Am I ready to look at myself, my childhood experiences and the impact of it upon my life?'

Ask yourself honestly if you have the resilience, self-awareness, time and space (physical, time-wise, mental and emotional) to embark on the training. You will never know for certain until you start, but asking yourself before starting is helpful to begin that process.

Self-awareness can take time to build and develop and not everyone may be in the right place to start training when they apply. If you do not get onto the course at first try, it is not a sign of failure; rather, it may highlight that you need to develop and build your self-awareness or resilience before starting on the training. It can often be a matter of first having personal therapy yourself to start that process of self-awareness, as the course is demanding and asks a lot from you.

Sometimes, having started the course, people discover that the process or what is being asked of them feels too challenging or painful. They may need to process those aspects of their self that come to their awareness before continuing on the course. People may leave or defer their training for these reasons.

Further reading recommendations from Myira

I would recommend the following three books to people considering embarking on psychodynamic psychotherapy training:

Howard, S. (2018). *Psychodynamic counselling in a nutshell* (3rd ed.). Sage.
This book is a short and very readable introduction to psychodynamic counselling, with an overview of psychodynamic theory and practice and the history of the approach. The book explains the key theoretical concepts of 'object relations' and the development of our internal world, how we develop our relationship patterns and how this gets created through our childhood experiences. It also introduces the key psychodynamic concepts and theories from Freud, Melanie Klein, D.W. Winnicott and John Bowlby, which form the foundations of psychodynamic thinking. You will learn how the theory is then translated

into clinical practice in the creation of a therapeutic space and relationship, and how the 'in here' therapeutic relationship is used as part of the work through the concept of transference. The book also explains the practical aspects and skills of offering counselling to clients, and answers common questions such as how to find the right counsellor, how to become a psychodynamic counsellor and what it is like to be a psychodynamic counsellor.

Gomez, L. (1997). *An introduction to object relations.* **Free Association Books.**
This book is foundational to understanding 'object relations', which is a central concept and theory in psychodynamic counselling. You will find a chapter on each major 'object relations' theory – Melanie Klein, Ronald Fairbairn, Donald Winnicott, Michael Balint, Harry Guntrip and John Bowlby – covering the 'school of object relations' and offering an in-depth understanding of core psychodynamic processes and thinking. These are followed by chapters on the clinical application and practice of psychodynamic counselling. This book provides a bridge between theory and clinical practice, and a 'map' to guide you through the work you are engaging in, brought together in one comprehensive volume. This is the core reading text I recommend to all psychodynamic counselling students.

Leiper, R. & Maltby, M. (2004). *The psychodynamic approach to therapeutic change.* **Sage.**
This book makes the link between psychodynamic theory, clinical practice and how theory translates into the actual process taking place in the room. Most importantly, it outlines the six core processes of therapeutic change, to aid understanding of what the change process is that the client and counsellor are going through during their sessions. It provides answers to the questions of 'What is going on in the counselling process?', 'What is the purpose of the counselling process?', 'What is the process you are facilitating for your clients?', 'What are you doing for your clients?', and 'What changes are happening in that process for the client?' I consider this book essential to understanding and contextualising the theory and clinical practice and explaining the changes going on and skills you are using to bring about those changes, and thus the purpose of counselling itself.

Experiences

Ambika Erin Connelly is a tutor in person-centred and experiential psychotherapy at the Sherwood Psychotherapy Training Institute, Nottingham. She introduces person-centred training.

Training in the person-centred approach (PCA) is an opportunity to foster awareness and skills that are highly transferable. Why? Because at the very heart of this approach is the person and the myriad relationships that a person might experience. Sometimes people associate the PCA with Carl Rogers' work from the mid-20th century, but that's only the beginning. The international community of person-centred and experiential therapeutic professionals has advanced Rogers' seminal work and this diverse and thriving collective continues to evolve the training and practice of PCA.

To even begin PCA training is to embark on a deepening exploration of who you are, what you believe and how this translates into your way of relating. All of these are assets in life, both professional and personal, whether you train to qualification level or not. This is because PCA training is not just about learning and applying techniques to use in therapy; it examines and encourages each person in training to consider themselves as a unique, multi-faceted and whole organism that exists in relationship with other interdependent systems. As you work through your training, you learn more and more about your 'way of being' in the world. A 'way of being' refers to living one's own identity, learning more about your intentions and their impact. Undoubtedly, the learning process will have a ripple effect through other professional and personal aspects of the trainee's life.

Recognising and being willing to develop who you are and what you believe are important anchor points in forming a picture as to whether PCA training might suit you. Beliefs and identity shape attitudes and assumptions, which in turn underpin expectations about relationships. It is often said that PCA is a values-based approach, so understanding your own values will help you be aware of how compatible this training feels for you.

PCA training is an invitation to hold an increasingly complex sense of yourself as a base from which to see the uniqueness of each person you encounter. The process of becoming more familiar with yourself in your training challenges your assumptions and beliefs about how people relate. In PCA training, this is part of the recipe – you need to have recognised your own attitudes and how you are living them before you can attempt to support another person.

PCA values in the therapy room are also core to the training. PCA training is likely to involve many iterations of what it means to be a person in relationship because the relationship, not the individual therapist, is crucial to all therapeutic collaborations. Training explores the complexity of you as an organismic whole, not just the intellectual concept of a 'self' or individual drives. Each person's differences and diversity are part of the interconnected social locations that we bring from our previous significant and influential relationships.

There is a rich philosophical, theoretical and research-based underpinning to PCA, both historical and current, which informs the training; all of these aspects come alive through the training experience. Therefore, PCA training will likely involve a blend of situations to foster a multi-layered sense of awareness. Learning may come through activities and discussions that offer ways to explore PCA tenets through the lenses of how you live. This includes practice sessions where all participants agree to bring themselves genuinely, not to portray a role or a reductive picture of symptoms or problems. The learning reflects the complexity of each person integrating the reality of encounter in all meaningful mediums of experience: cognitive, emotional, physical and possibly transpersonal dimensions.

This kind of training may not appeal if a moment-to-moment, dialogical style of education holds an unbearable uncertainty for you. It may not appeal if you do not see yourself as responsible for your education, or if you do not see yourself as part of a collective, co-creating the learning environment. However, if you feel that cultivating an understanding of yourself and how to be, see and work with people holds philosophical and even political coherence, the PCA may be a good start.

During training, it is very likely that difficult and necessary conversations will arise about how each person's inherent power and oppressions from relationships with significant others, community, history and society have shaped their identity. The PCA training environment is intended to foster the trainee's discovery of and familiarity with meaningful elements of their existence, pathways to self-acceptance and freedom to learn about experimenting with new ways of relating.

All of this is in recognition that the PCA works in a way that prizes a person and aims to meet the person where they are. In the PCA, to understand a person is to see them as wholly as they allow themselves to be seen, then accepting that it still is not possible to know exactly what it is like to be them. It is a radical stance. It is not grounded in diagnosing a problem or reducing a person to a pattern of symptoms to be treated, like a medical approach might do. It is daring to genuinely meet in each moment, and trust that the person, not the therapist, is the expert in themselves. The PCA therapist is professionally trained to accompany the person as they become better experts in themselves.

In PCA training, learning to trust each person's abilities and their potential to find their way, as well as learning to examine one's own motivations to 'help', is absorbed not through being told what to do but through witnessing the power of choosing for oneself. It broadens what it means and feels like to be accepting of the moment, of the relationship, of yourself and of those around you. And this is not without sharp, dark, strong questions of yourself and each other – how else could it be genuine or worthwhile?

One of many misconceptions of PCA and its training is that they are 'nice'. They might be better described as quietly fierce. To know your own values and stand in them, in the training room, in the therapy room and in life, also demands the willingness to be open to and changed by another person's truths. In PCA training, the opportunity for this is often called the encounter group or group process, which is a form of unstructured time shared together. This is where beliefs and assumptions are examined through authentically relating with fellow group members. It is another way that people involved in PCA training are encouraged to explore how consistent their values are with how they relate, internally and with peers.

As a trainee, some of the most difficult times for me were when I was confronted with how I did not trust myself, and its impact on how I related with fellow group members. One of the most powerful experiences was when a peer compassionately met me when I felt most unworthy of love. This challenged me to receive care and to perceive myself as a whole person, which made a lasting impression on my sense of identity. As a trainer, it is my intention to meet each person human to human, and with the belief that I will undoubtedly learn through being with them. As a person, I have come to learn the richness of stepping into relationship, although it still challenges me, and I strive to appreciate what it might take for someone else to step into relationship too.

Questions for you to consider in deciding if PCA (or another modality) is for you

- What motivates you to consider therapeutic training, and how do you see yourself working with people?
- When a person walks into a room for therapy, what beliefs might shape the way you see them and their reasons for being there, before they say anything?
- How do you believe therapeutic healing happens?
- What are your assumptions about the power a professional role like 'therapist' holds?
- What might challenge you to trust other people?

Further reading recommendations from Ambika

Here are some key texts for the beginner and why I would recommend them:

Tony Merry has written several books about the PCA, all of which communicate philosophy and theory in plain language and with personable warmth. Of these, ***Learning and Being in Person-Centred Counselling*** is a classic that encapsulates a wide range of classical client-centred and contemporary person-centred approaches in an accessible way. A new, third edition of this book is now available, updated by Sheila Haugh (2020), published by PCCS Books.

The PCA literature has an expanding repertoire of texts called 'Handbooks', which are edited collections of chapters written by a variety of authors. One of the most recent that covers the historical roots, contemporary perspectives and future directions of PCA, including considerations of diversity and power, is edited by Colin Lago and Divine Charura: ***The Person-Centred Counselling and Psychotherapy Handbook: Origins, developments and current applications.*** It is published by Open University Press (2016).

Finally, one of the best resources I know for PCA training is Keith Tudor and Tony Merry's ***The Dictionary of Person-Centred Psychology*** (2006), also published by PCCS Books. It provides a wealth of information in its succinct definitions and signposting to the sources where you can find out more about PCA terminology. It is a valuable compass to help navigate the nuances of PCA language.

ACTIVITY

An invitation to explore your responses to reading about these four modalities

You've just been offered a lot of information about these four modalities. Where has it taken you?

You might write in prose, make mind-maps, draw or perhaps record your words on your phone).

- What have you learned that you didn't know before?
- Has any of the material challenged you to think differently about anything you thought you already knew?
- Has any of the material deepened your commitment to a particular modality?
- Might any of the material have changed your mind about what you might study?
- Which modality most appeals to you right now, at the moment of writing, if you sense into yourself and see what's happening for you?
- What else do you think you need to check out before enrolling for training in a particular modality?

Question 4:
Where might I study?

Alongside making decisions about what you want to study and at what level, you need to consider where you would like to study.

It may be that you need to study somewhere near your home or work, which is likely to limit your choices. It may be that you want to study a course that is only available at a few places in the UK. It may be that your choice is more open.

Whatever your situation, if there are open days for the place/s where you might like to study, or are going to study, we recommend attending them. Take someone with you if you can – it's always helpful to get a second opinion.

At the open day (or any other such opportunity – some colleges/institutes will make other arrangements for you if you are unable to get to the advertised open days), you're looking for a sense of the people and the place (which we'll explore further in Chapter 2).

Some questions that might be useful at an open day

Course brochures, other publicity and talks at the open day/event will, no doubt, answer some of what's below, but think about what else you might particularly want to know, using some of these questions, if it feels right for you. We've developed the questions with particular attention to equality, diversity, inclusion and wellbeing, alongside academic matters.

This primacy of equality, diversity and inclusion is embedded within the national standards for counselling and psychotherapy training, and very explicitly in the most recent (2022) *Subject Benchmark Statement: Counselling and psychotherapy* produced by the Quality and Assurance Agency for Higher Education (QAA).[1] The statement, which applies to undergraduate and postgraduate study across the UK, states that 'programme providers have an ethical commitment to safeguarding students and clients through inclusive training which welcomes different perspectives, cultures and values and promotes cultural competencies. It can take a diverse range of therapists to work with a diverse range of clients. It also takes a diverse range of trainers and educators to work with a diverse range of students/trainee counsellors. Diversity of staff can play a crucial part in the ethical commitment to safeguarding students and clients and education providers are strongly encouraged to be moving towards having a more representative group of trainers' (p.5).

We quote it at length as it is so important. Indeed, these standards offer other useful ideas for question for you to ask of the course providers, so if you are going for a course at undergraduate or postgraduate level, it may be worth reading them, to have a clear idea of what course providers are expected to offer and find out if the one you are considering matches up:

---

1. The QAA is an independent body funded by the higher education sector and responsible for monitoring and advising on standards and quality in UK higher education. The 2022 Benchmark Statement can be found on the QAA website, under 'Quality Code', at **www.qaa.ac.uk**

- Who are the academic staff? What do they teach (and, in some cases, research)? How do they talk about what you'll be doing together? How did they respond to your questions? If there was a presentation, was it engaging? Was it clear? Could you follow it?
- With which professional bodies are staff registered?
- Does the course itself sound good? Is it missing anything you find important?
- Is the course accredited by a professional body? Is it going to be accredited? Do its contents align to the requirements of a professional body if it is not accredited?
- How are training days organised? Do they have a routine?
- When are the breaks so you can take a rest?
- If you wanted to walk and talk for some activities, is that possible?
- If an activity is not for you, are there alternatives?
- Are learning materials provided in advance, and if so, how, and what do they look like?
- What are the expectations of you outside of the classroom – for example, hours of private study, personal therapy, clinical supervision (ratios of client hours to supervision hours), number of placements, number of placement hours?
- Would you be expected to find your own placements? Is there an in-house clinic where you could see clients? What happens if you can't find a placement straight away – would you be held back a year or asked to leave, even if the circumstances were out of your control? Is there an alternative route to a qualification if you can't find a placement? What sort of jobs would that lead to?
- What do the students on the course say? (There are often student ambassadors or current students attending at open days.) What do they like and dislike? Would they choose this course if they were starting again?
- Where is social justice covered in the curriculum for each year?
- What does the course do to make the environment welcoming to ethnic minoritised, LGBTQAI+, neurodiverse and disabled staff and students, and staff and students of varying ages, classes and with different life experiences?
- What proportion of staff and students are ethnic minoritised, LGBTAQI+, neurodiverse, disabled, from different age ranges, from different classes?
- What is the teaching accommodation like – lecture theatres, general purpose teaching rooms, rooms for small group work? Modern and purpose built? An old building? Temporary portacabins?
- Where are the staff offices and do the staff have any private space where they can meet with students for one-to-one tutorials?
- Are all the teaching premises and facilities accessible for disabled people?
- Can you move the furniture, and sit or lie on the floor?
- Is there space to move around when you wish without feeling awkward?

- Do the rooms have lighting that suits you? Can it be altered in any way?
- Will there be traffic noise outside, or other disturbances – such as smells coming from the kitchens?
- Can passers-by look in? Can anyone hear what's going on in the room?
- Does the environment feel safe for your own needs?
- What does the training provider do to improve access arrangements/make reasonable adjustments for disabled people?
- What is the library like? Is it well stocked? Is there a good range of relevant journals? What happens if a book isn't held in the training provider's library? Can you get loans from other libraries?
- How easy/difficult will it be for you to travel to the venues?
- If it's a university course and you're going to live there, what is the living accommodation like, and how far are you likely to be from the teaching accommodation?
- What is the reputation of the course provider? (For instance, undergraduate courses will have a score in the National Student Survey.)
- Would you be able to continue your studies at higher levels with the same training provider?
- What career support is there?

When you leave the open day, how do you feel about what you have seen and heard? Inspired? Energised? Something else? Make a note, and trust your process.

Some notes about interviews

You may be asked to attend an open day in order to take part in an interview. Or the interview might take place another time, in person, or on the phone/online. Sometimes there is no interview.

If you are asked to participate in an interview, plan ahead for it and – as far as you can – relax into it on the day.

Your planning could involve:

- researching the course (reading the course materials online)
- getting an idea of the modality you've applied to study (see above)
- being clear what counselling and psychotherapy are (it's not 'giving advice', for instance)
- thinking about how you feel about the course content (how would you feel about being in a goldfish bowl (see page 83)?
- reflecting on what you bring to the course from your life so far (remember that you're coming into the course as a whole person).

Question 5:

How much is my training likely to cost, and how could I fund it?

Studying counselling and psychotherapy is not cheap. We want to say this up-front, in Chapter 1, so that we proceed with honesty about a matter that will be the key factor if you *do* finally decide to step in to study counselling and psychotherapy. We will also suggest some ideas here about how you might fund your training.

What a fictional MA student spends in one month

We thought about asking a student to write about how much they'd spent on their studies, but financial matters can be quite sensitive, so Deborah and Peter Blundell (who you met earlier) collaborated in creating a fictional student, Alex. Alex is taking a postgraduate course and just beginning a placement.

What follows does not include the course fees. We left them out as they are a fixed amount and you can easily find them out by searching for 'fees' on your training provider's website.

Our focus here is the financial aspects of studying counselling and psychotherapy that you *may not realise* before you begin. We think this much more pertinent to your decision-making. People do not always know how much spending they are signing up for by deciding to step in to studying counselling and psychotherapy.

Alex is 32, single, and currently lives with their sister, to whom they pay rent at a slightly lower rate than in the commercial private sector.

They have a small inheritance from their grandad that will help cover some of their costs. They also have a loan, an overdraft, and a minimum-wage job, and usually work four days a week. They've just reached the point in their studies where they are looking for a placement. Alex also has a hidden disability that limits their energy levels, so they need regular breaks and rests and have to balance how much they do in a day.

Let's see what Alex is doing, experiencing, and spending this month.

Alex is a student member of BACP, which costs them £82 per year – about £6 a month (2022 rates – see **www.bacp.co.uk/membership/student-membership** for current rates).

Alex applies and is invited to an interview for their placement. They decide to take a minicab there and back as it's a complicated journey by public transport and they don't want to be exhausted already before they even get to the interview. This costs £20.

The interview goes well and Alex is offered the placement.

Alex has their weekly therapy session that evening, which costs £50 for a 50-minute session, or £200 a month. Alex's course requires 40 hours of personal therapy each academic year.

The next day, the placement co-ordinator rings, offering Alex three clients on two afternoons. Alex has to cancel one of their work days (they'd asked for one afternoon and one evening). This means they lose eight hours' pay, rather than the four they had expected. On their minimum wage (£8.91 an hour), this means Alex is now losing around £285 a month while they are doing the placement.

On the first afternoon at the placement, Alex is meant to meet two clients. Neither shows up. Alex calls them and discovers that the placement co-ordinator didn't tell them about the appointments. The next day, the third client cancels 10 minutes before their appointment, when Alex has already travelled in. Alex will spend £160 a month travelling to placements but, due to client cancellations, will sometimes record no client hours towards their required total.

Although Alex hasn't seen any clients, they still have to have supervision. The day before the first supervision session (with an external supervisor), Alex's friend texts to say he's dropping out of the course – he was going to share clinical supervision with Alex. Clinical supervision is now going to cost Alex £80 a month for the 1.5 hour session, until Alex can find someone else to be in a group with them. The bus ride is £2.50 each way, totalling £5 a month. The supervisor declares that an upcoming CPD is a 'must' and so Alex signs up, spending another £8 for the online workshop. The supervisor also suggests Alex takes out their own professional indemnity insurance, costing £60 a year, working out at £5 a month.

Alex's course takes place one day a week (a day they don't usually work anyway). The university is within walking distance, so there are no travel costs. Meals and drinks each week cost around £10, totalling £40 a month. The tutor of the module Alex is taking this term suggests four books that are key texts. Since everyone on the course wants copies of the books, it's not possible to borrow them, so Alex spends £80 on books this month.

Alex's old laptop finally breaks down and it's £400 for a new one. They also buy some software to help with dictating essays, as they find too much typing physically painful. The software costs around £100, and is brilliant. Spreading the cost of the laptop and software across the year comes to around £40 a month. The legacy from Alex's grandad is now gone.

Alex's total expenditure (not including rent, heat, light and food, or course fees) is £644, and they have lost £285 in earnings on top of that. And the costs easily mount up, and can be unpredictable.

Some of what Alex spent may not be relevant to you – for instance, you may not be required to have personal therapy. (You could also look into low-cost or free psychotherapy, so long as the therapist you see is acceptable to your training course: they may be required to be accredited with a particular professional body. The Free Psychotherapy Network offers free sessions for people on low incomes: **https://freepsychotherapynetwork.com**

Supervision costs can also be considerably cheaper than Alex's (bear in mind that high supervision costs do not necessarily indicate a higher level of skill from supervisors), and some placements do provide free supervision (although they will expect you to attend the supervision at the time it is offered, whether or not that fits with your timetable, meaning you may have to make a special trip into the office).

Alex might have asked for accommodations/reasonable adjustments from the university due to their physical health needs. But Alex is anxious not to cause a fuss – in their experience, disability is not always accommodated by training providers and Alex doesn't want to get labelled as a trouble-maker.

Further reading

You may have already heard of Christine Miserandino's spoon theory. You can read about it here: **https://butyoudontlooksick.com/articles/written-by-christine/the-spoon-theory**

Essentially, spoon theory is Miserandino's way of showing that, if your energy is limited, you only have a certain amount of energy/resources ('spoons') available to get through the day, so you must use them wisely. Alex's minicab journeys meant they didn't waste the spoons (energy) needed to perform well at the interview.

Funding

David May is Student Finance Manager at Nottingham Trent University. Here he offers some advice about paying for your studies.

Further education funding

Further education courses are often free, but it can depend on your age and personal circumstances. If you are returning to studies after some time away, perhaps in full-time employment, it's likely that you will need to pay for your course. There is government funding available, but it is dependent on the type of course you are studying. Most funding is likely to be in the form of a loan, often known as an Advanced Learner Loan, which will help you cover the costs of your tuition. You will usually need to cover your own living costs.

There are non-repayable grants and bursaries available, too. Availability and amounts differ depending on where in the UK you live. These are usually available to students from low-income households and usually only available to students of particular ages. You can find the latest information on the respective national Student Finance websites:

- England: **www.gov.uk/further-education-courses/financial-help**
- Northern Ireland: **www.nidirect.gov.uk/information-and-services/education**
- Scotland: **www.studentinformation.gov.scot/students/further-education/funding-your-course-at-college**
- Wales: **www.studentfinancewales.co.uk/further-education-funding**

Higher education funding

Undergraduate funding

The UK government provides statutory funding for undergraduate courses via the Student Loans Company. The rules differ for each of the UK nations as student funding is a devolved issue. You generally apply through the funding system where you usually live, rather than the location of your chosen higher education institution.

Tuition fee loans cover the cost of tuition fees. Maintenance loans, and grants if you're from Wales, contribute towards living costs. Entitlement to funding is dependent on meeting certain personal and course eligibility rules. These eligibility rules change from time to time – for example, the UK leaving the European Union has made it more difficult, though not impossible, for students from the EU and EEA to receive funding to study in the UK. The latest rules covering the eligibility rules can be found at:

www.gov.uk/student-finance/who-qualifies
www.ukcisa.org.uk/Information--Advice/Fees-and-Money/Government-Student-Support

The cost of tuition is usually covered by a Tuition Fee Loan in full. The amount of maintenance funding can vary significantly from person to person. It also differs depending on whether you live away from your parental home while you study. If you're under 25, maintenance is usually determined by a parental household income assessment. You are exempt from requiring an assessment if you can show that you are 'independent' – for example, if you are, or have been, married or in a civil partnership, have care of a child, are irreconcilably estranged from both parents or have supported yourself financially for three years prior to starting your course. If you're over the age of 25, you will always be classed as an independent student, and if you have a partner, their income will usually be taken into account in an income assessment. Some students may qualify for an extra amount of maintenance, known as 'special support'. You generally qualify if you have an underlying entitlement to certain state benefits – for example, if you are a lone parent or have a long-term health condition or disability.

The Student Loans Company also provides supplementary grants for eligible students with children or adult dependants. They will also contribute towards the costs of computer software, equipment and non-medical helpers (for example, a British Sign Language interpreter or specialist note-taker) for students with disabilities, long-term health conditions and specific learning differences.

Navigating the funding rules can be a minefield. Your chosen institution will have a team of specialist advisers that can help you determine your entitlement for funding and support you in making any applications.

Postgraduate funding

The UK government provides statutory funding to support you while you study certain postgraduate courses, such as a Master's (MA/MSc) degree. As with undergraduate courses, the rules differ in each of the countries in the UK. It is important to note that the funding is not as generous as that for undergraduate courses. You will need to consider how to meet any shortfall between the amount of funding you receive and your course and living costs. The personal eligibility rules are broadly similar to those of the undergraduate system. The course rules are more complex, however – there are significant differences between eligible courses in each national Student Finance service.

Most national funding providers pay postgraduate funding to you directly, in the form of a single loan. This means that you control what you do with the money. You could use it to support your living costs, or you could use it to contribute towards your tuition fees – or a bit of both.

If you have a disability, long-term health condition or specific learning difference, you can receive the Disabled Student's Allowance, which you can use to pay for software, equipment and non-medical helpers.

You can find the latest funding information on the respective national Student Finance websites:

- England: **www.gov.uk/funding-for-postgraduate-study**
- Northern Ireland: **www.studentfinanceni.co.uk/types-of-finance/postgraduate/northern-ireland-student**
- Scotland: **www.saas.gov.uk**
- Wales: **www.studentfinancewales.co.uk/postgraduate-finance/master-s**

Repaying your student finance funding

Most people repay their student loan through the pay-as-you-earn (PAYE) tax system. Repayments are taken either weekly or monthly, depending on how and when you get paid. A percentage of your salary will be taken at source in a similar way to income tax or national insurance payments. You can find the latest information on repayment regulations and the interest charged on student loans on the government's repayment website: **www.gov.uk/repaying-your-student-loan**

The latest funding information can be found at:

- England: **www.gov.uk/student-finance**
- Northern Ireland: **www.studentfinanceni.co.uk**
- Scotland: **www.saas.gov.uk**
- Wales: **www.studentfinancewales.co.uk**

Scholarships and bursaries from institutions

Most, if not all, colleges and universities offer scholarships and bursaries. As a general rule, a scholarship is usually a discount on tuition fees, and a bursary is usually extra money that is provided to you as a non-repayable grant to help towards your living costs. The administration of scholarships and bursaries can differ significantly between institutions. Some may be offered on a competitive basis – you must make an application to an awards panel; some you may simply qualify for because of your personal circumstances. For example, a bursary will be automatically provided to you if your household income is below a certain threshold. Some awards are given if you can show academic, sporting or musical excellence. There is usually extra financial support, too, for students from particular groups – for example, estranged students and care leavers, who do not have any parental support. When weighing up which institution to choose, do spend time researching the scholarships and bursaries on offer. Some can amount to several thousand pounds or may even cover your full tuition fees.

External scholarships, bursaries and grants

External organisations, charities and trusts offer scholarships, bursaries and grants too. The eligibility criteria for these are incredibly varied. Some may be offered if you are from

a particular geographic location, have worked – or come from a family who has worked – in a particular area of industry, or if you have a health condition or disability. There are several websites that can help you find this extra funding. Most will ask you to pay a fee to search their databases. In the first instance, you should always ask the funding advisers at your institution of choice to help you with your search, as they may already have access and can also help you avoid any common pitfalls. They are likely to help you be more successful in your quest, too. Government advice can be found here:
www.gov.uk/grant-bursary-adult-learners

Support for those in financial hardship

Universities and colleges usually have a scheme to support students in significant financial hardship. Originally, the main scheme was funded by the government. This was known as the Access to Learning Fund. Recently, funding has been provided by the institutions themselves. As such, the eligibility criteria from institution to institution may differ. The premise is usually the same, however: the purpose is to ensure that students can meet their essential outgoings while they study. Financial support is provided on a discretionary basis and is usually paid in the form of a non-repayable grant. It is often prioritised to those students who may struggle the most – for example, students with children, disabilities or without family support. You will be able to find further information about the discretionary hardship support offered at your institution of choice on its website. Further government advice can be found here:
www.gov.uk/extra-money-pay-university/university-and-college-hardship-funds

> **TAKEAWAY MESSAGES**
>
> This has been a long and detailed chapter, so thank you for staying with us.
>
> As you will have seen, there's a lot to think about.
>
> You'll be making choices about whether to study, and if so, at what level, which course and modality, whether you can afford to do so, and sources of funding. The takeaway messages from this chapter are:
>
> - Take your time.
> - Explore what's on offer.
> - Ask questions, reflect on the answers.
> - Trust your process.

The next chapter…

In the next chapter we consider the learning relationships you're likely to find as you step in to, or think about stepping in to, counselling and psychotherapy courses and as you look ahead to the assignments and assessments you will find there.

2

Learning relationships in counselling and psychotherapy courses

In the previous chapter, we took the view that, in order to step forwards as sure-footedly as possible, we needed to take a step back. So, rather than launching directly into *specific* study-skills advice, we started by looking at some of what we think you might need to know in order to decide *if* you want to step in to a counselling and psychotherapy course. We declared that process to be a part of study skills.

Chapters 2 and 3 take the view that either you have now decided (and the answer is yes), or you want to know some more about what a psychotherapy and counselling course might be like for you before you make your decision for sure (you could see the whole book like that, of course). So, we're alongside you as you step into the counselling and psychotherapy training room for the first time and as you make your way in this new setting – or as you imagine what it might be like to do so.

You'll notice that in this book we're continuing to move at a careful pace, not rushing, aiming to set the ground for your studies and assessments, recognising that – just like everything else in the world – they do not exist in a neat, boundaried vacuum, but that they have wide-ranging contexts and connections, and they merit careful and respectful thought. If or when you start to meet clients coming for therapy, you'll often encourage them to go at their own pace. Offer that care to yourself too, as you make significant study and career decisions.

This chapter will explore some selected aspects of the learning *relationships* with 1) people, 2) organisations, and 3) power and politics (the wider landscape for these relationships) – relationships that are or can be present when tackling counselling and psychotherapy courses/training and readying yourself for assignments. Chapter 3 will then explore some selected aspects of learning *processes* that are or can be present when tackling counselling and psychotherapy courses/training and assignments, such as group contracts and the types of learning with other people that they seek to cover.

In these two chapters, we're hoping to help prepare you for at least some of what you may find as you start – or think about starting – your own learning journeys. We also advise expecting the unexpected, because that's very much the hallmark of counselling and psychotherapy, from the training room to the therapy room. Being in relationship, whether with people or with processes, is full of complexity, and almost always surprising in some way.

Learning relationships with people in counselling and psychotherapy training

In this first section of the chapter, we begin by inviting you to look at some learning relationships with *people* in counselling and psychotherapy training.

We start with you:

- your learning relationship with yourself. This is so that you can prepare yourself (as well as you can) for the challenges, and fun, of psychotherapy and counselling training.

Then, we consider some learning relationships with other people – relationships that you're likely to engage in as you progress through your training:

- your peers, tutors, lecturers or trainers
- your personal therapist (if you have one)
- your placement co-ordinators
- your clients
- your clinical supervisors.

You as a learner

> **ACTIVITY**
>
> **An invitation to respond personally to some statements about learning, teaching and assessment**
> You may be reading this book rather warily, ahead of signing up for a Level 1 taster course to see if you'd like to progress further in studying it, having not been in a classroom for years. You may be starting at higher level but haven't studied for a while, or have never studied counselling and psychotherapy before. You may be further along in studying counselling and psychotherapy and wanting to reflect on what its learning, teaching and assessment means to you.
>
> Wherever you are, we think you can take something from what follows.

So – the invitation is to read through the following statements and put down some of your responses, either in prose or mind-maps, by drawing, or audio recording (whatever works best for you).

You might want to reflect on all of these statements. You might recoil from all of them. Whatever you do, can you ask yourself what's happening for you?

We'll then share some of our thoughts with you.

Statements
- Learning is a natural talent – you either have it or you don't, and if you have it you don't have to work at anything you study.
- If you take studying really seriously, you have no fun.
- Being in a classroom is about being talked to by the teacher or tutor and writing down as much as possible of what they say.
- You don't talk about yourself in class, and you don't write about yourself in essays – it's irrelevant, self-obsessed and nobody wants to hear it.
- Teachers and tutors know best – only their opinion of your work matters.
- If you ask questions, you'll be seen as a troublemaker.
- If you're asked to learn something from another student, the teacher isn't working hard enough. They're being paid to teach the class.

Our thoughts

Our shared feeling was that the statements made us anxious. We felt their harshness. Some were, to us, so reminiscent of being at school that we could almost smell the floor polish. If they took you back to school too, and not in a good way, remember that most of us were at school a long time and it's no wonder that we often think back to it (and often the harsh bits of it) when we think of learning, even when we've done other courses (at work, at college, at university). Carl Rogers (1980, p.69) said ominously of the educational system: 'the teacher is the possessor of power, the student the one who obeys'.[1]

Please be reassured (we hope this is reassuring) that counselling and psychotherapy courses are going to be very different from the harsh bits of school (if that was your experience) – and very different, in fact, to many other learning contexts you may have experienced. Rogers continues, talking about person-centred learning:

> The leader or a person who is perceived as the authority figure in the situation is sufficiently secure within himself and in his relationship to others that he experiences an essential trust in the capacity of others to think for themselves. (1980, p.70)

---

1. Rogers, C. (1980). *Personal power*. Constable. An accessible, congruent, deeply political reading, whatever modality you're studying.

Even now, this is a radical stance. Take a moment to hear what Rogers is saying.

Whether person-centred or not, learning counselling and psychotherapy isn't about being told (by anyone), 'Here is the only way to be a counsellor and psychotherapist and this is exactly what you must learn and do.' Instead, it's, 'Here are some opportunities to explore who you are becoming as a psychotherapist and counsellor within your modality.' As such, you will be encouraged to ask questions, including challenging ones, of yourself, each other and tutors/lecturers/trainers, to work towards your own understandings. You won't be seen as a 'trouble-maker' for asking questions, but you may sometimes hear challenging feedback about 'how' you have asked. There's freedom here, but there's also intense work, both academic and personal.

You can and will talk and write about your own life and experiencing in some parts of the training – but only as far as feels right for you at that time, and whether it 'feels right' is something you won't always know until you've already left your 'window of tolerance' (that is, the limit of what is currently manageable for you). It isn't irrelevant and self-obsessed, it's part of bringing yourself, exploring yourself – the very basis of training to be ready to meet clients. In some of your work, you'll be asked directly to reflect on yourself. Check with your tutors whether the essay they're asking you to write can be written in the first person and can include your experiencing and your lived experiences, and how and to what extent. And never underestimate, for you and others, what that will take – to bring yourself genuinely to the work.

You may attend academic lectures in your training. In a university context, this may be in a large lecture theatre. In smaller training environments, you may remain in the same classroom where you do the rest of your learning. Nowadays, lectures often (but not always) involve interactive work, rather than you just listening/making notes, and the availability of PowerPoint slides and lecture-capture technology (even more widespread and polished since online learning became the only option during the Covid-19 pandemic) means that you don't have to write down everything a lecturer says or it will be lost forever.

However, most of your learning on counselling and psychotherapy courses is likely to be in smaller group exploration with others. You'll often sit in a circle or semi-circle, able to see each other, rather than in rows, all facing the teacher/tutor/trainer. The arrangement of the furniture says it all: you'll be learning from everyone. We all have something to teach (and learn from) each other, not just the tutors/lecturers/trainers. In encountering this way of working, we may be troubled: it's not what we expected or what we think we paid for, perhaps. We may ask, who is responsible for this learning? The answer is that we all are.

Likewise, rather than just being assessed by tutors/lecturers/trainers, in counselling and psychotherapy training you will also assess yourself, you will assess other trainees and other trainees will assess you. There will be assessment by clients – written feedback questionnaires as well as in-the-room responses to you. Clinical supervisors will evaluate you throughout your clinical placement work and write reports on your progress. So will placement providers, but less fully because they know you less well. It sounds like a lot of people assessing you, and it is. Everyone's assessment has a place in helping you ready yourself for relationship with others. It doesn't mean you have to agree with what anyone says about you, but you do need to hear it, and that may be hard at times.

How you'll feel about these sorts of learning relationships with yourself and others is something to reflect on. If it feels strange – and we appreciate that it might, particularly at the start – you'll need to work with that, at your own pace, within your own abilities, seeking support as you need it. Counselling and psychotherapy training is like this, although it should always be open to development and growth, particularly in how it responds to the equality, diversity, inclusion and wellbeing of participants.

After writing the harsh statements you just read and responded to, we then simply contradicted that harshness, wanting to encourage you in gently. But *just* contradicting the harshness didn't sit comfortably with us. (We're committed to showing you our workings – something very important in becoming/being a therapist, which is why we're explaining this.) There has to be both care and challenge in psychotherapy and counselling training. Meeting the other in the therapy room is about being in relationship; it's full of not-knowing, and anything could happen. Your training is aiming to ready you for that.

Finally, we don't see successful study as about having/not having 'natural talent'. Our view is that you can learn how to study successfully. To study psychotherapy and counselling seriously, we feel we have to be able to find the fun as well as the challenge/purpose – that's what we hope this book will, ultimately, offer.

ACTIVITY

An invitation to respond personally to some statements about training as a psychotherapist/counsellor

In the previous activity, we started with general statements about learning, teaching and assessment. Then, in sharing our thoughts about those statements, we started to weave psychotherapy and counselling training into the exploration.

The following statements take us on a step further. They are statements we think might be useful to you going into counselling and psychotherapy training.

The statements are not offered as an outline of what an 'ideal student' looks like and does. It's unlikely that anyone is an 'ideal student'. Instead, the statements are intended to name, bring together and hold the complexity of the world you're entering, with its new learning relationships.

So – the invitation here is to see how far any of these statements resonate with you as you read them. How would you rewrite any of them (even by just changing one word)? What might be missing from the list, from your perspective?

Put down some of your thoughts, either in prose, mind-maps, by drawing, or audio recording (whatever works best for you).

Statements
- I have enough of an idea for now of what the course is about, and I'll keep feeling my way through it. I appreciate that I cannot know everything before I start.
- As far as I know, doing the course fits in okay with my other commitments (I can make time to do it, even though this may be difficult at times).

- I have some/most of what I need (as far as I know now) to do this course (such as a space in which to study and enough money to pay for my studies).
- I have ideas about why I'm doing the course (such as developing transferable skills, making a career change, getting an award at a higher level of study). I think my ideas will develop as I do, and I'm open to that happening.
- Most of the time I enjoy learning about a variety of subjects – I don't see 'studying' as a boring chore.
- I like the idea of studying counselling and psychotherapy – it's attractive to me in some ways that I can identify.
- I like reading/listening to audio books; I don't see this as a boring chore.
- I like reading/listening to audio books about counselling and psychotherapy – I've enjoyed the reading/listening I've done so far in ways that I can identify.
- I'm likely to follow some of my own leads for reading/listening (for instance, by looking at the reference lists in articles), rather than just reading/listening to what's on the reading list. I want, to some extent, to find my own way.
- Most of the time, I like talking about academic ideas/practical matters with other students/tutors and hearing what people have to say (I know I don't need to be always speaking to show my engagement).
- I'm ready to be challenged by other people about my academic/practical ideas. I'm ready to see other points of view.
- I can hold my own carefully considered opinions supported by academic literature, even if others don't share my opinions.
- I generally enjoy writing or recording my thoughts – I don't see it as a boring chore.
- I want to improve my writing/recording of my thoughts – it's exciting to learn more.
- I might want to be a published author one day (maybe I am already!).
- I'm going to try to be present in group work with others.
- Although it is anxiety provoking, I am ready to be challenged by other people in a group.
- I'm prepared to be honest about how I am feeling (while being aware that there may be times when I don't feel safe enough).
- When I speak my truth, I will hold care for others as much as I can (while recognising I cannot always know the impact of my words).
- I tend to know when I've reached my limit. I tend to know when to take breaks. I can find things to do that help me switch off.
- I'm going to really try to be self-caring while I'm on this course as I know already that it's going to bring challenges.
- I think I can bring something to this course, as well as gain from it (my lived experiences, my personal identity, my way of being, who I am).

Learning relationships with other people

The first sub-section was headed 'You as a learner', but other people have already been present, because we as individuals are always and inevitably interconnected to some extent with other people.

So we turn now to look more directly at you in learning relationships with others.

Here's a reminder of who we'll meet here.

We begin with peers and tutors/lecturers/trainers in the classroom. Then, we will look at your learning relationship with your personal therapist (if you have one). After that, we will move on to some relevant relationships if you are on a course (now or in the future) that requires you to meet clients – relationships with counselling co-ordinators at placements, with clients, and with clinical supervisors.

Learning relationships with peers and tutors

As we'll describe more fully in Chapter 3, you'll find lots of learning in groups, experiential work, personal development work and academic discussions in a counselling and psychotherapy classroom – lots of 'being together'. Even when the immediate, apparent focus might be academic, there will be elements of the experiential and of personal development in the group. Sometimes material and interactions will flow over from earlier parts of the day, or previous days, where the group did experiential or personal development work. In some training organisations, a group will spend their whole time together; in other training organisations there will be different group formations during a training day, meaning that material that cannot be shared for reasons of confidentiality will be present for some members, bringing different complexities.

All this focus on the experiential, personal development and academic work with the personal intertwined, all in groups, means that, in contrast to some subjects you might have studied before, everyone (tutors/lecturers/trainers and trainees) will be encountering each other all the time – to some extent, at least, *as part of why we are there* – as both lovely and fallible human beings in the room. The training will never be detached from us as people. It is not meant to be. It is an intense process, to put it mildly, for all concerned.

That there are likely to be both intense highs and intense lows – and everything in between (including boredom) – is something we think most people aren't sufficiently aware of when they go into counselling and psychotherapy courses/training, even if they do expect their studies to bring self-awareness, perhaps including self-awareness of parts of themselves that they may be less content with. We wanted to make you aware, as you step in, that you must ready yourselves for a continuum of intensity. To reflect on why counselling and psychotherapy training might need to be intense, and why intensity is (to some extent) to be welcomed, look back at Ambika Erin Connelly talking about encountering the other (Chapter 1).

We've said that tutors/lecturers/trainers are alongside trainees in encounter. Of course, though, there will always be a power imbalance between you, the students, and your tutors/lecturers/trainers. Tutors/lecturers/trainers mark your work and attend Award/Progression Boards where decisions are made about, for instance, students' progression (or not) on a course, and what qualification they achieve. They are required to play a part in upholding standards for a demanding profession. (Note, though, that tutors/lecturers/trainers do not make the rules that govern Award/Progression Boards, and they do not control the regulations that govern so many educational processes, such as decisions about giving students extra time to complete an assignment.) It would be wrong, then, to regard tutors/lecturers/trainers as your peers (some may become your friends after the course, but not during it –you may 'get on' with one or more tutors/lecturers/trainers to varying extents).

But – with these matters understood – we are all there together in the training room, encountering each other, learning from each other. This may be very different from your previous educational experiences where teachers/lecturers/tutors may have been more detached and less likely to have brought themselves and their personal experiences into the room. Counselling and psychotherapy training is a place where you should be able to show curiosity about why those teaching/training you said or did particular things, if you are troubled by them, pleased by them, or just want to know more. Again, this may be very different from your previous learning relationships with teachers/tutors/trainers.

When you start to get a sense of the demands of being a tutor, you might also hold in awareness that many/most tutors/lecturers/trainers (with exceptions) will generally be trying to do their best, even though they cannot always succeed for everyone all of the time, and this is sometimes for reasons outside their immediate control. It is (or should be) part of counselling and psychotherapy training to be aware of the impact of the work on everyone concerned. We are all human beings.

Among peers in counselling and psychotherapy training, some very close friendships and relationships can arise, partly because of the depth of what is shared there. Sometimes we might find that we like people too much to be able to give them constructive feedback. There is also no rule that says we must get on with everyone on the course. That we might think there is such a rule is just part of a societal stereotype that counsellors are 'nice' people (fluffy and warm people who do no more than listen and nod sympathetically). Counsellors can be all sorts of things. We might have different views, beliefs and values from others in the room. We might fall out with peers and/or tutors/lecturers/trainers we used to like, or suddenly see the humanity in someone we previously hated. Someone might always remind us of another person we like or don't like. There's going to be material here to work with, to ready yourself to meet whoever your clients happen to be. There's a purpose in sensing how you interact with the variety of other people that training presents to you. That really is something to hold in mind as you take part in your course.

Sometimes, learning relationships (between students, between tutors/lecturers/trainers and students, and vice versa) will involve discrimination, harassment and microaggressions. It's not different from what happens in the everyday world, but here it is played out in an intense setting with educational/career consequences intertwined with personal ones. Phoenix, an interviewee in Deborah's study of survivors of sexual violence training as psychotherapists (Lee, 2020, p.116),[2] encapsulates some of what we are pointing to. Phoenix said:

---

2. Lee, D.A. (2020). Survivors of sexual violence training as psychotherapists in the UK. In Lee, D.A. & Palmer, E. (Eds.). *#MeToo: Counsellors and psychotherapists speak about sexual violence and abuse.* PCCS Books.

> We had been [studying] trauma… I sort of came into the group talking about it from a personal experience… I could have just sat there and wrote it in my journal, but what's the point?… There's people in our room… I know that it's been uncomfortable for them to hear on two different levels… because they don't want to listen to that sort of thing… and because it's happened to me and not them… Almost like they are pissed off they haven't got that much drama… I saw my supervisor, the words I used were… emotionally raped.

When we read situations like the one Phoenix describes, where her peers in training were so hostile, we can see that this will impact on people's experiences of a counselling and psychotherapy course, and being assessed, particularly by peers who have behaved in discriminatory ways. There can also be a loss of trust in those who have not done what was felt to be needed – particularly tutors/lecturers/trainers.

Tutors/lecturers/trainers need to be alert to discrimination, harassment and microaggressions, and ready to intervene. They may be working with a sense that difficulties may be worked through, but bullying, harassment and microaggressions are not part of the process of counselling and psychotherapy courses. Staff training and supervision need to centralise social justice. That social justice is not always centralised is a consequence of a) the limited exploration of social justice from counselling and psychotherapy training tutors have themselves taken, and b) the ubiquity of discrimination, harassment and microaggressions in our wider society. In a profession like ours, it is vital that there is change across the board.

We consider some ways forward later in this chapter, and in the next chapter we start by considering how far a group contract (an outline of what a group wants its learning experience to be like) may help in holding the complex relational work that must necessarily take place in counselling and psychotherapy classrooms. Our contention is that reflection on discrimination, harassment and microaggressions must be part of group contracting.

A learning relationship with your personal therapist (if you have one)

As we saw in Chapter 1, if you're on a UKCP-accredited course, you'll be required to be in personal therapy. BACP-accredited courses and NCS-accredited courses require personal development opportunities, but personal therapy isn't mandatory.

What this means for you in practice is that, if you are on a BACP/NCS-accredited course, or a course that is not (or not yet) accredited, you might be required by your course to have personal therapy (a small amount or many hours each year), or you might be required to acquire your personal development by another means, such as personal development groups – which will be described in Chapter 3.

If you are in personal therapy that is required by your course, your therapist will be asked to certify the hours that you have attended. Your personal material discussed in sessions will not be shared with your training providers. It is confidential (other than the usual caveats), just as it is for any client. A therapist you see while in training is not there to attest (or not) to your fitness to be a counsellor/psychotherapist. But if you are in training, you may wish to check who your therapist's clinical supervisor/s is/are, so that you can be sure you will not, at some point, be taught by someone who knows your personal material. Your safety, your boundaries matter.

We've said that some courses will require personal therapy and some will not. So, it is useful to say that there are certainly questions, disagreements and tensions among psychotherapists and counsellors about whether personal therapy should be required of trainees – arguments that are beyond the scope of this book, but that we note in passing so that you might consider where you stand. Where you stand might change as you make your way through your course and beyond it. David Murphy and colleagues' research (2018)[3] offers interesting perspectives on this.

What we will say, without taking sides, is that, in our opinion, when you are in personal therapy you learn a good deal about what it means to be a client and what it means to be a therapist. You can use this in tackling counselling training and course assignments. You may see practice that you'd love to be able to emulate, and practice that you hope you'd never inflict on your own clients (and everything in between) – maybe even from the same therapist. We would also say – as we're seeing already in this book – that counselling and psychotherapy training has its very challenging times and it is governed by confidentiality – meaning that you can't talk about personal material belonging to other people outside the training room. So having a therapist allows you to process what's happening in a setting that doesn't break confidentiality.

> ### ACTIVITY
>
> **An invitation to reflect on personal therapy**
>
> If you are in personal therapy while you are training (or you have been in the past), take some time to reflect on and write about/draw/record what the process is (or was) like for you and what it brings to mind now as you think about becoming a counsellor or psychotherapist yourself.
>
> - What does it tell you personally about being a client?
> - What does it tell you personally about being a therapist?
>
> If your experience of therapy was/is a harmful one, or less than ideal, which can certainly happen, you may choose to do this carefully, or come back to it later when you feel ready, or not do it at all.
>
> Below you will find two further readings that we recommend. Irvin Yalom is a very respected psychotherapist, and *The Gift of Therapy* is a book many people read early on in their studies and find inspiring. Anna Sands (a pseudonym) writes of being harmed by her encounter with psychotherapy, as well as how it helped her.

---

3. Murphy, D., Irfan, N., Barnett, H., Castledine, E. & Enescu, L. (2018). A systematic review and meta-synthesis of the qualitative research into mandatory personal psychotherapy during training. *Counselling and Psychotherapy Research*, *18*(2), 199–214.

Further readings

Sands, A. (2000). *Falling for therapy: Psychotherapy from a client's point of view.* Palgrave.

Yalom, I. (2003). *The gift of therapy: An open letter to a new generation of therapists and their patients.* Piatkus.

Learning relationships with clinical placement co-ordinators

If your course asks you to meet clients, you will do so at a placement. The placement will be in a service that has been approved by your training provider to offer clinical experience to its students.

We're going to begin this section by looking at some aspects of learning relationships with placement co-ordinators that get little published attention but we know people *do* encounter – i.e. less-than-good learning relationships.

We state up-front that, while we hope none of what we cover here is or will be your experience, securing a placement and being line-managed by placement co-ordinators are not always straightforward and comfortable matters. We started to touch on this in Chapter 1, when we talked about Alex's experience of being allocated clients and the placement co-ordinator not informing clients of their appointments.

Some courses will have their own placement arrangements (an in-house clinic, perhaps), so looking for an external placement will not be necessary, at least at first (you may be required, or you may want, to experience more than one placement, or to volunteer in one or more particular areas of counselling).

Where that's not the case, some trainees get the first external placement they go for (as we allowed fictional Alex to do). Then the placement co-ordinator allocates them a client within days, and they're off – accruing hours towards their qualification.

For others, it's not like that.

One of us (Deborah) made many applications for placements. Many placement co-ordinators never replied at all. Some rejection letters arrived the day after the application had been sent (never with any feedback). One placement offered an interview in a faraway place, then a placement, but was never heard from again. By the time she secured a placement, some of her fellow trainees had been seeing clients for three months.

Once underway, some placement co-ordinators were not respectful of Deborah's full-time work – wanting attendance at peer group meetings and CPD events, asking her to come into the office just to be read a potential client's assessment form, offering clients who could only come on different days, or who wanted to come fortnightly…

What we take from experiences of difficulties securing placements, and difficulties with some placement co-ordinators (Deborah also had good placements and great relationships with placement co-ordinators!) is that there are lots of trainees looking for placements and there is limited time for placement co-ordinators, who are often working part-time, to engage with applicants. Placement co-ordinators are doing a highly responsible job, matching trainees with clients and holding the possibility that something might go badly wrong. Not all placement co-ordinators will have experience, or sufficient experience, of managing people, including trainees.

If you find your relationships with clinical placement co-ordinators tense, you may want to check in with yourself about what this means for you: is it telling you anything you need to know (beyond the structural issues just outlined)? Is the situation prompting connections with your past, for instance? There can be some learning from tricky relationships with placements co-ordinators. Try to take up all opportunities for reflection that your learning relationships offer to you, even where this is challenging. It is part of personal development.

At their best, your relationships with clinical placement co-ordinators will support your training journey. At the least, they're providing you with the opportunity to see clients, and they're allocating you clients, some of whom will appear, with their permission, in your course assignments. We can see care for trainees here, alongside care for clients; this is ethical practice. It's so important that trainees are not asked to meet a client who is – in some way – needing something that the trainee is not yet able to offer. That can cause harm to the client and can harm the trainee's confidence and thus their ability to meet other clients, impacting their studies and their learning journey. A good clinical placement co-ordinator will be able to sense who might work well with whom, as Dwight Turner explains here. We'll meet him again in Chapter 5, as a clinical supervisor assessing trainees.

Experiences

Dr Dwight Turner is a UKCP registered clinical supervisor, as well as a psychotherapist and a writer interested in intersectionality, difference and diversity. Dr Turner has assessed trainees to work in clinical placements, so we asked him to talk to you about how he works as a clinical placement co-ordinator.

When I'm assessing trainees to work with clients, I consider the level of experience of the trainee: what year of their course are they on, how are they finding the work thus far, what placements or voluntary work have they done already. This method of trying to get to know the trainee helps me to gather some knowledge, intuitive and literal, about their strengths, and allows me to better pitch the right clients for them to work with, given their level of experience.

Further reading

For a more detailed description of securing and working in a clinical placement, we suggest you read:

Oldale, M. & Cooke, M.J. (2015). *Making the most of your counselling and psychotherapy placements.* **Sage.**

Learning relationships with clients

In a section on relationships with clients, we could easily start talking with you 'about counselling', and digress for thousands of words from the main purpose of our book, which is to look at tackling counselling training and course assignments. We've managed to hold back from that, and suggest you instead look at another of Pete's books, *First Steps in Counselling*.[4]

Tackling counselling and psychotherapy training at Level 3 and above and doing your course assessments *does*, of course, involve learning relationships with clients. We are all people, and we are all impacted by and learning from each other, as two individuals in the room, all the time we are together and long afterwards. Many in our profession know this. You will, though, at some time or other, certainly more often than is acceptable, find an 'us' and 'them' narrative in some placements and among some therapists, some supervisors and probably in quite a lot of books/articles you'll read, to one extent or another (even up-to-date books/articles). We state, unequivocally, that we see this is disrespectful and wrong. Let's draw attention to some ways of seeing differently.

> **ACTIVITY**
>
> **An invitation to read and reflect about 'borderline personality disorder'**
> 'Borderline personality disorder' ('BPD') is a contested diagnosis (that's why we have placed it in quote marks). People (largely, but not exclusively, women) who are given this diagnosis are too often treated very badly – without compassion and human dignity – by people working in mental health.
>
> Here are two online articles by Rachel Rowan Olive about her experience of this:
>
> - Olive, R.R. (2019, September 16). We can discuss mental health care responses, but leave my personality out of it. *Mental Health Today*.
>   www.mentalhealthtoday.co.uk/blog/diagnosis/we-can-discuss-mental-health-care-responses-but-leave-my-personality-out-of-it
>
> - Olive, R.R. (2018, November 1) The complaints I never made. *Mental Health Today*.
>   www.mentalhealthtoday.co.uk/blog/awareness/the-complaints-i-never-made
>
> Have a look at them if this feels right for you.
>
> As you tackle your training and course assignments, you will hear and read disrespectful comments about people coming for therapy – about particular personal identities, psychiatric diagnoses, life events, survival strategies. This is one reason why we cannot stress enough the importance of taking seriously the reading/listening lists for your course. You cannot know how to counter what feels wrong (or perhaps even know it should feel wrong, or why) if you have not engaged widely

---

4. Sanders, P., Williams, P.J. & Rogers, A. (2021). *First steps in counselling: An introductory companion* (5th ed.). PCCS Books.

with current discussions and debates in this arena. Taking reading and reflection seriously in the field of counselling and psychotherapy is never just about passing assignments. People's very lives may be at stake.

Further reading

You might like to take a look at *Asylum*, the radical mental health magazine: **https://asylummagazine.org/**

You might also like to explore the Soteria Network's aims, values and ways of working: **www.soterianetwork.org.uk/**

Learning relationships with clinical supervisors

When you start seeing clients, you will also start seeing a clinical supervisor (or more than one clinical supervisor, if you give your time at more than one placement and those placements require you to meet with their own in-house supervisors). This will be a relationship that you will not have had before (although you may have had experience of relationships like it).

Experiences

Let's hear from experienced clinical supervisor Caz Binstead about her thoughts on the learning relationship between trainee and supervisor. Caz is also co-lead at #TherapistsConnect, an online platform with a thriving Twitter and Instagram community, which trainees and qualified therapists can join just by using the hashtag. She is founder of its first project, #TraineeTalk – a weekly facilitated discussion group for trainees to explore themed topics (mindful of confidentiality).

I've been asked to write to you as an experienced clinical supervisor of trainees and newly qualified therapists. Indeed, I specialise in the transition from student to private practice and have written for BACP on setting up in ethical and successful private practice (including looking in depth at appropriate use of supervision). You can find some of my work at: www.bacp.co.uk/news/news-from-bacp/blogs/2021/29-july-inspirational-private-practice-tool kit

Supervision is a core element of being a therapist, a core element you'll first encounter as a trainee as soon as you begin seeing clients. Supervision is a regular, consistent, facilitated space where the therapist – trainee or qualified (you have supervision through your whole career) – can explore their work in an open way, with an experienced practitioner.

As a student entering supervision, a simple way to think about it is that supervision focuses on the learning and development of the supervisee, is rooted in best-practice principles related to ethical work/decision-making and accountability, and also provides a nurturing, supportive and reflective space.

You are expected to prepare before a supervision session, to identify issues you wish to explore, and then, in the room, present client work of your choosing, and certainly to raise any concerns you have, for instance in relation to risk (very importantly, make sure you know how to contact your supervisor in an emergency). You and your supervisor explore your work together, in a way appropriate to your modality, level or longevity in practice. You may find yourself in a supervision group rather than a dyad, where this process will then be opened out to all participants (with the supervisor as the overall facilitator).

In my experience, often the best ethical and creative work comes from the supervision space that provides an environment of safety, where openness and honesty and flourish. However, supervisees who are trainees might find this difficult, for a number of reasons, not least that their training institutions require the supervisor to complete mid-term and/or final reports about them. From worries around perceived mistakes in the work to feeling vulnerable if they share personal experiences and feelings, for the trainee, supervision may not always feel, or indeed be, straightforward.

An important part of clinical supervision for me, then, is the work that the supervisor and supervisee do together to try and create the safe and trusting space that is needed for client material to be adequately reflected on. Tending to the space via informal and formal reviews can foster curiosity about the process of supervision, the supervisor's way of working, any learning needs or style of the supervisee, as well as the relational dynamics between both parties. As a student, you may be restricted in whether you have a choice of supervisor, as many supervisors are employed in-house by placement providers or on training courses. So it is important that the supervision space is one where a functional working alliance can be both established and regularly reviewed.

If you're already thinking beyond your training or are reading this as a newly qualified therapist entering private practice, it is good to become accustomed to the benefits of supervision. Your supervisor really does have the potential to be your ace card, given the likely isolation of therapists in private practice and the levels of responsibility involved in running a private therapy practice.

If you are choosing a supervisor, either as a trainee (bearing in mind any professional registration requirements associated with your course), or once you are in private practice (you may wish to change supervisors at various points in your career, as you grow and develop), I would recommend checking out some of the well-known therapy directories, which usually have a search option for qualified supervisors. Discuss your needs and wants with your potential supervisor to determine compatibility, and perhaps try out two or three initial sessions with different people before you choose.

Supervision will accompany you throughout your career, and the best advice I can give you is to approach it – as with anything new – with curiosity and gentleness. Embrace learning how to be a supervisee, as much as you do learning how to be a therapist!

Further reading

Shohet, R. & Shohet, J. (2020). *In love with supervision: Creating transformative conversations.* **PCCS Books.** The Shohets are key authors in the field of supervision, and this book encapsulates much of their thinking and practice.

> **ACTIVITY**
>
> **An invitation to explore Twitter**
> If you're on Twitter, have a look for #TherapistsConnect and #TraineeTalk. Might you want to join in, or watch what happens? There's lots of learning available via this online forum.

Learning relationships with organisations

Now we turn to your relationship with some organisations you'll encounter during your counselling and psychotherapy training.

Here are the organisations we will discuss:

- your training provider – rights and responsibilities
- professional bodies (whether or not you are a student member) – with a particular emphasis on ethics.

Learning relationships with your training provider

Many training providers take your rights seriously by providing a contract. It is a list of what they promise to provide and what they expect from you. If you haven't been given such a document, check it out with your course team. A contract is important in showing you that you have responsibilities, and you have rights too – that you're working in partnership with your training provider.

Training providers will have a range of policies and procedures, some of which you'll probably only become aware of if you need them. If you are encountering discrimination or harassment from any member of the learning community, there should be complaints and grievance policies and procedures you can use to report your concerns about what has happened/is happening and seek a response. Some matters can be responded to relationally without the need for formal procedures.

Courses may have community meetings – informal places where students can encounter each other and explore what's happening. Your course may elect student representatives (and some modules may choose to have module representatives). Student representatives, evidently, take the role of representing their fellow students. They will attend course committees – places where all staff (academics and professional services staff – such as librarians and careers consultants) associated with the course meet to discuss course-related matters and give feedback on behalf of the cohort they're representing. You might yourself want to volunteer for such a role. It should not be too time consuming. If you are the course representative, take care to report back positives and constructive comments, and to be clear about how many of your colleagues are raising any issue you take to a course committee. If you wish to raise issues about the practice of a particular staff member, you should usually have already discussed it with the person concerned and you should also speak with your course leader before the committee. A course committee is not a place for shaming individuals. There are better ways to proceed, particularly for students entering counselling and psychotherapy.

All students will be asked to be involved in quality assurance and enhancement mechanisms via student feedback questionnaires (and for students on undergraduate and postgraduate degrees, external surveys such as the National Student Survey and the Postgraduate Taught Experience Survey respectively).

> **ACTIVITY**
>
> **An invitation to research bias in student evaluations of learning and teaching**
> Before you fill in module and course questionnaires (which you can usually do anonymously), or object to the way of being of a particular member of staff, you could search online for research showing how bias enters into students' evaluations of members of staff who are not white, male, heterosexual, middle-class, cis-gendered, able-bodied and neurotypical. We may think we judge fairly, but we all live in a society with social injustice woven deeply into its fabric.
>
> What we're saying overall is, let's be respectful of each other as we study and work in counselling and psychotherapy – a profession where we must be respectful of the people who will come to meet us (clients). The learning journey is never separate from its destination.
>
> This never means accepting harassment, bullying and microaggressions.

Learning relationships with professional bodies

Depending on your course, its level, and whether or not it is accredited, you may be required – or you may wish – to join one or more of the professional bodies in the field of counselling and psychotherapy.

Joining professional bodies brings membership benefits to students (such as access to professional development support and journals and, once you are qualified, registration), and it brings another expense (look back to Chapter 1 and the section on costs).

Whether or not you're a member of any of the professional bodies, you will be asked throughout your studies to read and reflect on their ethical codes and the ethical code of your university/training organisation.

Codes of ethics are not just rules you have to follow. They should be read and reflected on. Like everything else in the field of counselling and psychotherapy, it should not be mechanical or straightforward.

We encourage you to really engage with ethical codes, interrogating the meanings of everything you can find in them. In this way, you find out where you stand and why you stand there. You can also see, if you keep some notes from time to time, if and how your views evolve.

The UKCP Code of Ethics and Professional Practice can be found on its website at: **www.psychotherapy.org.uk**

The BACP Ethical Framework for the Counselling Professions can be found here: **www.bacp.co.uk/events-and-resources/ethics-and-standards/ethical-framework-for-the-counselling-professions/**

The National Counselling Society Code of Ethics can be found here: **https://nationalcounsellingsociety.org/about-us/code-of-ethics**

Further reading

Ethics is a huge topic that has filled many whole books. A full discussion is beyond the scope of this book. Try one of the most recent:

Reeves, A. & Bond, T. (2021). *Standards and ethics for counselling in action* (5th ed.). Sage.

Writing about clients on social media

We've decided to look at ethical learning relationships with clients by considering what we post on social media – how learning relationships can be compromised. We chose this as it is so important and seemingly so poorly understood.

Scenario 1

You've just seen your first client, and it was great! That was after months of searching for a placement. You also failed your ethics essay last week, so success in one area, at least, is absolutely thrilling.

You're waiting for the bus home, scrolling through Twitter. You see a few therapists are active online and you think – or you don't think… You want to tell someone what's happened. It hasn't happened until someone knows, and someone puts a 'like' on it.

So, you type out: 'I saw my first client today, and it was fabulous! She said she'd never had a therapist as good as me! And it was MY FIRST TIME!'

The bus turns the corner, so you push your phone into your bag, where it buzzes pleasingly as you hop on the bus. You're definitely getting likes, even if you can't see them yet.

Scenario 2

You've done 100 client hours now. It took ages. You're tired out.

Today you were allocated a client who said she'd had a really bad therapist last year who didn't respect her boundaries. You felt really angry, as all the therapists you know – especially you – are trying their best, particularly trainees who are rushing from one commitment to the next. You managed not to say anything.

As you lie in your bed that night, unable to sleep, you open up a Facebook group for therapists that you've recently joined. People often type there to ask advice about clients. It's peer supervision, isn't it? It must be, since so many therapists post.

So, in the dark, you type out: 'Colleagues, I had a client who I think really hates therapists. It made me feel so angry. She said she'd had her boundaries disrespected. We're just doing our best. I couldn't connect with her because I was feeling so angry. I don't know what to do next. Will she make some sort of complaint about me? Do clients who complain about one therapist complain about the next therapist? Can I ask for some advice?'

Two therapists are online and chat with you (in this group with 1,000+ members). They're so friendly and helpful, asking where you are in the country, and what placement you're at. You type back. They then wonder about the client's history. You know a few things about that, so you tell them about that too.

Our responses to the scenarios

We've offered these scenarios as, unfortunately, as we intimated above, therapists (in training and qualified) posting about their clients on social media isn't rare; in fact it's regular. Clients honour therapists by sharing their lives. When therapists break client confidentiality in this way, it undermines learning relationships between clients and therapists and brings dishonour to the profession. You, our readers, are just starting out on your counselling and psychotherapy journeys, and so this book is a good place to be clear: never talk about clients on social media, even if you think you've anonymised them; even if you think (wrongly) that only other therapists will see what you've written. It is part of tackling counselling training and readying yourself for assignments to remember at all times that, *whatever* is happening for you in relation to your client work, *take it to supervision*. This is a learning we can and must note from the very start. If you can't take it to supervision, ask yourself why not?

The wider landscape of learning relationships: Power and politics

In this final section of the chapter, we reflect on the wider *landscape* in which all of the above relationships with people and organisations sit, focusing on issues of power and politics in the field of counselling and psychotherapy.

This wider landscape is included here for two reasons:

- First, while there has always been political activism in pockets of counselling and psychotherapy, we feel that more people are now moving beyond an apolitical stance and are realising that, if we don't study and reflect upon the personal identities and experiences people bring to training rooms and therapy rooms, we do not have at hand what we need in order to encounter others, and we risk doing them harm. It is increasingly recognised, at least in some quarters, that this is too important an area of work to leave for post-qualification CPD courses, although it is fair to say that therapy training is quite slow to centralise social justice.

- Second, this chapter is, evidently, about your learning relationships. You, as learners, will always bring your own intersectional (more than one) socio-political contexts from your wider world – you will have a variety of identities, some very central to who you are right now, some perhaps less so, and you will have areas of allyship and interest, some just emerging. All of this will be present in the training room and in the work you do outside of it. When you are entering into a new field of study or progressing within it, it's useful to be aware of some of the books, people, networks, and communities that can (if you wish) be alongside you as you bring your whole selves to your work, and as you study and tackle your course assignments.

Even just knowing there *are* thoughtful activist counsellors and psychotherapists out there who are concerned about personal identities and lived experiences can nourish you and help you along. You don't have to join them yet, or come out with any part of you that you're not ready to share.

Further reading

We just mentioned the concept of intersectionality – a term coined by Kimberlé Crenshaw. So, we offer you a reading suggestion about it.

Hill Collins, P. & Bilge, S. (2020). *Intersectionality: Key concepts.* **Polity Press.**

A note about coverage of power and politics in this chapter

Please note that in what follows we make no claims to have included 'all' of the wider landscape of power and politics in counselling and psychotherapy. Our omissions are not deliberate, suggesting that we think some areas matter less. What we are aiming for is a flavour of social justice in the field. You are likely to know of people, organisations and networks that we haven't covered. We find it very encouraging to see that new people, organisations, and networks seem to be emerging all the time. Maybe your organisation or network will be next? This section will also note what is, at the time of writing, a very live issue in relation to power and politics in our field – SCoPEd.

Our list for consideration in this section is:

- *Mentoring schemes*
  The Black, African and Asian Therapy Network (BAATN) 'Each One Teach One' mentoring scheme
  The Pink Therapy mentorship scheme

- *Valuing lived experiences*
  Notes about #MeToo and other lived experiences

- *Organisations and networks*
  Counsellors Together UK
  Association of Neurodiverse Therapists
  Psychotherapists and Counsellors for Social Responsibility (PCSR)

Mentoring

In this section, we hear first about the BAATN mentoring programme, and then Pink Therapy's mentoring programme.

Experiences

Sheila Balgobin created the Each One Teach One (EOTO) mentoring programme for the Black, African and Asian Therapy Network (BAATN).

The EOTO mentoring programme wasn't born out of lofty ideals, but from real frustration with my own psychotherapy training. Remarks such as 'I understand how you feel – I was the only Jewish girl in my village' or 'You didn't do the exercise correctly' (despite my white exercise partner stating I did EXACTLY as was requested!) made my blood *boil*!

I found myself killing off my tutors regularly in my dreams – which my training therapist encouraged me to keep bringing to my sessions – 'Just keep doing it in your dreams, please,' I was told. I nearly came to acting out my feelings during an experiential weekend – despite a warning received early that very morning in a dream. I was quite unprepared for the unjustified attack launched against me by the tutor. What hurt the most was that *not one of my fellow students – all white – said anything*. By the end of my course, I was angry, frustrated and felt I had wasted £7,000 and two years of my life – I was definitely NOT pleased! But then someone who, to this day, I believe was an angel, in the form of another student on a different psychotherapy course where I was studying, suggested I attend the Black African and Asian Therapists Network (BAATN) annual conference.

I never saw that student again – despite being in the same small building – but what I did see at that conference, and even more importantly *felt*, changed my life. That conference made me realise that I wasn't crazy or imagining things; I wasn't alone – others were experiencing the same things; I was sick and tired of constantly battling with people who had no true interest in or understanding of who I was, and I needed to be around others of my profession who thought and looked like me. Something lit up in my heart that day and I issued a call at that conference; several senior BAATN members answered that call, and EOTO was born. In the ensuing 11 years, as I built the programme, some 300 students have passed through it – and made my dream, born of anger and frustration, come true for others.

If you're training or thinking of training, and what I say here speaks to you, here's our website, take a look:
www.baatn.org.uk/student-support

Further reading

These are some recently published books around 'race'.

Charura, D. & Lago, C. (2021). *Black identities and white therapies: Race, respect and diversity.* PCCS Books.

Cousins, S. (2019). *Overcoming racism: Building resilience and wellbeing in the face of discrimination and microaggressions.* Jessica Kingsley.

Ellis, E. (2021). *The race conversation: An essential guide to creating life-changing dialogue.* Confer Books.

Turner, D. (2021). *Intersections of privilege and otherness in counselling and psychotherapy: Mockingbird.* Routledge.

And some websites to explore:

Black Therapy Matters – **www.blacktherapymatters.com**

Community Trauma Conference UK – **www.communitytraumaconf.com**

Experiences

Martin Fisher (who we heard from in Chapter 1) is a bi-friendly, kink-friendly, poly-friendly, attachment-based psychotherapist. He is currently mentoring his first group of GSRD trainees through the Pink Therapy mentoring scheme, which he describes here.

I've always gravitated towards outsiders. When I was in psychotherapy training, there were Muslim trainees who were not part of the 'in group'; I wanted to be friends and to make them feel included. I mixed with kink and poly people. My first client was gay, poly, living in a thruple. A whole world of gay, sexual and relationship diversity (GSRD) opened up. People who are GSRD come to therapy for therapy, but they get judged. If you're poly, you're diagnosed with insecure attachment and told that, to 'get well', you need to be monogamous. If you're kinky, you're told the problem is your lifestyle and you need to change it. It's liberating when people don't encounter that, when they're able to talk without worrying about the therapist's reaction. I'd read books by Dominic Davies (founder and CEO of Pink Therapy). In lockdown I was able to participate in some of the Pink Therapy training courses. So much had opened up online that extra training was easier to do. Then, when I received an email asking for therapists to be mentors of psychotherapists-in-training, I decided to offer four places for people to join together in a group.

The current participants are all on MSc courses, from the foundation year to the final year of training. We met up, and agreed to have eight sessions, meeting every three weeks for six months. We had a first session to agree our group contract – to keep confidentiality, to be respectful, to listen, and to be open to challenge. What happened after that was decided by the group – we've looked at self-disclosure, self-descriptions and advice-giving. We've had some group supervision within the sessions. Sometimes people just want to talk with me as a fellow therapist, rather than about GSRD, and that's important too. Therapy can be an isolating profession because you don't get to bounce ideas off other people. I have a strong commitment to building in opportunities to counter that isolation. Pink Therapy mentoring is part of that commitment.

Further reading

These are some books about GSRD, and two websites.

Barker, M.-J. & Iantaffi, A. (2020). *Life isn't binary: On being both, beyond and in-between.* Jessica Kingsley.

Barker, M.-J. & Scheele, J. (2016). *Queer: A graphic history*. Icon Books.

Burgess, R. (2021). *How to be ace: A memoir of growing up asexual.* Jessica Kingsley.

Davies, D. & Neal, C. (1996). *Pink therapy*. Open University Press.

Easton, D. & Hardy, J. (2009) *The ethical slut: A roadmap for relationship pioneers, a practical guide to polyamory, open relationships, and other adventures.* Celestial Arts.

See also Meg-John Barker's website: **www.rewriting-the-rules.com/meg-john-barker** and the Pink Therapy website: **https://pinktherapy.org**

Valuing lived experiences

Now we turn to the politics of lived experiences. There is quite a theme of some psychotherapists and counsellors (and some clients/potential clients) thinking that therapists (qualified and in training) shouldn't have particular lived experiences (such as when we say '#MeToo') – they worry that it makes them 'unfit for practice'. While researching the course landscape for this book, we came across one course (at Level 3) that was seemingly fearful of even admitting trainees who were in personal therapy or having psychiatric treatment. While there are, of course, instances where therapists (qualified and in training) may not be fit for practice, or where people applying for therapy courses are not ready to begin training, we see such a trend as problematic and in need of challenge in that it denies the humanity of therapists and dismisses their lived experiences as having anything of value to bring to their work. We believe this is very much not the case.[5]

Experiences

As mentioned above, Deborah has worked on #MeToo for a co-edited book with Emma Palmer,[6] and guest edited a special issue of *Psychotherapy and Politics International*[7] on therapists' lived experiences.

All of you reading this book will have a range of lived experiences. During your training, and after, you'll hear people declare that some lived experiences are 'not okay' for therapists to have, some are 'okay if you've recovered' (whatever that might mean), while others might be 'okay'. All of this is simplistic. We are whole beings. Some days some of what we've experienced in life will be very live for us; sometimes we won't be thinking about any of it. We have to honour all of what we are, and all of what other people are. How else will we be therapists? The message I want to convey to you here is: Don't be put off from training by what other people say about your lived experiences. Look for some community – through reading, joining groups, finding fellow travellers in training and outside of it (or something else that feels right for you). It's a political act to bring all of who you are. Maybe the tide is starting to turn, and therapists (qualified and in training) will be able to speak and write their truths.

---

5. See, for example, Adams, M. (2013). *The myth of the untroubled therapist: Private life, professional practice*. Routledge. Marie Adams disputes this notion of the therapist as untouched by human vicissitudes and troubles.

6. Lee, D.A. & Palmer, E. (Eds.). (2020). *#MeToo: Psychotherapists and counsellors speak about sexual violence and abuse*. PCCS Books. Fourteen people, largely therapists, talk with conversation partners about whatever they want to say about their own experiences of sexual violence and abuse.

7. Lee, D.A. (Guest editor). (2020). Therapists' lived experiences. *Psychotherapy and Politics International*. Peer reviewed articles, arts and poetry, book reviews and opinion pieces covering areas including dual training in sex work and psychotherapy, loss and bereavement, menstruation, sexual violence, self-harm scars and more. (Some of the articles are open access, others will need to be accessed via an institution.)

Further reading

We've foregrounded #MeToo in this section. Let's follow that thread for a moment. Being a student frequently brings excitement and growth. It is also not rare for students to encounter interpersonal violence. Rape culture is rife in society, and in education. You may have heard about Everyone's Invited:

Everyone's Invited – **www.everyonesinvited.uk**

At the time of writing this book (summer 2021), more than 50,000 testimonies from students and graduates reporting interpersonal violence had been posted on its website.

Some contacts in the UK
Rape Crisis Scotland: **www.rapecrisisscotland.org.uk**
Rape Crisis England and Wales: **https://rapecrisis.org.uk**

Organisations and networks

In this section, we look at three organisations and networks.

Experiences

Counsellors Together UK introduces itself on its website in this way:
UK Counsellors, also known as Counsellors Together UK (CTUK), started in July 2017 as a Facebook group discussing the prevalence of qualified counsellors being expected to work for free. The discussion has continued to grow into working together to campaign and bring an end to unpaid work in our profession. Today, the group comprises more than 7,200 members.

Tara Shennan (also a #MeToo book contributor) works for CTUK. We asked her what she'd like to say to trainee counsellors and psychotherapists. Tara said:
Start by getting to know the sector. People say clients find counselling mysterious, and that's the same for people joining the profession. Arm yourself with as much knowledge as possible. Have a look at Counsellors Staffroom on Facebook.[8] My view is that it is really worth becoming a counsellor and psychotherapist. It's not about getting rich. But counselling and psychotherapy can be viable as a profession. The work is there. There's no reason it can't be viable. We're wanting to get the basics in place so that qualified counsellors and psychotherapists aren't working for free, so that they can put food on the table and pay the bills, and then they can think about doing the job they love, and what they want it to be like.

This is why we're doing the work we are doing at CTUK. We want counselling and psychotherapy to be seen less mystically and more honestly. I'm working class, and we want training in counselling and psychotherapy to be viable for working class people. You don't need to go on a BACP-accredited course, you can do the BACP's Certificate of Proficiency when you've finished your studies if you want to join its register. You can get involved with CTUK, and other organisations, if you'd like. CTUK's goal is

---

8. www.facebook.com/groups/counsellors.staffroom/about/

for all of us to be able to do the job we love. I'd like to see more co-operatives of counsellors and psychotherapists. At first, people talked about the issues facing counsellors and psychotherapists in an ideological way. Now, changes are really happening, albeit slowly: people are noticing problems and wanting to take action. I've put forward a resolution to BACP to make accreditation free, for instance. It's okay, by the way, to feel a mix of feelings – wanting to change the system and needing to work within it.

You can find Counsellors Together UK at: **https://ukcounsellors.co.uk**

Further reading

Kearney, A. (2018). *Counselling, class and politics: Undeclared influences in therapy* (2nd ed.) (Proctor, G. (Ed.)). PCCS Books.

Experiences

Lesley Dougan is one of the founders of the Association of Neurodiverse Therapists (ANDT).

In Spring 2021, the ANDT was founded to provide visibility/advocacy for neurodivergent therapists (qualified and in training). ANDT is an international organisation based in the UK. ANDT welcomes any therapist or trainee identifying as neurodivergent because:

> A neurotypical person is rarely going to have a lot of reasons to believe they're neurodivergent, or to wish to be recognised as neurodivergent. (Callie, 2019).[9]

ANDT rejects the notion that an individual's neurodivergence should be dependent on whether a clinician thinks you meet their tickbox criteria for a specific diagnosis, rather than their lived reality. Applied behavioural analysis (ABA) is built upon an ableist premise, resulting in internalised ableism, impacting the sense of self and self-acceptance (McGill & Robinson, 2020).[10] From a neurodivergent lens, ABA is seen as an example of ableist conversion therapy. ANDT is against conversion therapy and all forms of discrimination. A small group of neurodivergent therapists (qualified and students) whose diversity includes autism, Tourette's, ADHD, neurofibromatosis and dyslexia, founded ANDT to give neurodivergent qualified and trainee therapists a voice, and to highlight and challenge the micro and macro aggressions that are perpetuated in a profession based on neurotypical assumptions.

You can find the ANDT at: **https://instalker.org/ANDTherapists**

---

9. Callie. (2019, April 9). *Autism: The (self) diagnosis debate.* [Blog.] Neuroclastic. www.neuroclastic.com/2019/04/09/autism-the-self-diagnosis-debate/

10. McGill, O. & Robinson, A. (2020). Recalling hidden harms: Autistic experiences of childhood applied behavioural analysis (ABA). *Advances in Autism, 7*(4), 269–282.

Experiences

Psychotherapists and Counsellors for Social Responsibility (PCSR)

PCSR introduces itself on its website as follows: We are committed to locating counselling and psychotherapy in its social, political, ecological, and economic context; recognising the impact of the political dimension on the client-therapist relationship; developing ideas about how social, economic, political, ecological and cultural issues can be integrated into theory and practice; identifying and challenging adverse discrimination at all levels within our profession and in the wider world; generating action, launching campaigns, and seeking to influence political processes.

Deborah says: I joined PCSR while I was a trainee and, when I saw a call for new steering committee members, I tentatively threw my hat into the ring. The welcome was warm and I was soon also the Editor of the in-house *Transformations* magazine, which then led me onwards to becoming an associate editor with *Psychotherapy and Politics International*. PCSR has a buzz and it has tenacity. It asks the hard questions and doesn't flinch from its political work.

You can find PCSR here: www.pcsr.org.uk

Further reading

Andrew Samuels co-founded PCSR with Judy Ryde. You might want to take a look at some of Andrew's work, maybe starting with:

Samuels, A. (2019). *A new therapy for politics?* **Routledge.**

Nick Totton, a PCSR steering group member for many years, has also written a body of work that is very well-worth exploring. Maybe start with:

Totton, N. (2012). *Not a tame lion: Writings in on therapy in its social and political context.* **PCCS Books.**

The Scope of Practice and Education (SCoPEd)

We are including the SCoPEd project here because we feel it embodies the debates and tensions around counselling and psychotherapy as political activities, not simply therapeutic, and it also demonstrates the battles for power within the profession and between different professional groupings within the mental health sector generally in the UK.

Catherine Jackson, who as former editor of *Therapy Today* has reported extensively on SCoPEd, briefly outlines the project here and the arguments around it.

SCoPEd is a joint initiative involving (at time of writing) six of the main membership organisations representing counselling and psychotherapy in the UK: BACP, UKCP, NCS, the British Psychoanalytic Council (BPC), the Association of Christian Counsellors (ACC) and the Human Givens Institute. Together, they are developing a framework that will position all qualified therapists and councillors according to the levels of their core competences and standards of practice.

SCoPEd is contested heatedly by some organisations, including PCSR, because it is seen as establishing a hierarchy within the counselling and psychotherapy professions.

It proposes three 'columns', into which counsellors and psychotherapists are categorised, depending on their levels of entry qualification training. Column A and B are populated by counsellors, primarily, and Column C by BPC and UKCP registered psychotherapists, and some members of BACP and NCS who meet its higher standards of qualification but are not distinguished by professional title. Effectively, Column C comprises the most highly qualified practitioners with the longest, most in-depth training, deemed capable to work with very challenging clients, and Column A comprises counsellors trained at diploma level, whose training is seen to least equip them to work autonomously and with complexity.

Critics say SCoPEd essentially carves into stone the primacy that psychotherapist and psychoanalytic practitioners have always claimed over counsellors on grounds of length and depth of initial training. Interestingly, this is a total change-around by BACP, which previously declared there was no difference between counsellors and psychotherapists (and it is in this spirit that the terms are used together in this book).

SCoPEd has also been criticised for discounting the post-qualification experience and CPD that therapists accrue over their years of practice, and for ignoring the value of lived experience. SCoPEd is also seen to be a further manifestation of the creeping professionalisation of counselling, which has long been criticised by person-centred counsellors in particular, who question the way the profession is being turned into a highly regulated, self-policed, formalised, formulaic practice. This, they say, is counter to its values and principles and constrains the professional autonomy of the practitioner and creative working with the client in the room.

In response, BACP says SCoPEd would:

> create a shared framework agreed by different Professional Standards Authority accredited register bodies [the PSA is a national scheme that accredits health and social care practitioners who do not have a statutory national register, like counsellors and psychotherapists], bringing greater credibility to the profession. It will also give employers and commissioners a single framework to use, which will help the profession become better understood, valued and trusted by those who employ therapists and commission our services. SCoPEd would allow us to better articulate and advocate what our members can do as part of our overall work to represent them. It would enable BACP to more effectively promote the skills and abilities of our members in a way that hasn't been done before, and we believe this means our members would have access to more paid opportunities.[11]

You can read more about SCoPEd here:
www.bacp.co.uk/about-us/advancing-the-profession/scoped/scoped-framework/

And what some of its critics say here:
Binstead, C. (2019, August 26). *Open letter regarding SCoPEd project by Caz Binstead. Psychotherapists and Counsellors for Social Responsibility.* pcsr.org.uk/resources/12

---

11. See the BACP website pages: www.bacp.co.uk/about-us/advancing-the-profession/scoped/scoped-framework

Murphy, D. (2019, January 31). *The questionable evidence base of SCoPEd*. The Alliance for Counselling & Psychotherapy. https://allianceblogs.wordpress.com/2019/01/31/the-questionable-evidence-base-of-scoped

The Alliance for Counselling & Psychotherapy (2020, October 16). *Open letter from person-centred community calls on BACP to halt the SCoPEd project*. The Alliance for Counselling & Psychotherapy. https://allianceblogs.wordpress.com/2020/10/16/open-letter-person-centred-calls-on-bacp-to-halt-scoped/

Experiences

Seeing therapy as political may be new to you as you enter this new field of study. So we asked Hannah Jackson-McCamley, who is studying for an MSc in Transactional Analysis at the Metanoia Institute, to talk with you about politics in therapy. Hannah graduated from the London School of Economics in 2006 with a BSc in political science and history and now works in funeral ritual and bereavement care.

My psychotherapy training started in early 2020, against a backdrop of Brexit, climate crisis, #MeToo, Black Lives Matter and the Covid-19 pandemic. If Harold Wilson thought a week was a long time in politics, what would he make of the past few years?

The impact of these outside forces on my fellow trainees and my own engagement with my foundation course was underscored by this massive exterior noise. We quickly went from classroom to Zoom, and – despite our distance – the intensity of world events could not be denied.

Learning about unconditional positive regard when Covid alone exposed stark inequality in the UK, and transactional analysis's 'ok-ness' when a War on Woke was underway brought the political into the therapeutic in a dynamic and real way. Many of my peers were uncomfortable when wider political conversations started, especially following George Floyd's murder in May 2020. Matters of injustice and oppression are rarely polite conversation. But, as trainee therapists, we must be aware that our future clients may present with issues outside our comfort zone, and politics is just one of many potentially triggering topics for client and counsellor alike.

'The personal is political' may have been a rallying cry of second-wave feminists in the 1960s but it feels just as pertinent today. As I move forward in my training and begin to work with clients, I cannot separate off the wider social and political context from the personal experiences discussed in the therapy room, consciously or otherwise.

My undergraduate degree was in political science, and politics remains a particular interest. Over the years it has got me into many lively debates, especially around election times. However, for me, politics is not about parties and partisanship. I understand politics to be about how we navigate the world in relation to our gender, sex, 'race', class, location and culture, as well as institutional and systemic impacts on individuals. As I made my transition into the world of counselling, I wondered how my world view and that of my future clients would affect the work.

But even before I invite anyone to sit on my couch, we need only look at the gender, 'race' and class imbalance reflected in faculties and the student body of many training institutions to see politics at work. Reading lists are dominated by male scholars. The profession itself is monopolised by white, middle-class women. Why is that? And where is the intersectionality? Everyone has mental health, so why is the field not more diverse? What socio-economic factors prohibit a wider racial or social mix on the courses? Are these questions not based on politics?

And beyond the classroom, in my placement at a low-cost counselling service in London, my clients are presenting with concerns about climate change, the stresses of lockdown and worries about racial tensions and homophobia – not just down to personal experience but concerns about how they fit in the current world order. Alienation and oppression cause distress and are often engendered by outside, systemic forces. External pressures have meant increased demand for mental health support in the last year. Yet the provision of therapy is not equally available. Waiting lists are long, especially if you cannot afford to go private, with demand on the NHS overwhelming. Is this again not politics?

I am learning that counselling transcends the therapy room. The work does not end as the clock strikes 10 minutes to the hour. We walk alongside our clients and aim to bring them into awareness. Amidst that awakening may be enhanced consciousness of inequalities that they have faced, oppression they may be under, injustices suffered. Our clients are not molded in a silo. They are products not just of their caregivers but of the society they developed in and the choices that they may, or may not, have had or made. Choice itself is often evidence of the haves and have-nots, and we may muse that the reason for that inequity is, yet again, influenced by the political sphere.

Counselling students are often encouraged to be in therapy themselves, so it may be worthwhile for those who are uncomfortable with politics' role in psychotherapy to investigate their aversion. Politics in the therapy room does not necessarily mean a therapist's disclosure. It is about being attentive to our clients and the world they inhabit.

As a trainee, I am often asked why I want to be a psychotherapist and my answer is that I am interested in individuals. To be interested in an individual is to be curious about their whole narrative, forged by political and social introjects and the endless nuances that form how they relate to the world and inform the work you do together.

Further reading

If you're interested in exploring the historical debates around registration and regulation of counselling and psychotherapy, we recommend:

Mowbray, R. (1995). *The case against psychotherapy registration: A conservation issue for the human potential movement.* **Trans Marginal Press.**

These are two books that explore some of the politics around counselling and psychotherapy as healthcare professions:

House, R. & Totton, N. (Eds.). (1997). *Implausible professions: Arguments for pluralism and autonomy in counselling and psychotherapy.* **PCCS Books.**

Bates, Y. & House, R. (2003). *Ethically challenged professions: Enabling innovation and diversity in psychotherapy and counselling.* **PCCS Books.**

> **TAKEAWAY MESSAGES**
>
> This chapter began by looking at people, places, and organisations in counselling and psychotherapy learning journeys. What we hope to have conveyed, overall, is that there is much complexity in such learning relationships.
>
> We then looked at the landscape in which people, places, and organisations are located and operate. We focused on power and politics. What we hope to have conveyed, overall, is some of the vibrant ways in which our field is developing, its activism, the debates that inform its development, and its growth.

The next chapter…

Chapter 3 turns to learning processes you'll encounter in counselling and psychotherapy training.

3

Learning processes in counselling and psychotherapy courses

Introduction

Chapters 2 and 3 form an introductory package to accompany you either as you step into the counselling and psychotherapy training room for the first time and make your own place there, or as you imagine what it might be like for you to do so, and decide whether to take that step.

Chapter 2 explored some aspects of learning *relationships* with people and organisations – and with power and politics (the wider context for these relationships) – that can be present in counselling and psychotherapy training, and readying yourselves for course assignments. We wanted to start with that broad picture so that you could gain a sense of the field, and how (over time) you might place yourself in it.

Now, in Chapter 3, we're narrowing our focus to the immediate environment you're likely to experience when or if you start studying – the classroom/training room. You may find it comforting to reach this more narrowed-down, boundaried terrain. Check in with yourself and see how you're experiencing the journey.

Our particular focus in this chapter is on some selected aspects of learning *processes* in counselling and psychotherapy training that are also part of readying you for course assignments (which we come onto later).

We start with an exploration of group contracting (sometimes the term 'ground rules' is used, which means roughly the same thing). Group contracts are agreements to prepare the classroom for the work that needs to be done there. Group contracting is a basis for learning.

Then we discuss that learning. We focus on types of learning that are usually encountered in counselling and psychotherapy training rooms/classrooms: learning in groups, experiential learning, and personal or self-development (PD).

In the chapter, we'll hear from learners and teachers, bringing a variety of voices, but all approaching learning processes (and relationships) as our whole selves, bringing our whole histories. We hope you will find points of connection with the experiences of others, but *your* personal counselling and psychotherapy learning journey will always be unique to you, because you are unique. We encourage you to recognise and respect your own process and to think about how the process may be for your colleagues, so that you're taking up an opportunity to think about the socio-political. We end with some perspectives on neurodiversity and the learning experience, and what to do if something does go wrong in any of your learning relationships.

Introducing group contracting

As we have touched on already in this book, bullying, harassment and microaggressions do occur in the classroom/training room. It is distressing for those involved and seems particularly wrong when those same people will go on to work with clients in the therapy room. Just as in the therapy room, these behaviours have no place in the counselling and psychotherapy classroom/training room.

We've also discussed the likelihood of encountering and grappling with many other examples of interpersonal difficulties when we are being congruent/genuine with others and seeking to learn to be ready to meet people in the therapy room.

So, you've probably already got a sense then that there may be a need to have processes in place that seek, as far as possible, to hold the counselling and psychotherapy classroom safe enough for the work that is to be done there. (We're using the term 'safe enough' deliberately, in an echo of Winnicott's concept of the 'good-enough mother'. We believe the classroom should be safe enough for us to do our work there, while accepting that it cannot ever be completely safe – and if we aren't exposed to some adversity, how do we ever learn to cope with life outside that safe-enough environment? Following Jacobs' (1995, p.50)[1] analysis of Winnicott's work, we believe that, while a classroom doesn't need to be perfectly safe, there can also be a 'not safe-enough classroom'.)

We've heard, too, of course, from people talking about supportive relationships with fellow students and tutors – relationships that flourished in classrooms/training rooms and developed over time as people qualified and progressed to being in practice as counsellors and psychotherapists. These experiences will also have developed in the context of the safe-enough counselling and psychotherapy classroom.

An important ongoing process in holding the continuum of all that can happen in counselling and psychotherapy training is group contracting. A group contract sets down what one group wants their learning experience to be like (and every group's ideas are likely to be quite different from those of another).

In some courses, you may work with just one group all the time, so group contracting at the start of the academic year happens just once. In other training, you may participate in different groups for different activities, and so you would need to contract in each group.

---

1. Jacobs, M. (1995). *D.W. Winnicott*. Sage.

Creating a group contract is a collaborative exercise involving students and tutors/lecturers/trainers – a task that can be both immediately practical and intellectually stimulating, if we are all open to that. There may be a text for us to interrogate (as we'll see below), or we may be working with a completely blank sheet of paper.

In our experience of teaching, few students have encountered group contracting before. Or, if they have, they've not had experience of serious engagement with the process of group contracting. When groups are asked to write down ideas for what might go into a group contract, they often struggle. They might manage, 'We will treat each other's opinions with respect', before stalling a few minutes into the time allocated for the activity. Sometimes people get frustrated when asked to create a group contract, believing what the learning environment needs to be like is obvious, and that the group should be getting on with the 'real work' of studying and learning.

We believe the group contract and the process of creating it are a vital part of the learning process in counselling and psychotherapy training and of readying yourselves for course assignments. The group contract underpins the 'real work' – it makes the group context safe enough to do what is often very challenging work. Moreover, it is itself part of the 'real work' – making a successful group contract is an opportunity for both personal development and the development of the group: a learning process of how to work together with care, community, challenge and complexity from the first day of training. Counselling and psychotherapy itself – including completing course assignments – demands that we engage in personal development and that we work with care, community, challenge and complexity. There are serious and meaningful purposes to being asked to write (and review) a group contract.

Here's one example of why it is so important to approach the task with that serious engagement we call for.

Working on a group contract is an opportunity to consider what we mean and what it might imply when we make the statement (which groups quite often do) that: 'We will treat each other's opinions with respect.' If we're serious about this, we have to consider what we do if someone holds an opinion we seriously disagree with – say, a racist belief? If we've already agreed, without working it through, that we will 'treat each other's opinions with respect', where does that leave us? Might we then have to respect that racist view?

Clearly, we cannot respect racism. To do so would be to act with a lack of integrity, directly in contravention of the ethical codes of all our professional bodies/training institutions. The BACP *Ethical Framework for the Counselling Professions* (2018),[2] for instance, states that a fundamental value of counsellors/psychotherapists is 'respecting human rights and dignity' (p.8). It also states: 'We will… accept we are all vulnerable to prejudice and recognise the importance of self-inquiry, personal feedback and professional development.' (p.15).

But, clearly, our contracting has to be carefully considered. We cannot assume that everyone in the group is going to share our views and beliefs and value systems.

Let's look now at a sample group contract.

---

2. BACP. (2018). *Ethical framework for the counselling professions*. BACP.

Sample contracting

This sample group contract particularly relates to a module about interpersonal violence and abuse.

> We all agree to the following group contract:
>
> We recognise from the outset that material that might be considered intense and difficult is covered here. While the module leader seeks to hold the class, to offer as safe as space as possible, we are in fact all responsible together for working carefully. The class is co-created.
>
> Anyone in the room may have personal experiences that relate to any of the issues we are exploring – experiences they already know, or that they re-evaluate and see differently in studying these areas. Given the prevalence of interpersonal abuse and violence, this is to be expected. To be aware that knowing about interpersonal abuse and violence from personal experiences is not surprising or unusual is part of the underpinnings of the module. The module is organised with 'survivors' [other terms are available] at the heart of the work, not as an aberration from a norm.
>
> Whether we identify personally with the material being explored, completely, to some extent, to a lesser extent, or not at all, all students are all equal in the room. There is a place for all of us here.
>
> We will always seek to behave respectfully towards each other, and in our responses to materials, and comments we make in large or small groups, seeing all our work here as about behaving ethically. There's a lot at stake in talking about sensitive topics. This should not be taken to imply a non-critical stance.
>
> We recognise that there are likely to be times when, influenced by the society in which we live, we say things that need some respectful challenge. We will seek to do this carefully, with the support of literature as appropriate, recognising that not to do so may feel unethical. We may need to spend some time processing any issues that arise, so that we can leave them in a state that feels right to all of us.
>
> If we are expected to read something, we recognise that it will have been chosen for a good reason. Everything is here to build on developing knowledge and understanding of these areas. We are so infected with societal stereotypes around interpersonal abuse and violence that wide reading is crucial.
>
> We recognise that at times reading a particular piece may not be appropriate for us at the time we are asked to read it. We will try to keep an open mind about people not reading what has been requested of us, and try to assist each other in exploring the issues raised, nonetheless.
>
> When talking in class, we will carefully consider the words we are using. Words, in the field of interpersonal abuse and violence, are contested – for example, 'victim' and all the other alternatives. This care will be replicated in essays. We need to know why we have made particular word choices.
>
> It is okay to make mistakes and learn from what may have gone wrong.
>
> We also recognise that it is possible to be creative and light-hearted at times with what may be intense and difficult topics.

> Where personal experiences are shared in a group, either in a small group discussion or in the wider group, we will receive such sharing as gifts, and keep confidentiality. No personal material will be brought back from a small group to a main group without explicit permission. This contracting around keeping shared personal experiences confidential is non-negotiable. (Note: the module leader may need to check in with student/s after a class.)
>
> Where personal sharing takes place, the person sharing will decide if they ever want to say anything further. No person who has spoken will be seen as an open book, a 'representative' of a particular 'group' of people, or expected to share whenever someone else feels they want to ask. This is also non-negotiable.
>
> If we need to debrief about anything that has happened, we will seek the module leader's advice.
>
> STOP is our code word when a debate needs to stop immediately.
>
> If we decide as a group that we need to take a break and do something else for a while during the class time, we can do so.
>
> Anyone who wants to leave the room can do so without needing to alert anyone in the group (unless they feel they need company, and then they may choose to speak to someone in the group before leaving).
>
> We will check in with each other at the end of sessions, to make sure everyone is okay after exploration of intense material.
>
> It is okay to work through materials in our own time if anyone feels they may find the content of some sessions particularly difficult. There is no need to signal a reason for non-attendance unless the person wants to do so.
>
> We will, though, need to keep in mind professional body attendance requirements in our attendance on the course as a whole.
>
> This is a module belonging to all of us, so we all may want to bring in our choice of materials at different times. Where someone is not sure if the material is too graphic or distressing, they are welcome to discuss this with the module leader first.
>
> If we have any concerns about anything to do with the module, we will raise them constructively with the module leader at the time they arise, or soon afterwards, rather than waiting for an end-of-year student feedback questionnaire.
>
> We will keep this group contract under review while we are learning together.

We are sharing this group contract with you as it foregrounds the intensity of studying sensitive topics like interpersonal abuse and violence and the need to work sensitively. As psychotherapy and counselling trainees, you'll often be working with this kind of material, as you will when you qualify and work as psychotherapists and counsellors. As mentioned already in this book, you need to ready yourself to manage intensity from the very beginning of your training, and to work with the utmost sensitivity. Taking group contracting seriously, and making sure the contract is clear about how the group will handle sensitive and difficult matters that are likely to arise, is a fine way of starting this process.

ACTIVITY

An invitation to do some journalling about group contracting

We'd like you to record your reflections on group contracts through some journalling (writing, or mind-maps, or drawing or recording your words).

You could choose one or more of the following prompts:

- How do you feel about the contents of this sample group contract? You might like to consider the term 'non-negotiable'. How does it sit with you? What would be 'non-negotiable' for you? Are there other terms, or items, in the sample group contract that you find interesting to explore?

- What might you add/remove/phrase differently for: a) a module on loss and bereavement; b) a module on professional ethics, and/or c) a group supervision?

- Some practical matters were included in the sample group contract. There are many other practical matters that could be included in a group contract. For example: lighting, temperature and seating arrangements of the room – how can they be made to suit everyone? And lunch and rest/comfort breaks – liminal spaces (the spaces in-between, like breaks and lunchtimes), with fewer obvious rules, can be more anxiety-provoking than the more structured nature of the classroom/training room. Some will need some space away from the overwhelm of other people. Some may need to take some physical rest. Does everyone bring their own food, and if you agree to go out to eat together, what kind of venue will people find comfortable? Do not assume that everyone will feel able to explain why they have particular needs or preferences, and they should not have to.

What are your responses to the practical matters in the sample group contract, and above? Can you think of other practical needs or other areas that might need consideration? What might you need?

You should note that some needs of students/tutors are not open for negotiation. We'll talk about access arrangements/reasonable adjustment plans in the next chapter, so you might want to come back to these questions again once you have explored that material, to deepen your exploration.

- How do you feel when you read and think about group contracting? Strong emotions can arise from trying to decide what you want your learning experiences to be like, including that you may not have been shown respect by other students, teachers/tutors/lecturers/trainers in your previous educational experiences. We're all likely to be able to remember times when others, particularly those in positions of power, have humiliated us, when our needs have not been met and have even been ridiculed. How can we ensure our counselling and psychotherapy classroom (and its liminal spaces) is different? How can we all play a part, through our group contracts, in achieving this?

> If you have felt impacted by this activity, be gentle with yourself; and remember that people's needs, including yours, matter. They should always have mattered.

Notes about group contracting for triad work or goldfish bowl work

In the course of your studies, you're likely to take part in triad work – working in a group of three (client, therapist and observer, and then rotating the roles), or doing this work in a goldfish bowl (literally, you sit in the middle as therapist or client, while the rest of the group, including the tutor, observes) – to learn about being in each of the roles, and about giving/receiving feedback on being a therapist. This learning activity can be stressful for all involved because it directly involves judging and being judged.

For a group contract for triad work or goldfish bowl work, you're likely to need to agree how you (when you're being the therapist) want to receive feedback from the observer/s.

The client may sometimes need to tell you things you may find difficult to hear.

Of importance to note here is that the person being the client (who is likely to have spoken about their own personal material, although in some cases they may have acted a role given to them by the tutor) decides what happens to any recordings made. They can require a recording of a whole session to be deleted, even if the person in the role of therapist was hoping to use the recording for one of their case study assignments (see Chapter 5). Adopting this principle in triad and goldfish bowl work readies you for the potential for clients from placements agreeing to and then changing their mind about you using recordings of sessions in your case study assignments. Sometimes this can happen late in the day. Whenever the client decides, it must be honoured.

As with group contracts for work in the classroom, personal material that is shared in triads and goldfish bowls must be kept confidential to the triad and to whoever is in the goldfish bowl for that particular session, and not shared with other people (that includes absent members of the group, trainees from the main group or another group, and people outside of the course), and must not be raised again in the triad or goldfish bowl on another occasion, except by the person who originally shared it.

Being clear about the importance of confidentiality of each other's material is an excellent starting point for keeping client work confidential, and for thinking about how you will present client material when you write case studies for assessment.

Re-negotiating group contracts

Even when a group contract looks to be working and has been working for a while, it may soon need more attention. The self-development of trainees during a course means that people's views about what they want the group to be like can change and evolve rapidly and even radically. Needing to re-negotiate the group contract is a good thing. It shows the group contract is being taken seriously, that it really is live, and not 'just a piece of paper' gathering dust that no one bothers to think about.

A particular point of change may be if new members join the group so, effectively, a new group is formed – such as when one or more people return having taken a year away from their training. Of particular note for groups like this is that much personal material may already have been shared in the previous group, so decisions have to be made about what of that will be shared in the new group, by whom, when, where, and in what ways. It's not straightforward. Some people may be content to share anything they've said already. Some people may want to share nothing from past sessions until they are more comfortable with the new group. While we've said that a 'new group' emerges with the arrival of new people, people joining a group after time away from training will bring their own worries about doing so, and about their place in the group. A delicate renegotiation will need to take place, again keeping the contract live.

Try to see re-negotiation, as well as the initial negotiation, as offering more opportunities to work positively with complexity and be alongside others. All of the work you do on being open to the expressions of each other's needs and desires in the classroom/training room will assist you to be ready to meet clients where they are, and to write about clients sensitively when you complete course assignments. We encourage you to see the wider import of group contracts for the profession you're studying to join.

Learning in groups, experiential learning and personal development

We've said that group contracting is a learning process that seeks to make the counselling and psychotherapy classroom/training room safe enough for the work that needs to be done there. We turn now to the sorts of learning this involves – essentially, learning in groups, experiential learning and personal development.

Experiences

Some of these ways of learning may be new to you, and even the words themselves (experiential, personal development...) may make you feel uneasy. So let's begin by hearing from Nicky Young, a student on the MSc in Counselling and Psychotherapy at the University of Salford. She (like many of us) describes herself as 'naturally shy', and says this about this new ways of learning.

Learning in groups, learning experientially, are important parts of counselling training and take many different shapes and forms. On my course, this has included 1) offering our personal experiences of and thoughts and feelings towards subjects taught during lectures, 2) practising our skills peer-to-peer in skills groups, and 3) discussing our vulnerabilities and personal obstacles while in personal development (PD) groups.

I recall in the first year being asked to bring something that had deep personal meaning to present to the group in PD – something that expressed our emotion in any other way than simply speaking it. I wanted to challenge myself and to push my boundaries, so I wrote a very personal song and performed it to the group while attempting to play along on the ukulele. It transpired afterwards that I had mistaken the brief and that all we had to do was to bring in a song or poem that had personal meaning for us, and the rest of my peers just played a song or read a poem that was special to them. I initially felt mortified that I had got it wrong and done something I felt was hugely embarrassing. However, on reflection, I felt a huge sense of accomplishment and pride in my courageousness. I had allowed myself to be vulnerable; I had shown myself that I can do things that make me feel uncomfortable, which made me a bit braver in my everyday life. It also made me realise there is no such thing as 'wrong' in experiential learning: anything goes, and this gives the opportunity for freedom of expression.

I'm a naturally shy person, and I found group work an uncomfortable process – one that stretched me so far out of my comfort zone that I felt the elastic had snapped. The prospect of speaking in front of a group of people – in any of the settings I described above – terrified me. I still find it challenging having all eyes on me when I talk, and I find I go into 'fight or flight' mode, which can make it difficult to articulate what I want to say. However, I have found that confidence is a skill that can be developed through experiential learning – the more I challenge myself and practice speaking up, the easier it gets, and this process is helping me to become a stronger, more confident person.

It can still be daunting bringing issues into the group; there is always the fear of saying something 'stupid' or bringing something that I worry may not be 'important enough' to discuss. An example would be during check in – is it appropriate to mention the stressful morning I had prior to the session, and the distraction I now feel because of it? I have found that being open and honest with the group, asking 'Is this relevant?' and listening to the feedback from my peers, has been the best course of action.

The journey has allowed me to step out of my own box. Hearing a variety of different perspectives has opened my eyes to different ways of thinking. This has broadened my capacity to meet people where they are. It has taught me to drop my defences and to become more aware of and accepting towards others' opinions and perceptions, and I feel this has been essential for my personal growth.

As you go into your own training, I'd suggest remembering that counselling training gives you the rare opportunity to be surrounded by a group of people who are invested in developing a non-judgemental attitude and who are willing to listen with open minds. This has allowed me to find my voice, to push myself and to bring things to the table.

Learning in groups

You will spend most of your time in psychotherapy and counselling training learning in groups, in some of the ways Nicky has mentioned. Most of us have experienced sitting in a classroom, seminar room or lecture theatre with some or many other people when we were at school, college or university, or on a work-related course. There is, though, a significant difference between learning *in the presence of others* – as we are likely to have done in those settings (primarily being connected by being in the same room and having a similar experience), and *learning with, through and in relationship with others*, where the connection between people is both the medium for, and the content of, the learning. Learning in groups on counselling and psychotherapy courses is more often the latter type. It involves listening, speaking, sharing ideas and self-disclosing personal experiences, feelings and thoughts; it also involves being present, taking some risks and sitting with some uncertainty.

There are many tensions in being a member of such a group – speaking or not speaking, how much to say, what to say and when, how much to listen, how much to show of ourselves...

One thing about groups, however, is that the majority of the people present are having to wrestle with much the same tensions as you are. The other participants are likely to be just as worried about what is happening for them as they are about what you are saying.

Let's think here in more detail about some of the processes involved, so you can explore how you might feel about what is being asked of you.

Sharing in groups

Sharing is offering our thoughts, feelings and experiences, not in order to argue a point so much as to cast light in the darkness or make and strengthen connections between group members. We can learn from the views and lives of others if we listen openly and without judgement. Sometimes another group member may say something that stirs strong feelings in us – great sadness, anger or joy. Then we need to be honest and open in our responses, as far as we can be, so that we are genuine and not, for example, pretending to feel comfortable when we are not.

Sharing in groups can have several beneficial learning outcomes, for example:

- Sharing our thoughts in groups helps us solve problems and get new perspectives on issues. This 'many heads are better than one' effect is most noticeable when contributing views and experiences in order to make sense of a difficult theoretical point.
- It can help us 'ground' our ideas or make them concrete rather than abstract in our own or other people's experience.
- Sometimes our thoughts and feelings seem to 'free up' when we are in the presence of others, and we think and feel more expansively.
- Ideas have a better chance of 'evolving' or developing when many contributions are made; it's easier to get stuck in a rut when we are on our own.
- We can gain support for our position or feel less isolated when other people describe similar feelings and experiences to the ones we have. We feel less of an 'island'.

Being silent in groups

Many of us have difficulty contributing to group activity, and there can be many reasons for this. Most of the reasons originate within us; it's rare that we can honestly say there simply wasn't time to have our say.

The trouble with this sort of difficulty is that the learning process in groups does require many different contributions in order to work effectively. At a very basic level, some people are simply more talkative than others. Even when everyone in a group is relaxed, we might not make absolutely equal contributions to a group discussion. But again, this doesn't explain why some of us hardly ever speak at all. Here's an opportunity to explore that.

ACTIVITY

An invitation to explore sharing and silence in groups

What do you think about the following points? Make some notes, or mind-maps, or draw or record your words.

- I get just as much out of being silent as I do from talking. Groups need people to listen, just as much as they need people to talk.
- Some people are afraid to talk because they think that they have nothing sensible to say.
- It is difficult to say something if everyone else sounds cleverer and more articulate than you.
- Some people are crippled by embarrassment and completely 'dry up' at the prospect of speaking in a group.
- Everyone's contribution is helpful and of value, regardless of what it is.
- If you haven't got something sensible to say, it's best not to say anything.
- I don't find it easy to speak in groups and if I can take the risk and do it, then everyone should.
- If I have a problem speaking in groups, I should, as a trainee counsellor, address it and work on it, not just accept it and say, 'It's just the way I am, I can't change.' Counselling and learning about counselling is about change, after all, and I should be 'up for it'.
- Everyone should say something because it shares the responsibility of doing the work of learning, and it shows that we are committed and active, not just passengers along for the ride.

Some of our thoughts

- Groups are not deliberately set up by tutors to be an ordeal, even if sometimes it can feel like that. Groups are used because they are believed to be a good way of learning counselling and psychotherapy.
- You have every right to speak. (How does it feel to hear that?)
- Try not to feel intimidated by others' apparent ease when speaking in groups. They're probably quaking too.
- It often helps to say how you're feeling: for example, that you're nervous about public speaking or that you don't know what to say. Saying it can bring your nerves down a notch and can encourage others to say they feel like that too, normalising these feelings in the group and humanising and connecting everyone.
- Showing something and passing it around – a photo, a page of a book that you've

photocopied – can be useful in taking people's eyes off you while you speak. Obviously, what you show has to relate to what you are talking about!

- Don't wait until you have a brilliant point to make. You will wait forever. Group discussions move very quickly, and by the time you have organised your words to express this wonderful idea, the emphasis will have shifted and moved on.
- It is better to engage in the discussion in a natural way. Don't be too ambitious; make some lower-key points and you will begin to feel relaxed. This is the way group learning happens, in small steps that everyone can follow and feel part of, rather than in a few amazing bounds that leave most participants behind.
- Don't be afraid to ask questions of the tutor or other group members. (It may well be that others don't understand something that has been said, either.) Asking questions can be a good way in to speaking aloud.
- Keep it simple and straightforward whenever possible. And, paradoxically, don't worry if you can't organise your thoughts and feelings into a simple coherent statement: 'getting it out', even in a jumble, can help.
- The statements in the section above include some harsh words – about 'passengers along for the ride' – and harsh attitudes ('if I can take the risk… everyone should'). We might also want to complicate positions like that, by asking how sharing and silence have arisen for some people in the group. Is it a consequence of something happening in the group? And why must everyone be the same, and/or move at the same pace?

Experiential learning

You'll be doing a lot of experiential learning in groups (and also on your own) on your counselling and psychotherapy course.

Although we might think that the term simply means 'learning through experience', experiential learning has many different meanings. The term is probably most frequently associated with the experiential learning cycle described most fully by Kolb (1984).[3]

This general and rather abstract model has been used to help us understand how best to arrange learning experiences for adult students, in particular. There have been many attempts to add to the ideas or tailor them to specific learning situations, but we include it here so that you can think about you as a learner and how you learn best.

Experience

Experiential learning requires personal and practical involvement in the thing being learned. That is to say, it is *learning by doing* rather than learning by simply *knowing*. This makes the experiential learning model admirably suited to counselling. So, the first stage of experiential learning is to have an experience of some kind – maybe an activity or structured exercise, or the experience of being a client or psychotherapist and counsellor. This then provides fuel for the next stage of the learning cycle.

3. Kolb, D.A. (1984). *Experiential learning.* Prentice-Hall.

Reflection

It is important to provide opportunities for personal reflection on the experience – even if you simply ask yourself, 'What happened there?' Sometimes this is helped by sharing your experiences in groups.

Generalisation

This is our attempt to apply what is learned in one rather narrow setting (such as in a five-minute exercise on your course) to a wider set of contexts (such as practice as a counsellor and psychotherapist in a variety of settings).

Testing

Finally, we try out our new learning – sometimes in real life – and that provides us with a new experience, so we start the cycle all over again. Experiential learning becomes a permanent state of learning and development.

There are many types of activities that might be involved in the experiential learning of counselling and psychotherapy, such as:

- *Prior learning and prior experience*: Assembling a portfolio of qualifications and experience, assessing competencies.
- *Personal development and/or personal therapy*: Group and individual therapy, creative/expressive approaches, visualisation, setting personal learning goals, keeping diaries and journals.
- *Autonomous learning*: Setting personal learning goals, negotiating learning contracts, challenging power dynamics of learning relationships.
- *Client work or work placement*: Setting up your own co-counselling with another student, client sessions, professional relationships with other helpers, placement, supervision, mentorship.
- *Problem-solving in class and in the real world*: Exercises, brainstorming, generating, testing and evaluating action plans.
- *Project work/research*: Surveys, experiments, case studies, field work, interviews, presentation of results.
- *Awareness-development exercises*: Simulations, role-plays, games.
- *One-to-one skills practice sessions with peers*: Listening, giving and receiving feedback.
- *Community meetings and other learning groups involving interaction*: Group discussion – listening and speaking in groups, evaluation, giving and receiving feedback, challenge.
- *Presentations of student work and student-led workshops or seminars*: Presenting ideas and experience, demonstrations, feedback from group sessions, recordings of work with clients.

There are many opportunities for experiential learning in counselling training; the list above is not exhaustive, it is just for illustration. You may well be able to add some new categories or activities of your own.

Experiences

We heard from Nicky Young earlier, primarily talking about starting out on an experiential learning journey and bringing the shyness many of us feel. Now let's hear from Phil Jackman, a fellow student on the MSc Counselling and Psychotherapy: Professional Practice at the University of Salford, reflecting back on learning in groups through experiential learning and personal development.

When I reflect back on the course I've studied, I've found experiential learning to be an overwhelmingly empowering experience. It offers an opportunity in academic learning to bring your own personality to your theoretical framework, to bring and develop your own style and flavour. It's learning by doing in a live and lively environment. As a person-centred psychotherapist-in-training, for me the realisation offered by experiential learning has been that counselling in a person-centred way is about the encounter, being open to it and letting it happen to you, as opposed to avoiding encounter by deploying tactical interventions. It's about sacrificing the comfort of a predetermined journey and destination in favour of being present in the unpredictable world of the other, the client. The classroom of experiential learning is the dress rehearsal for the main event of the encounter within the therapy room.

I've said it's been 'overwhelmingly empowering', but it was, at first, frightening and uncomfortable – it was a loss of control and the associated comfort. But through doing, I learned it was okay to be in the encounter, to trust myself and the other – whether client, student or lecturer – and to observe how belief in the Rogerian necessary and sufficient conditions transforms into an experienced knowledge of their power and utility.

Through the process of experiential learning I've explored my relationship not only with theory and practice but with myself. In particular, I find it valuable being given live feedback and observing my resistance and attachment to my perception of my efforts, especially in 'skills' sessions. For me, there was transformation, an increased openness to the opinion of others and the value to be gained from these alternative perspectives.

A key part of what I consider to be experiential learning has been the learning after the event – the subsequent offerings the mind provides as it chews over what has happened, specific feedback or exchanges with clients (experiential learning is not just in the classroom).

Overall, I think the processes of experiential learning brings life to the theory. That view sounded somewhat idealistic and lofty to me when I first read about it. However, through the process of doing and observing the subsequent power that comes from the person-centred 'way of being', life and meaning *is* brought to the theory. Through doing, theory became knowledge, thoughts became facts.

This journey of experiential learning led to the somewhat humbling realisation that my thoughts and perspectives aren't static; they change and this change happens to me, almost in spite of me. I feel I am a better person as a result of the experiential learning I have encountered so far. It has given me a willingness to change, to step back and let it happen to me.

Personal or self-development (PD) groups

PD groups are a feature – and for some counselling and psychotherapy approaches, the central focus – of the vast majority of counselling and psychotherapy training. There are some slight differences in the meaning of the term, depending on a number of factors, including the theoretical approach of the course. These differences can lead to the personal development requirement of training being met in different ways.

Courses will provide or require one or more of a range of PD opportunities, including:

- personal therapy
- small group work
- large group work
- home groups
- community groups.

These methods can be provided by the course itself or may occur outside formal course contact time. Each course provider will have their own way of organising, timetabling and verifying PD.

How does your course meet the PD requirement and what is the rationale behind it? There should be a clear rationale, explained by tutors at interview/open day, and/or in the course documentation. If you have any concerns at all about the PD component of the course you are applying for or currently on, we encourage you to ask your course leader to explain it.

What exactly does PD involve? An experience on some counselling courses is that the PD component is never explained to students. You may be left to find out for yourself, and this can often feel like a struggle, especially when tutors seem perversely to withhold information as though there is some great 'truth' to discover. Not all courses are like this. They give a varying amount of information to facilitate the PD process. How does your course approach PD? How do you feel about what's required?

In our view, there is something to be said for both ways of approaching PD. If there is no information, a group has to find a way that suits (to some extent) the people in it. If there is information, then 'What are we meant to do here?' is partly answered. However, it cannot be completely answered, because groups are always going to be fluid and shifting entities.

Experiencing the PD component of training can:

- help trainees understand the client role. This gives us exposure to, and insight into, the range of possible feelings experienced by clients, including an appreciation of the power dynamics of helping relationships.

- give evidence that we trust the counselling and psychotherapy process. Would you go to a dentist who 1) only went to the dentist when they had raging toothache, 2) didn't trust dentists, and 3) thought that dentistry was only 'okay for those who need it in an emergency'?

- help trainees develop an increased awareness of their *self* as an individual. We are better helpers if we understand ourselves better, with fewer 'blind spots', unhelpful attitudes and prejudices.

- secure commitment to ongoing personal and professional development. It is a requirement that professional helpers continually maintain their 'fitness' to practise (like an athlete being in training to maintain peak performance).

- further our understanding that helping has a social and relationship context, and that counselling and psychotherapy has to work with complex socially constructed meanings, not just individual worlds. Skills of negotiation, appreciation of consensus, and group vs individual needs can all be explored.

When PD is done in a group setting, all of the issues, both positive and negative, that arise in group learning will also be present. This means that the whole experience can add up to something quite momentous, or it can be, at times, over- (or under-) whelming. Skilful facilitation of this group work is essential, yet at the same time, all group members must remember that there is a collective and individual responsibility for what happens in the group.

In our exploration of learning relationships in Chapter 2, we encouraged you to hold awareness of the demands on lecturers/tutors/trainers. These demands are perhaps nowhere more apparent than in PD. Let's hear from a very experienced PD facilitator.

Experiences

Amanda Ryding is Programme Leader for the BSc Counselling and Psychotherapy: Professional Practice course at the University of Salford. Amanda is researching PD. She gives a tutor perspective, and also shares her own understandings of personal development groups for you to consider.

Skinner (2010)[4] explains how counselling and psychotherapy trainees are not only expected to develop new skills and understand theory, but they must also adapt their personality in line with new skills and knowledge. Therapy training, by its own admission, is a process of deconstruction of the self to meet the needs of clients and the profession. It is no wonder that I meet students who are reluctant and fearful to engage in PD. We can read about deconstruction of the self but, in practice, acceptance of vulnerability is threatening.

Lehman (2006)[5] explores how transformative learning (Mezirow, 2009)[6] is a contributing factor to the development of self-awareness. As a part of this awareness, old values and beliefs are questioned and challenged. Transformative learning must bring the negative aspects, otherwise it is pointless learning, as it has no psychological movement or developmental capacity. The PD group provides an opportunity for transformative learning.

As trainers in PD, it is our responsibility to consider the power differential between us and trainees, and to attempt to minimise it – the

---

4. Skinner, D. (2010). *Effective teaching and learning in practice*. Continuum International Publishing Group.

5. Lehmann, J. (2006). Telling stories. In White, S, Fook, J. & Gardener, F. (Eds.), *Critical reflection in health and social care*. Open University Press.

6. Mezirow, J. (2009). Transformative learning theory. In J. Mezirow & E.W. Taylor (Eds.), *Transformative learning in practice: Insights from community workplace, and higher education* (pp.18–32). Jossey-Bass.

reasoning for this is that self-awareness cannot operate where power dictates the agenda (see Johns, 1996[7]).

Heron (1990)[8] suggests that facilitators may be cathartic, catalytic or supportive, and we need to be mindful of our positioning. I feel that I am all three, depending on the individual, group dynamic or level of training. By my own admission, I am aware that I hold the power – I'm the tutor – but I attempt to create influence and impact rather than control of groups (Rogers, 1961).[9] The all-seeing, all-knowing trainer who is empathic and sensitive all of the time to students' needs is a creation of students' desires (Johns, 1996[7]).

Running a personal development group is a challenging task. Thorne (1987)[10] points out that it is exhausting and demanding work – trainers require the ability to be therapist, teacher, and facilitator, all at the same time.

My own experience of facilitating PD groups is a mixture, from wonderful expressions of what it is to be human to the ugliness of fear manifesting itself in the group. On occasions, I am irritated by students' attempts to 'play games' and hide behind a professional façade that they have created for themselves. I am fully aware that my nurturing nature is seen as a weakness by some and, as a result, I am confronted by disapproval. At one end of the scale, I witness students' anguish about speaking, for fear that they may 'get it wrong', and at the other, complete dismissal of me. This 'acting out' takes time and patience on my part to overcome. I fully understand the difficulties of wishing to pass the course, coupled with experiencing the 'rawness' of an unstructured group dynamic (Dexter, 1996).[11]

Moller and Rance (2013)[12] discuss the 'good', the 'bad' and the 'uncertainty' that trainees experience in a PD group. Personal development, by its very nature, has the potential to be a distressing experience – participants in their study cited words such as 'painful, fear, intimidating and scary' to describe attendance at a PD group. I cannot imagine for one moment that any facilitator of a PD would wish for any student to feel this way, but there are tasks that the group must participate in for the progression of the students. Ieva and colleagues (2009)[13] discuss how participants in the PD group felt uncomfortable at times but allowed themselves to take risks, resulting in their own personal growth and professional growth.

I feel sad that this process is not made easier for students and that I am unable to ease a lot of the personal pain they will inevitably endure. But they need to be ready to go into the world of work; therapy is a lonely profession and

---

7. Johns, H. (1996). *Personal development in counselling training*. Sage.

8. Heron, J. (1990). *Helping the client: A creative practical guide*. Sage.

9. Rogers, C.R. (1961). *On becoming a person*. Constable.

10. Thorne, B.J. (1987). Beyond the core conditions. In W. Dryden (Ed.), *Key cases in psychotherapy* (pp48–77). Croom Helm.

11. Dexter, G.L. (1996). *A critical review of the impact of counselling training courses on trainees*. Unpublished PhD thesis. University of Durham.

12. Moller, N.P. & Rance, N. (2013). The good, the bad and the uncertainty: Trainees' perceptions of the personal development group. *Counselling and Psychotherapy Research, 13*(4), 282–289.

13. Ieva, K.P., Ort, J.H., Swank, J.M. & Young, T. (2009). The impact of experiential groups on master students' counsellor and personal development: A qualitative investigation. *The Journal of Specialists in Group Work, 34*(4), 351–368.

students need to be equipped in understanding their own psychological health (Irving & Williams, 2001).[14]

In my own mind, I am clear I have a job to do. I have a responsibility to the profession and the wider public to uphold the ethical values, to act as a 'gatekeeper' (BACP, 2018).[15] The tension that exists between a facilitator and trainee is natural – the facilitator acts as 'mirror' to the trainees' behaviour, expression and values, and at times there will be conflict and disagreement (Johns, 1996).[16]

In essence, I am fascinated and moved by the energy of the PD group. It grants the power to be human in all our complexities, and provides the environment to examine this with empathic acceptance (Rogers, 1951).[17] The PD group is a process, not a learning objective.

Experience

By contrast to Amanda Ryding's positive exploration of PD groups from her perspective as an experienced facilitator who loves the work, here is an account from a student. They published it anonymously in *Therapy Today* magazine,[18] to protect the identities of all those concerned, and because they did not want to personalise the experience to a particular course.

They are writing after qualifying, reflecting back on their experience, and their words support Amanda's appreciation of how hard it can be for the trainee, particularly when the group is not well facilitated by the tutor. Anonymous begins by saying: 'Whisper the words "group process" [PD] to any counselling student or recently qualified counsellor and watch the fear appear in their eyes.'

Anonymous doesn't object to group process/PD itself, but highlights the potential outcomes and impacts if it is badly facilitated. They felt their own experience of PD was 'almost entirely manipulated'. Their personal therapist tells of students in PD 'being actively encouraged to prod each other until they snapped'.

Anonymous describes group[process as 'like being in a boxing ring. Punches are thrown and it's up to the tutor/referee to keep all parties safe… [But] there are counselling tutors who are not outstanding, ethical referees and, because of this, some very vulnerable people are out in the ring on their own.'

Anonymous feared complaining. They wrote the article after the revised BACP *Ethical Framework*[15] was published in 2018. In particular, they welcomed points 79 and 80, which state:

---

14. Irving, J.A. & Williams, D.I. (2001). The path and price of personal development. *European Journal of Psychotherapy and Counselling, 4*(2), 225–235.

15. British Association for Counselling and Psychotherapy (BACP). (2018). *Ethical framework for the counselling professions.* BACP.

16. Johns, H. (1996). *Personal development in counselling training.* Sage.

17. Rogers, C.R. (1951). *Client centred therapy.* Constable.

18. Anonymous. (2018). Do no harm. *Therapy Today, 29*(9), 36–37. www.bacp.co.uk/bacp-journals/therapy-today/2018/november-2018/articles/do-no-harm/

> 79. Trainers and educators will model high levels of good practice in their work…
> 80. Trainers and educators will encourage trainees to raise any concerns at the earliest opportunity and have processes and policies for addressing any trainee's concerns.
>
> The takeaway message from the article in *Therapy Today* is:
>> If something has happened as part of your training that is causing you undue stress or anxiety, don't assume it is normal and don't accept that you have to put up with it.

> **ACTIVITY**
>
> **An invitation to consider your thoughts about PD/group process having read Amanda Ryding's contribution and the *Therapy Today* article by Anonymous.**
>
> You might do some journalling (writing, or mind-maps, or drawing or recording your words) about where this material has taken you.

Further reading

Rose, C. (2008). *The personal development group: The student's guide.* **Routledge.** We have only been able to offer you a taste of PD, and we recommend this book if you want to explore the topic further.

Neurodiversity and group work, experiential learning and PD

We said at the beginning of the chapter that your experiences of learning processes in counselling and psychotherapy training will be unique because you are unique. We've heard so far from students and tutors navigating their ways through the learning processes of group work, experiential learning and PD – the central parts of classroom training. We also want to highlight equality, diversity, inclusion and wellbeing, and in particular how neurodiversity impacts upon all that we've explored.

> *Experiences*
>
> **Zoë Stephens is co-founder and student member of the Association for Neurodiverse Therapists (ANDT). Zoë writes here about neurodiversity in the classroom from the student's perspective.**
>
> If I asked you what comes to mind when you think about your first day at a new college, what would you say? Would you be nervous? Would you think about the journey there? How might it feel to walk into that classroom, full of people

you may never have met before? Would you think about what you'd be doing all day? Sit with what comes up, in your mind's eye, before you read on…

On the first day of a new college course, I wake up and run through the plan of how to get there. I have my whole day written down in a visual timetable so I know what will happen and when. I have already decided the clothes I will wear to make me appear 'smart yet fashionable'. I take the bus approximately 30 minutes before the one that, if it is running to time, will arrive at my destination when I need it to. I do this because I need to make sure I'm the first person to arrive at the classroom. If I get there first, others will naturally strike up a conversation with me and won't notice how nervous and shy I am. Do you do that? If I have to walk into a classroom with students already seated, that coping strategy has been compromised and I have to mask how I'm feeling.

'Masking', which means pretending to be somebody you are not, as though you are wearing a mask to prevent anyone seeing the real you, is something that neurodivergent students need to do a lot of the time. It's not that neurotypical students (those who don't have any disabilities that are classed as 'neurodiverse') are likely to be particularly nasty, but they may not understand, and that worries me.

I like to sit at the front of the classroom. Where do you like to sit? One of the big issues with neurodiversity is that routine helps and not being assigned a particular desk to sit at means I won't necessarily be able to sit at the same desk every week. When I don't have routine or when my coping strategies are compromised, I start to feel a build-up of pressure in my body, and it feels like the feeling that comes (especially in your hands) when you're squeamish and catch sight of blood. Sitting there, I wonder if other students realise my discomfort. If the tutor writes the running order up on the whiteboard, with approximate times of when each segment will start and finish, I feel a surge of relief. But when they don't, I have to mask again and pretend that the sudden changes don't affect me. I wish all tutors knew how important this is. I remind myself this will surely prepare me for times when clients don't show up to their appointments in my future practice.

When the class begins, we have a theory session. There is so much information to take on board. I shout out when I have a question or when I have some knowledge I wish to share. I wonder if people sit there silently cursing me for being so bolshie. In truth, I'm just trying to make sense of all the information, and I forget that other people are even in the room. My mind is on just that one track and I have to continue that thought process until the end of it, or the physical feeling gets worse. I don't mean to be so annoying, it's just my way of learning.

In skills practice sessions, I find it exceptionally hard. Working in triads just doesn't work for me. I understand why we do it – we're supposed to observe how others practise and use that knowledge to implement changes in our own style so that we develop more and more as the course progresses. 'Performance-related anxiety' is often found in people who identify as 'neurodivergent'. In skills sessions, I find the physical presence of another person really hard to bear, to the point where either my mind goes blank or I say something that I'm aware isn't for the benefit of my client, it's more for my observer. I wonder if that has ever happened to you? What would you do if it did?

Working remotely via an online platform such as Zoom or Microsoft Teams is reportedly harder for some counsellors than working in a face-to-face environment, yet those platforms have settings that allow the observers to be in the 'room' in a much more discreet capacity. For example, when the settings are changed to Speaker View, the only people that appear on screen are the counsellor and the client, as they are the only two speaking during the session. This gives the simulation of a 'real' counselling environment. How do you find working remotely online? Do you have a preference between online and face-to-face working?

Break-times… are you the one that everyone wants to be around or the one that everybody knows but everybody forgets to talk to? I'm the latter. I'm the most vocal but I sit there and wonder if anyone would actually care if I wasn't there. Sometimes I wish I could be like everybody else and not be seen as the troublemaker, but when I get frustrated, it's my disability that does what it knows to do.

The technical term is 'executive functioning'. It happens with stress, so if I know I have to work in a triad for a skills session directly after a theory session, for example, I will be likely to have a 'meltdown' in the theory session. This might look like huffing and puffing or making a noise, but that's just me showing that I'm stressed and scared. I feel like I'm the only left-handed person in a room of right-handed people that have just been told to cut a circle out of a piece of paper and there are only right-handed scissors in the box.

Thinking about the experiences you've had, or conjured up in your mind's eye at the start of this section and deepened as I've talked with you, how do your experiences compare with mine? Are there any similarities and differences? How does that make you feel? Is this something for your reflective journal?

ACTIVITY

We invite you to take up Zoë's invitation.

We also invite you to go back to the earlier material on group contracts, which we've said are there to make a classroom safe enough for the work that needs to be done there. In what ways might a group contract make a classroom safe enough for *all* learners? What else is needed, in your view, for other groups of learners – groups that you personally belong to, and groups that you don't? (The latter will involve doing some reading, and we've given examples of readings you can do around aspects of equality, diversity, inclusion and wellbeing on pp.67–71.)

You might write in prose, create a mind-map, draw, or record your responses.

What to do if something goes wrong in your learning relationships

There may be times when one or more relationships in your learning experience go so badly wrong that you feel unable to deal with it on your own. You may even contemplate leaving the course because of it. You may need an independent third party to provide advice and support.

One option open to you is the Psychotherapy and Counselling Union (PCU): www.psychotherapyandcounsellingunion.co.uk

The aims of the PCU are to campaign for 'true diversity and equal opportunities in the therapy world, and to support individuals who are discriminated against'. It works for all counsellors, psychotherapists and other practitioners, 'from every corner of the field, including trainees, on an equal basis'.

It is like a trade union, in that it supports its members in protecting and campaigning for their rights with regard to training and workplace issues, including health and safety, discrimination, harassment and bullying, and professional issues such as terms and conditions of employment, especially in the voluntary sector; complaints procedures; closure of courses and agencies, and the use of therapy to get people off benefits.

It is not a professional association, and it works alongside bodies like BACP, UKCP and NCS.

To access PCU support, you need to have been a member for three months. You can find details about membership rates on its website (above), and there are special reduced rates for trainees and for members of Black Therapy Matters and BAATN.

Experience

To learn more about the PCU and what it can do for students and trainees encountering difficulties, Deborah interviewed Phil Cox (Complaints Support Worker), Sasha Kaplin (Member Support Co-ordinator) and Richard Bagnall-Oakeley (a member of the PCU Executive Committee). These are key points from the conversation.

Psychotherapy and counselling training is unique in how much your very being is subject to scrutiny. It's taking you apart and rebuilding you. You're uniquely vulnerable. Know this from the start, and be aware of the personal impact it may have.

When you begin training, it's also important to know that problems can easily arise there – that's because the training is relational; it's about people and relationships. The relational is never straightforward, how could it be? People can come into training with an assumption that everyone in the therapy world is self-aware, that we're all 'good guys', when actually what we see in the world plays out in training. Be ready for this.

If you feel strongly about an area, particularly if you are a member of a minoritised group, be careful about bringing that to the fore while you're training. You may find yourself positioned as an ambassador, and you may be asked how you will work with people who are not in that group. Be careful what you're passionate about during training. Hold down strong passions until you're doing research or until you're post-training. Be open but not too open. Think in terms of self-care. Pass the course first. Be an activist later. Speak once you're safe. Get into a position of power so you can impact change from the inside.

You may be used to the idea that, if problems arise, you could transfer to another university/ training organisation using Accreditation of Prior Experience and Learning (APEL). You can do that sometimes in therapy training, but it's not so straightforward as in other subjects, especially at later stages of training. If you're going to go, go early.

If a problem arises for you that is your error,

start by getting some advice. You can feel very isolated if you're going through a disciplinary. PCU can put you in touch with someone to talk to for support, somebody who is on your side. Try to head off problems before more people become involved. When you're trying to head off a problem, face-to-face meetings are better than emails. Avoid going to meetings on your own. Keep a written record of what's happened. If it's your error, after taking advice, own what you did. A denial will finish your training. Show you're able to reflect and to learn from your error. That's often enough to resolve the problem. Be willing to accept a warning that is not put on your record. PCU has often negotiated this for people.

A denial is appropriate if you did nothing wrong.

If a problem arises that is not your error, that's about a university/training organisation, course or lecturer, it may well be something we've already encountered at PCU. In our work, some institutions, some courses and some lecturers are mentioned to us time and time again. There is work happening that you won't necessarily know about. There are paths from internal complaints to the Office of the Independent Adjudicator for Higher Education (OIAHE).

Discrimination is the most common issue brought to us.

On an issue that's affecting your group – perhaps racism from a tutor – be wary of becoming a spokesperson for the group. You can end up standing alone. You'll look like a difficult trainee. Speak to someone before you put your head above the parapet. PCU is there to give you advice and support and to help you think things through.

We've seen cases where marginalisation is clear, and others where it's difficult to prove. Don't say a course is racist unless you can evidence it. Be wary of saying anything that you can't evidence. The course won't want someone damaging its reputation. Keep emails, keep marks and feedback, let organisations dig the hole for themselves. Unless what's happening is outrageous, be patient. If an organisation wants to exit you and they can't do it on marks, they will do it in other ways and act outside their own guidelines. However, you can end up winning the battle but losing the war – one person for whom we acted won their case and got their fees back, but then they didn't get their training and it was difficult to get into another course.

We've seen cases where training organisations have agreed access arrangements/reasonable adjustment plans (RAPs), but have not provided what they've agreed. Some people realise they are neurodiverse during training, and institutions are not as good as they should be at responding to neurodiversity. Our advice is to speak to someone and get advice early: don't let problems with RAPs/access arrangements drag on. Sometimes people get in touch when it's already been a problem for a few months.

In clinical placements, you're doing work, but you're volunteering; it's a grey area as to whether you have rights. If your clinical hours aren't signed off, your course may be over. You need a third person involved to help facilitate a dialogue. PCU can do that. And there's the wider problem of exploitation. The long-term aim of PCU is the problem of trainees and qualified therapists not being paid for their work. Creating a Code of Practice, with minimum standards for placements, was a campaigning piece of work PCU undertook in 2018. You can find it here: **www.psychotherapyandcounsellingunion.co.uk/codes-of-practice**

Whatever the issue is, how you raise it is key. If you get angry, that will not go well for you.

> It will be seen as a red flag'; you'll be regarded as unable to deal with anxiety; your ability to become a therapist will be questioned. When you receive an email that you don't like, pause, don't just reply. It's the replies that are used against students. Try to be collaborative and reasonable. Always be co-operative, as far as possible. Be prepared to bend. How you present yourself will impact how people respond to you. Act in a way that shows who you are, not who they think you are. You're not a projection. You're not a scapegoat.
>
> PCU has overwhelmingly had good outcomes for people we've supported. Some students are disaffected after what's happened, and they choose to leave training early. Very few students have been unable to go back to their training.

Some websites offering advice to students

The Office for Students (OfS) is the executive arm of the Department for Education, which states that it 'works with higher education providers to make sure that students succeed in higher education'. Its web pages for students offer sections including support for disabled students, student mental health, tackling harassment and sexual misconduct, and suicide prevention:
www.officeforstudents.org.uk/for-students/student-rights-and-welfare

The National Union of Students (NUS) website explains: 'The National Union of Students does not handle complaints against educational inductions and cannot represent individual students. If you have a complaint against your institution, we would suggest getting in touch with your local students' union at your place of study, so they are aware of the issue and can provide support. Then you will need to raise the complaint internally to your place of study… If you then wanted to raise your complaint further, you have every right to do so'. Note that if you're training at a private institution, you're unlikely to be fully covered by the NUS:
www.nus.org.uk/more/faqs/complaints-about-your-institution

The Office of the Independent Adjudicator for Higher Education (OIAHE) is 'an independent body set up to review student complaints about higher education providers in England and Wales'. It is a free service for students. However, like the NUS, it 'normally expects students to follow their higher education provider's internal procedures to their conclusion before complaining to us':
www.oiahe.org.uk

Further reading

Casement, P. (2019). *Learning along the way.* Routledge.
Casement writes: 'If a student persists with a complaint, that persistence may not be recognized as a sign of health. Rather, a student may come to be pathologized because of it' (p. 46). He continues: 'It is not pathology to feel disturbed by mistreatment, but it can be pathological to accept it' (p.49). Read this as an antidote to the mainstream and for some positive reinforcement of your sense of injustice.

Ahmed, S. (2021). *Complaint!* **Duke University Press.**
Feminist writer Sara Ahmed examines what we can learn about power from those who complain about abuses of power, drawing on oral and written testimonies from academics and students who have made complaints about harassment, bullying, and unequal working conditions at universities. A thoroughly refreshing take on complaints systems and why they are weighted against the complainant.

> **TAKEAWAY MESSAGES**
> - Take creating group contracts seriously – they're an opportunity to collaboratively think and feel through how you want to be with each other (peers and tutors/lecturers/trainers) as you all encounter the challenges of psychotherapy and counselling training in your particular group/s.
> - Openness to exploring each other's needs in the training room (and beyond) can contribute to your thinking about how you'll work with clients. Thus, writing group contracts has wider meaning than what happens in the training room and its liminal spaces.
> - Learning in relationship with other people (tutors/lecturers/trainers and peers) through group work broadly, experiential learning and PD is central to counselling and psychotherapy training because being a counsellor and psychotherapist (whatever modality or approach you're studying) is about being in relationship with the other (clients).
> - Being in relationship is not the same, or even a similar experience for everyone – equality, diversity, inclusion and wellbeing are all very important to work with in the classroom and in the therapy room. We are reminded of the need to acknowledge that people have different learning styles and needs.
> - We've heard PCU strongly encouraging you to be careful when raising concerns while you're studying. We've also heard Anonymous (2018), who feels that you should raise concerns if you feel concerned. What we have tried to do is present you with more than one way of seeing. As with so much in our field, we make our own ways forward, working with the particular circumstances in which we find ourselves. We reiterate that harassment, bullying and microaggressions are never acceptable.

The next chapter…

In the next chapter, we explore some skills and techniques for effective study.

4

Skills and techniques for effective study

This chapter is intended to accompany you as you begin to immerse yourself in studying and as assessments and assignments appear on the horizon, or as you consider what it may involve for you to do such work.

You'll be studying and anticipating your first assessments and assignments while acclimatising yourself to some or all of the learning relationships and processes we explored in Chapters 2 and 3. Those learning relationships and processes, as we've said, will often be intense, and much of what's happening may be new to you. Be sure, then, to make time to notice and celebrate all of your efforts. That's part of study skills, too.

In this chapter, we've chosen the following skills and techniques to explore with you to help you make the most of your studies:

- reading module handbooks/online learning environments, learning outcomes, assessment criteria, assignment titles, formative feedback, and keeping the assessment requirements in view
- learning the language and widening your vocabulary
- reading and keeping useful notes
- getting the most out of libraries.

In Chapter 5, we'll move on to a broad overview of the sort of assessments and assignments you're likely to be doing in your counselling and psychotherapy training. Chapter 6 will drill down into two common forms of assignment: essays and case studies.

Before we turn to any of the above, we begin with access arrangements/reasonable adjustment plans (RAPs). We want to let you know, as you begin to think about effective study for assignments and assessments, that there is support available (or there should be – we heard from PCU in the last chapter that students have approached them to say that support has not always been forthcoming).

Student support services and access arrangements/reasonable adjustments

You may have had access arrangements/RAPs when you've previously been in education. If you have, you will know some of the terrain as you move into studying counselling and psychotherapy. We say *some* of the terrain purposefully – counselling and psychotherapy training brings some particular issues to consider, as we'll see below.

You may, however, be moving into these new studies with needs that have never been met in educational settings, among other places – perhaps because you have not wanted to say that you needed support (like Alex in Chapter 1), or you may not have known much about what might be on offer or how asking for it might be received.

We know that seeking support is not a straightforward matter. Society is currently organised around a set of norms that nobody actually meets. Disabled people, people with mental health conditions and neurodivergent people (among others) are often treated badly and thoughtlessly. Counsellors and psychotherapists will regularly hear clients telling us all this and more, and will know some or all of it from our own lived experiences and those of people close to us. We don't underestimate what it takes to say what you need and why.

It's important to know that universities have an 'anticipatory duty' and must make 'reasonable adjustments' to ensure that students can access their studies, as outlined in the Equality Act (2010). This means they must not to wait to be asked to make their services accessible to disabled people, and must make the necessary changes to remove obstacles to a disabled person accessing their courses and facilities.

As you think about starting counselling and psychotherapy training (or as you move through it), you may begin to think that some support might be useful. So, we felt it important to invite a specialist in the field to contribute to this chapter.

We created three fictional students – Tom, Craig and Sam – and asked Louise Kidd, Disability Advisor at the University of Salford, how she would advise them.

Craig

Craig is a first-year BSc counselling student. He's always suspected he might be dyslexic, but his parents object to 'labels', so he held back while he was living with them. Now he's left home, he feels able to seek advice from the student support service. Louise says:
We'd speak with Craig about having a referral to an adult educational psychologist assessment via the university, with a specialist service called the Educational Guidance Service (**www.egs.org.uk**). Students pay a contribution towards an assessment like this – it's £50 currently – and the university pays the rest (currently around £290). Craig can keep the adult educational psychologist assessment and use it after university, when he in employment, as well.

While Craig is waiting for his assessment, we'd suggest he has a look at group and one-to-one sessions offered by our Skills for Learning service in the library. Other universities will have this too.

We also have a neurodiversity group at Salford, and Craig might benefit from connecting with the group and meeting with other neurodiverse students. Other universities are likely to have similar groups.

If the assessment says Craig is dyslexic, we'd work with him to set up a reasonable adjustment plan. This could include things like one-week extensions to deadlines, coloured paper for reading materials and voice recording of lectures – our inclusive teaching and learning framework at Salford outlines that students can voice-record the taught theory aspects of their course. If Craig's processing speed is impacted, we'd consider with Craig whether there might be adjustments around group work and presentations – for instance, how many people would be in the group/audience.

Under our inclusive teaching and learning framework (which will be similar to other universities), no student is marked down on spelling/grammar unless these are core competencies for a specific assignment. If something is a core competency for a course, then the assessment brief has to state this explicitly. Spelling/grammar are only usually core competencies in medical areas, where spelling of medical language needs to be correct and exact.

With the diagnosis in place, we'd suggest Craig applies for the Disabled Students' Allowance (DSA) for specific learning difficulty. This could enable him to get a laptop (for which he'd also pay a contribution), voice-recording software, read-aloud software (to help with proofreading), and to have one-to-one study skills support. Study skills support would usually be one hour a week, focused on assessments, and would provide guidance on note-making strategies, support with organisation and time management, and guidance on the production of work and academic writing for higher education. This support would be in place throughout the course, to discuss what assignments are asking for and to make sure Craig is doing what's being asked, to look at the structure of his written work, and to offer guidance on referencing. The intention is to continually help Craig develop his study techniques.

Given what Craig has shared about his parents and labelling, he might want to a referral to our wellbeing services and to discuss the impact of receiving a diagnosis.

Tom

Tom is a final year MSc counselling student. He has decided he wants to disclose his health condition, which is one where his energy is limited. Louise says:

We'd advise Tom to apply for the Disabled Students' Allowance (DSA). With the DSA, like Craig, Tom could get software that could help him. He could also get some ergonomic equipment for use at home, such as a supportive desk and chair, or equipment to use to work from his bed or sofa, like a lap tray, so he can be more comfortable while he studies. He could potentially get taxis to and from university and to and from his placement, if travel was a barrier to accessing education.

Tom's reasonable adjustment plan could include one-week extensions to assessment deadlines, attendance catch-up meetings if he misses some classes due to low energy levels, and building rest breaks into classes. If Tom has physical pain, we could provide a more robust chair than a standard classroom chair, to support his back and arms.

We're likely to discuss with him whether he experiences flare-ups in his condition – if it's worse in cold weather, for instance, and if it affects him cognitively – does Tom experience brain fog because of energy levels and pain? The reasonable adjustment plan would make the department staff aware that flare-ups might affect his attendance and engagement.

Tom might not have a formal diagnosis. You do need that to get the DSA, as it is part of the government Student Finance scheme. However, even if he doesn't have a formal diagnosis, he may still be able to get support from the university. We ask for medical evidence, but we can accept prescriptions for pain medication, a letter from a psychotherapist/counsellor, or a referral letter that shows Tom is in the process of seeking a diagnosis. We check in six weeks after the reasonable adjustment plan appointment and again three months later. If a student requires a review of support after this point, they can contact our service for an appointment to review and extend their support. We don't leave people without support, but we do need some form of evidence to put in either a temporary or full reasonable adjustment plan.

Sometimes what people want most is for lecturers to be made aware, so that they don't look like they're simply not paying attention when they're actually too tired to concentrate.

We'd also offer Tom a referral for wellbeing support. He may find it useful to talk through how he's feeling, perhaps particularly about what it's like to access support in his final year of study.

Sam

Sam is a first year MSc counselling student who has cerebral palsy and uses a wheelchair. They also experience anxiety and depression. Louise says:

As for Craig and Tom, we'd suggest Sam applies for the Disabled Students' Allowance (DSA). The DSA could be used for ergonomic equipment, such as a height-adjustable desk to use at home, equipment/software to help them dictate their assignments, a voice recorder to use in class, and read-aloud software. It could also be used for accessible taxis to get to and from university and placements.

Sam could also have a mental health mentor who would meet with them for an hour a week, to help with motivation, organising their workload, time management and a general wellbeing check-in in relation to university and life in general. The mental health mentor isn't a counsellor but has a mental health qualification or experience. We'd also signpost Sam to wellbeing support for anxiety and depression.

We'd talk with Sam and see if they require practical support. If so, the university would look at providing them with a practical support assistant. The practical support assistant could support Sam by setting out their equipment in class, such as their voice recorder and laptop. If Sam isn't able to use a voice recorder, the practical support assistant could scribe for them. It's a challenging role for a note-taker to work with a counselling and psychotherapy student. They have to take down the theory, not the student's personal information. They are given clear advice about how to do this. Equally, if Sam is using a voice recorder, the practical support assistant will turn it off when personal information is being shared in a skills group, for instance. Sam would also have a personal emergency evacuation plan, so that if there is an emergency they can exit safely from the premises.

We'd talk with Sam about a reasonable adjustment plan. We could arrange one-week extensions for deadlines if they find they are much slower at studying than other students. If Sam finds it anxiety-provoking to speak in front of others, arrangements can be made to reduce the number of people in the audience – for instance, just the teaching staff could attend. We'd hope to review this with Sam as they progress through the course. They might be able to present to more people later on. For group work, we can say that Sam should work in smaller groups, or work with someone they know. We know counselling and psychotherapy requires people to be able to work with a range of people, so again, we'd hope to be able to review this with Sam over time, and the mental health mentor would work with them to develop strategies to work with other people.

Further reading – websites

The following websites are useful sources of information and advice. The list covers wider issues than just those mentioned in the fictional vignettes above:

Anxiety UK – **www.anxietyuk.org.uk**

The Care Leavers Association – **www.careleavers.com**

The Dyscalculia Association – **www.dyscalculiaassociation.uk**

Dyslexia Action – **https://dyslexiaaction.org.uk**

Dyspraxia Foundation – **https://dyspraxiafoundation.org.uk**

Mind – **www.mind.org.uk**

National Autistic Society – **www.autism.org.uk**

RNIB – **www.rnib.org.uk**

RNID – **https://rnid.org.uk**

Stand Alone (support for estranged adults) – **www.standalone.org.uk**

Tourettes Action – **www.tourettes-action.org.uk**

There's also a highly recommended #TherapistsConnect interview with Deaf therapist Victoria Nelson at **https://therapistsconnect.buzzsprout.com/1091903/4827413**

ACTIVITY

Review one of the above websites/podcasts
Choose a website/podcast (or more than one) from the list above, and explore what you find there. It might be a website that relates to your own lived experience, or one talking about a topic you know little or nothing about. Consider what you have learned from your reading/listening, and how you might use it in your counselling and psychotherapy studies, in relating with others in the classroom and in meeting with others in the therapy room. Remember, when you meet clients, they are not

> there to teach us. We need to be informed and ready to encounter a variety of difference and diversity in our work.

Our thoughts about access arrangements

We want to say a few words about our views on access arrangements/reasonable adjustments, as lecturers and psychotherapists. We believe in an individual, careful response to people's needs (people are individuals and deserve care). We also feel that many of the access arrangements that are seen as 'reasonable adjustments' should be standard practice so that nobody needs to go through a formal procedure to get them. There's no reason, for instance, why *any* student (or lecturer/tutor) shouldn't get up and move about during a class. And if we're giving a student written feedback, we'd expect to write it clearly, with specific advice for feed-forward, for *all* students.

You might like to reflect on your own responses to what we've said here. What might help you study more effectively, even if you feel you don't have any specific learning support needs?

Laying the foundations for effective study

We are going to start by looking at module handbooks, online learning environments (courses often use sites like Blackboard or Moodle to house learning materials, to host online classes/discussions and to receive assessments for grading), learning outcomes, assessment criteria, assignment titles, formative feedback and keeping the assessment requirements in view. These all form part of the ground for effective learning, teaching and assessment.

We begin by noting that there are students who never read module handbooks and never explore the online learning environment (if there is one). They work with what's immediately to hand (whatever arises in a class) and what absolutely has to be done (an assignment).

This is one way of operating, but students who don't read the documents on offer miss out on lots of important information, and often don't do as well as they might. Students who do read the preparatory material provided and take time to explore the online environment tend to do better. They know what's going to be happening in a module week to week, and they know what's going to be asked of them there. They're able to see more of the nuances and, where they've not understood something, they've been in a position to ask informed questions.

Sometimes there can be errors in documentation. No one's perfect – not even course tutors! Where students notice errors, this is also a learning opportunity, as it can lead to unexpected discussions.

Obviously then, our advice to you is to take some time to read your module handbooks and explore your online learning environment (if there is one). We genuinely believe you will profit from the time you give to this.

Modules have learning outcomes. These are set out in a short set of bullet points indicating a) the knowledge and b) the skills you should have acquired by the end of the module, if you have passed. You'll find learning outcomes in the module handbook, and if there is an online learning environment, they are likely to be described there (among many other things).

Tutors/lecturers/trainers (who may or may not have written the learning outcomes themselves) use a module's learning outcomes to structure the learning and teaching offered in a module, and to make sure that you'll be in a position to evidence that learning in assessments.

You should receive details of the assignment title/s for a module as soon as you start studying it. That's good practice: it means that you can start to think about where your work in a module is leading immediately you start studying it.

You might be asked to evidence learning outcomes in your work, or you may be asked to evidence a set of assessment criteria developed from the learning outcomes, or you may be asked to evidence both learning outcomes and assessment criteria.

To 'evidence' something in your work means to show that you know and/or can do what is being asked of you. A typical skills-based learning outcome/assessment criterion for an essay would be 'to evidence, or show, that you can communicate in writing'. A knowledge-based learning outcome might be, if we take the example of an ethics essay, 'to evidence, or show, your understanding of a professional body's ethical framework'.

Whatever the exact requirement, you have to meet it in order to pass the assignment. You can submit an otherwise brilliant response to an assignment title, but if, in the course of making that response, you haven't met the assessment criteria and/or learning outcomes, the marker will have no choice but to fail the piece of work.

There should be opportunities throughout modules for you to ask questions about what the learning outcomes and assessment criteria mean.

In particular, as assessment deadlines draw closer, there should be opportunities for you to check out that how you are approaching the assignment title is meeting the learning outcomes and/or assessment criteria.

Courses/modules/module leaders will have different views about whether you can only ask questions in class (which might be the case if a class is very large), or whether you can also show tutors/lecturers/trainers your assignment plan (or part of an assignment, such as its introduction). Check out what is available on the course/module you're taking.

Worryingly, some students never take up opportunities to share work with lecturers/tutors/trainers and receive feedback. This includes students who are struggling, who then don't have an opportunity to say they are finding it hard and ask for help.

If you're feeling in any way unsure about what you're doing and advice is available (and you feel comfortable approaching the tutor/lecturer/trainer concerned), we strongly encourage you to take it up. Getting feedback on a draft is an example of *formative feedback* (feedback that does not result in a grade), ahead of *summative feedback* (which does result in a grade).

However content you feel about your work, it's always useful to get some formative feedback – a second pair of eyes looking objectively at what you're doing before it's submitted can be helpful.

While you're working on the assignment question, have it and the assessment criteria/learning outcomes printed out on a piece of paper beside you, or pinned up on a board (or whatever works for you, to keep it in mind and readily at hand), so that you can check from time to time, and especially as you reach the editing phase , that what you are writing matches up with the question you're responding to and the assessment criteria and/or learning outcomes you need to evidence in order to pass.

Learning the language and widening your vocabulary

As you enter into a new field of study, or progress to a new level of study within it, you'll find language in use that you haven't heard before. Widening your vocabulary in general is also an excellent idea during counselling and psychotherapy training.

Learning counselling and psychotherapy language and widening your general vocabulary can help you in the following ways:

- In the training room – it can help you follow counselling and psychotherapy material and arguments more easily.
- In doing assignments (written and spoken) – it can make you more able to select the shade of meaning you require in your expression, both in relation to counselling and psychotherapy and more generally, and this can make your writing more interesting to read and your presentations more interesting to listen to.
- In the therapy room – widening your vocabulary can enable you to understand a wider range of words that a client might use, reflect back more effectively, or clarify the feelings a client is sharing with you, and convey ideas from counselling and psychotherapy in ways that a client will understand and find most helpful.

Next time you are in class, maybe you could ask the tutor/lecturer/trainer if they can explain unfamiliar words as they come up (bearing in mind it isn't always straightforward for anyone to do this on the spot, particularly with words that are quite familiar to us). You could also ask if they can recommend a dictionary explaining the terms used in the approach you're studying.

Asking questions about words in the training room can also lead to a wider discussion in your group around the meanings of many words, and the power of language.

You might decide, at the beginning of a new course, new module or new topic, to collect words that are frequently used and write your own definitions for them, based on the information gleaned from class, from a good dictionary, and from other set readings and material you access for yourself. You can learn as many new words from your peers, in class and socially, as you can from your tutors/lecturers. The most valuable way of learning anything is by being actively involved in it, by engaging fully with everything on offer.

Along the way, you will hear therapy words/phrases that don't appeal to you and that you don't want to use (most therapists have a collection of these). Learning how *you* want to express yourself in the language on offer is an important part of your development as a practitioner.

A thesaurus will be useful for widening your vocabulary. Unlike a dictionary, a thesaurus will not tell you what a word means but it will give you lots of alternatives to that word. You can buy a thesaurus in book form, or you can search on the internet for alternatives to particular words. Just be careful it is being used in the way you also want to use it. 'Congruent' in Rogers' terminology will not necessarily be adequately replaced with 'coinciding' or 'identical'.

We all have favourite words we stick to (once you start listening back to recordings of your client work, you'll see how much you over-use some words and expressions). A thesaurus will give you some alternatives and add variety to your expression.

Be careful not to use a thesaurus all the time, though; there's nothing wrong with using everyday language. There will certainly be alternative words to use, but they may not be ones that people *would* use, and they can sound and look strange sometimes. 'She said she was going out' sounds very odd if written as, 'She expressed that she was departing'. Use your own judgement about whether an alternative word works and is readily understood: words are not always interchangeable.

ACTIVITY

An invitation to use an online thesaurus (and your own pre-existing vocabulary) to make a list of alternatives to a range of feelings often talked about in counselling and psychotherapy

You might start with these words and then progress to others that come to mind:

- I'm angry
- I'm sad
- I'm happy
- I'm hurt
- I'm afraid
- I'm in love
- I hate
- I'm curious
- I'm jealous
- I'm excited
- I'm bored
- I feel nothing

So, for example, rather than saying 'I'm angry' you might say, 'I'm furious', 'I'm enraged', 'I'm incandescent', 'I'm beside myself', and so on. (If you are feeling angry, or can imagine it, choose a word that captures the nature of your anger just now.)

Reading texts and making useful notes

Reading

Before you read anything, ask yourself 'Why am I reading this?' and 'How well do I need to understand and remember this material?'

This will ensure you read with a purpose. If you are not sure why you are reading any book, or what you are wanting to do with the learning you gain from the material, your reading will be less effective, and maybe not even be useful at all.

How to read a book for study

Many readers will be familiar with reading fiction for fun or intellectual stimulation. But this kind of reading is perhaps the only occasion when you read a book by opening it at page 1 and reading it word by word from cover to cover. For textbooks and the materials you will have to read for your course, your first step should be to preview what is to be read.

When buying a book, most people try to get a feel of it by quickly flicking through the pages, reading the back cover notes and going through the table of contents and any endorsements. This is more or less what we mean by previewing the material: it helps you find out which bits of the material will be most useful to you.

We suggest you consider using a preview checklist like this, in which you approach reading the book more systematically by looking at:

1. The title. This tells you the general subject area (is it what you want or need to read about?). A subtitle will also give you clues. Make a note of the title, the author(s), the publisher(s), the publication date.

2. The author. Check out their biography (most books include this, either at the front or back). How qualified and experienced are they? Their biography may also include a list of their other publications, which may also be useful to look at. Remember, though, that new authors emerge all the time and have just as much of interest to say (if not more) than 'big names' in a field, so don't discount someone out of hand because this is their first book.

3. The publisher. Are they noted for the quality counselling books they publish? What type of counselling books do they usually publish? Mainstream? Critical? Authoritative?

4. Date of publication. The page that backs the title page will tell you when and where the book was first published, how many reprints it has had (the more there are, the more popular the book is, and therefore it may be more useful for you). It will also tell you if the book is a new edition, meaning that it will have been revised since it was first written. Always try to get the latest edition, so you can benefit from any new material and be confident it is up to date. Don't dismiss older books – they may be classic texts, and you can use them in that way in your writing. So don't chuck Freud or Rogers in the bin, but do check that your latest 'Introduction to counselling' text really is the most recent and relevant to today's contexts.

5. The cover notes or blurb. These should state the level at which the book is pitched (introductory course, certificate, diploma, degree or postgraduate) and how the subject is treated. You'll also find on the back cover (and often at greater length in the opening pages of the book) what other people in the field think of the book (obviously only good reviews appear there, but the endorsers have to be able to stand by what they've written, so reading the endorsements can be helpful).

6. The table of contents. Do the chapter headings relate to your reason for reading the book? Make a note of the chapters you might find useful.

7. Preface/Introduction. This should tell you the scope and purpose of the book, provide a brief summary of the chapter contents, and suggest how the book should be used to get the best out of it.

8. Index. The subject index (at the back) lists key words that represent important themes in the content. Check for words that reflect your learning interests and needs. Does the book suit your purpose? There may also be a separate name index, listing who is mentioned and quoted in the book. Are these authors/authorities you have heard of and are they relevant to your interests and needs?

9. Conclusion. Unlike when you're reading a novel, it is not a bad thing to read the end of a textbook first. The conclusion should sum up the key points in the book. Similarly, the opening and/or closing paragraphs of each chapter should introduce and summarise the contents. Some authors helpfully offer brief bullet-point summaries.

10. Bibliography/References. This is the list of publications the author has consulted and/or quoted from. The dates of these sources will give you a good idea of how up-to-date the author's work is. Are they quoting sources from the current decade? Any older, unless they are classic texts, and you should question whether it is going to be useful to you. You can also find ideas for your own further reading here, especially if you agree/disagree with what the author says about these books (and some authors provide 'further reading' lists).

Having done this, you will have a fair idea what the book is about without having read much of the text at all. Keep a record of all the titles, authors, publishers and contents of the books you have previewed in this way. It will be invaluable when planning assignments.

The next stage is to approach the text, but not necessarily at page 1.

First, using your preview, select the part/s you are interested in, the part/s that suit your purpose. (You might, of course, like the look of the book so much that you want to read all of it, or every chapter looks ideal for your purpose. If you're doing a book review, you certainly have to read all of the book.)

Second, skim over the whole book, noting the structure of the material, subheadings, tables, diagrams, overviews and summaries. Make notes if you need to.

Third, read the overviews and summaries (if there are any) for each chapter, and make notes on the central ideas that the author is trying to convey.

Fourth, read the text. Jot down notes as you go along, remembering to note page numbers as that will help you locate material for future reference. It is very frustrating to find you have noted an important point but you have no clue as to where you read it.

Having done this, do you understand the material? Can you remember it? Now is the time to review what you have just read. Think back over the text and, without looking at the text and in your own words, see if you can describe the main ideas expressed in the material. Again, it is better if you write this down (or type it, of course) at this point, because the more you become actively involved in the material, the more you will learn and remember of what you have just read.

This progressive elaboration of the material means that you can read to the depth that suits your purpose – from last minute cramming before a class to reading an entire book to gain deep understanding.

Making useful notes

As we saw in Chapter 3, most counselling and psychotherapy courses are based around group work and the personal experience and input of the participants. However, some of the input from your tutors/lecturers/trainers will be in the form of lectures (short and long, formal and informal, online or in person).

Even though the majority of your learning will not be from lectures, note-making is still essential. It is another way of interacting with the material you're studying, and can be used with books, journals, radio and TV broadcasts, as well as lectures, tutorials and group discussions. You'll even find some things worth noting down in informal discussions. People often forget to do this, and learning from informal discussions is then lost.

Notice that we're using the term 'note-making' rather than 'notes', indicating that the activity is as important as the content of the end product. Also, we have called it note-making, not note-taking, to emphasise that we're talking about a creative activity – you are in interaction with the material. You're never aiming to record word for word what someone says (unless they are dictating a passage to you); you are aiming to capture in your own words the main points they are making.

Note-making is also a good way of ensuring you concentrate throughout a lecture, and can ask pertinent and relevant questions at the end, if you feel there are areas where you would like more clarity or explanation.

There are two broad categories of material from which it is useful to make notes: written material and spoken material, which we will now discuss in turn.

Making useful notes from written material

Your aims in making notes from written material are:

- to locate the exciting ideas and quotes in what you're reading, to find what calls to you in it – material that you agree with/disagree with/want to consider more
- to condense the material, maintaining its essential meanings
- to cross-refer it to other notes (such as a workshop you attended, or a reading on a similar topic)
- to relate it to an assignment (such as what it offers to an essay/presentation question you're working on), and

- to demonstrate to yourself that you understand what you're reading because you can put the information in your own words – rather like the skill of reflecting back what a client says in a counselling and psychotherapy session.

In your notes, be sure to distinguish between quotes from the book and your own notes. Be sure to put all direct quotes in quote marks and make a note of the author, date and page number, so you can easily find it again when you write your assignment. This is important to avoid accidental plagiarism (when you claim something written by another author as your own work).

Making useful notes from spoken material

No two lectures (and lecturers) are the same. This is to be expected rather than criticised: part of your learning as a counsellor and psychotherapist is to work with differences, rather than requiring everyone to be the same.

If you are returning to study after several years, practise your note-making skills before you start attending lectures. One way of doing this is to make notes from radio programmes (try BBC Radio 4) or podcasts. Make some notes and then reflect back to yourself (or to a long-suffering other) what the key points were.

People's style of note-making ranges from the verbatim account (if you do shorthand or write or type very fast) to the barest of outlines.

Good lectures (and lecturers) use repetition, multiple examples and re-emphasis so that the audience has more than one opportunity to understand the purpose of the material. There's an old saying: 'Tell them what you are going to say, say it and then tell them what you've said.' It does work. It is useful to know this before you attend a lecture, so that you know you won't need to write or type everything that is said, unless you choose to do so, and that what the lecturer says very briefly at the start will be expanded on later in the lecture, and summarised at the end.

The amount of notes you need to make will depend on the content of the lecture (lectures that have a heavy factual content may require more notes – and this is where PowerPoint slides are invaluable); how familiar you are with the material; whether there are alternative sources where you can retrieve the information, such as PowerPoint slides, a recording, a detailed handout, and/or the full text of the lecture, or if the lecturer is talking about a paper they wrote (which you could then read beforehand, and just focus on your impressions in the lecture).

Here are two suggestions for making notes at in-person lectures: use abbreviations wherever possible to save time, and leave plenty of space between points so that you can go back if needed to expand on a point made earlier.

After the lecture, check you can read your writing – if you can't, you may need to re-write your notes while the lecture is still fresh in your memory. However, these days students tend to type their lecture notes directly onto their laptops and annotate the slides as the lecture goes along. This removes difficulties with handwriting.

It is notable that the move to online lectures during the 2020/21 Covid-19 pandemic was helpful to many students. And it seems the practice is likely to persist (to an extent).

You can pause a recorded online lecture whenever you need to, to think through the material, make some notes and annotate lecture slides. You can also listen again whenever you wish – for instance, if you need to clarify in your head and rephrase in your own words what the lecturer is saying.

Another category of lecture that you may encounter is a presentation at a conference or workshop where the presenter is reading from a prepared paper. Sometimes participants will be given an abstract or summary of the paper before or after the presentation. It is not usual to ask the presenter to slow down or repeat themselves on such occasions. You will just have to do the best you can.

Overall, when making notes, the most important questions to ask yourself are, 'Why am I making these notes?' and, 'What am I going to use them for?' You must make your notes fit your needs.

Getting the most out of libraries

Sharon Potter is Research Support Librarian, Nottingham Trent University, and Ellie Lupton was at the time of writing a BA sociology student at Nottingham Trent University. Here they discuss how to make best use of the library.

Ellie: I have to write an assignment on 'Empathetic approaches in counselling with people experiencing mental health issues'. Where would you recommend searching for useful academic sources?

Sharon: If you're looking for books, search your library catalogue first, as that's the best place for those resources. You can extend your search using Amazon, the British Library catalogue and a collection of academic and research catalogues called Library Hub Discover. If you want to search more widely, or if you're studying at MA/MSc level, you need to include journal articles. I would recommend you search your library catalogue for those, if it includes journal articles. There are other places you can search, too. Start with Google Scholar (**https://scholar.google.com/**) – it will give you a good overview of what's available for your topic. It also includes publications before they are added to library catalogues and databases, so it enables you to find resources that are very recently published. Then check which databases your library subscribes to (databases are collections of journal articles from a wide range of journals). You don't need to know which journals are relevant for your research topic because the database search will bring together all the relevant articles from any source, and that's very useful if you haven't studied a subject before – if, for instance, if you're moving to counselling and psychotherapy for your postgraduate studies. Check which databases are relevant, and make a note of those that you find retrieve results that are the most useful.

E: What would you suggest to ensure that I'm searching effectively?

S: First of all, you need to think what it is you're searching for. Don't just type the title of your assignment into the database, as people sometimes do. You need to break it down into the different elements or concepts. For example, there are three concepts in your assignment – empathy, counselling, and mental health. Then, within each concept, think of different keywords. Some concepts may not have alternative keywords so there will just be one keyword (or phrase), but, if that's not the case, try to think of as many synonyms and alternatives as you can for each concept. Make a note of them so you don't forget them and have to do the thinking again. Then you build up your search based on the keywords and phrases for each concept. You might consider creating a concept grid so you can see how your search will be constructed, as in the table here:

Table 4.1: Concept grid

Concept	Keyword 1	Keyword 2	Keyword 3
1. Empathy	Compassion	Empathic engagement	Emotional intelligence
2. Counselling	Psychotherapy		
3. Mental health	Mental illness	Mental disorders	Mental distress

With a database, you should be able to enter the search terms for each concept as one line, with AND and OR linking them, like this (I'll explain the inverted commas below):

    empathy OR compassion OR 'empathic engagement' OR 'emotional intelligence'
    AND   counselling OR psychotherapy
    AND   'mental health' OR 'mental illness' OR 'mental disorders'

When you have several relevant references (or 'records'), look at the titles, abstracts and keywords for them, because they may suggest additional keywords or, in some instances, the correct terminology to use for more effective searching.

Other techniques you can use include phrase searching. So, for instance, putting the inverted commas around the phrase 'mental health', as in my example, means the search will retrieve references that include the phrase 'mental health', rather than just the separate keywords 'mental' and 'health'. This is useful in any database, but particularly in those with a multi-disciplinary coverage, and in Google Scholar. It's a quick and effective way of filtering out lots of irrelevant references.

You can also limit your searches to different fields in databases. This is helpful if you get too many references and can't think how to narrow them down by using further keywords. You can limit your search to the abstract, for example, because the abstract condenses the key elements of the article. If your search terms are in the abstract, the article should be relevant. You can also truncate keywords: instead of typing all the different variations of a word, type the stem and then an asterisk – for example, behaviour*. This will look for behaviour, behaviours, behavioural and so forth. You can also limit the search by publication type, depending on your research. You may want to limit your search to peer-reviewed journal articles, as these are in scholarly journals and have undergone a rigorous review by experts in the field before they are published, but in counselling you would probably also want to include professional journals, which will have qualitative research articles as well.

E: You were saying you can search in the abstract. How would you do that in a search engine? I've searched using keywords, but I didn't know how to refine it so that the words come only from the abstract.

S: In most databases you have an advanced search option. Some databases default to this screen but if it doesn't and the default is the basic search without the option to specify which field to search in, you need to go to a screen where you can select the field. The default in most databases is to search everything, which is why you can end up with far too much. If that's the case, select 'Abstract' from the drop-down menu. You can also limit your search to the keywords or descriptor fields, but your search terms have to match the keywords that have been assigned to the records in those databases.

E: Thank you. I'm wondering how I decide which are key papers and who are the key authors in a field?

S: Most university libraries will have either Scopus or Web of Science, which are citation databases. They cover all disciplines, and when you search either of them, you can reorder your set of references by the number of times they've been cited by other journal articles within those databases. If the author has been highly cited, that's a good indication that they have been influential in that area of research. You just have to be aware that very often the top-cited paper is a review article and not primary research. To identify the authors, both these databases have an analyse function, so if you select all those references and click on Analyse, it will quickly tell you how many papers each author in that reference list has written and you can see if one or two authors have been more prolific than the others in that area. Remember also that key papers/authors don't have to be the most established 'names', so you shouldn't disregard new writing and work that interests you, even if it hasn't yet been widely cited.

E: You mentioned review articles, should they be ignored?

S: It can be useful to read a review article because it might lead you to other journal articles that perhaps you haven't picked up through your searches.

E: What about other types of publications that aren't books or journal articles? Are there any other sources I should be looking for?

S: In counselling/psychotherapy, there will be reports, statistics, policy documents and other types of publications you won't find through the databases, which are known as 'grey literature'. These are likely to be produced by government departments, medical bodies, professional associations, societies and organisations that work in counselling – such as BACP. Conference proceedings can also be an important source, as research is often presented at conferences ahead of publication. Some databases, like Scopus, Web of Science and Zetoc, include these.

E: When searching the library catalogue, I've found some dissertations, but I'm not sure if

I can use them, as they've been written by another student. What do you think?

S: That's a good question. You can use them as long as they're relevant and add to your writing. If you think about it, when you use a journal article, that's work done by someone else.

E: I've sometimes heard that I should only cite peer-reviewed work. Would dissertations be classed as peer reviewed?

S: Not really, but they will have gone through an examination-type process. That's interesting because, as I mentioned earlier, you can limit your search to peer-reviewed articles and that's good in terms of finding good quality research, but in an area like counselling/psychotherapy, there might be other work that is relevant that isn't peer reviewed. You need to think about the type of source that you're using and what it's adding to your research – is it relevant? For example, if the article is from a professional journal and it's in a curated database (some databases include professional magazines), it should be safe to use. The tone and content will be different to that of an academic peer-reviewed journal but that doesn't mean it won't be good or relevant – it's just different. But if you rely solely on that kind of information, you are unlikely to get high marks, so be sure to include peer-reviewed articles predominantly.

E: What if the library can't provide copies of everything I've found?

S: Your library won't have access to everything you find, so you need to check your library's arrangement to obtain resources externally – primarily from the British Library, but sometimes from other libraries, and sometimes directly from the publisher. This service is generally referred to as an inter-library loan. First, check if your level of study qualifies for inter-library loans, as some universities limit this service to final year undergraduates and MA/MSc students. Then check if there is a limit on the number you can request, because if there is, you need to prioritise your requests. Also, check if there's a charge.

E: I can see I'll amass a lot of resources. How would you recommend keeping track of everything?

S: Consider using a reference management system. Check which one your library has a licence for. It's likely to be RefWorks or EndNote. There are also free packages, such as Mendeley and Zotero. They all work in a very similar way: you'll export references from the databases or Google Scholar into the software, which will create a record of your references. You can set up folders to organise them by theme or by different assignments, and then, when you're ready to write up, you can use these systems to integrate with your Word document to generate a reference list in the appropriate reference style. Remember to check which reference style your coursework should use. You have to be consistent with your referencing. When you look at a reference list at the end of a journal article or book chapter, you'll see that there's a consistency and they're presented in a certain style and will have all the elements in a set order.

E: Students often wonder why referencing is so important.

S: You need to reference for two reasons. One is to acknowledge the fact that you are using somebody else's work, and the second is to enable whoever's reading your work to locate the original source to see where you've got your information from. You might have found some articles that your tutor hasn't come across, so they're going to want to read those when they mark your work, or they might want to check something that you've said about the reference. Referencing is part of good academic practice, and if you don't reference, or even just forget to add a reference, that will look as though you've plagiarised, so make sure you reference everything you've used that isn't your own work.

E: There's new literature being published all the time. What do you think is the best way to keep up to date with it?

S: This can be tricky because research *is* being published all the time. It depends how long you have to do your research and write-up. If it's a short assignment, you probably don't need to worry about that because you haven't got time, but if you're working on a dissertation, then you're going to conduct your research over several months, which is plenty of time for new literature to be published. One way to keep up to date is to set up search alerts in the databases. When you have decided which search terms return relevant results, you can save those searches in the databases you are using, and set alerts so you receive an email maybe once a month telling you when new publications have been added that match your search terms. You can also set alerts in Google Scholar. You may also want to consider signing up for email lists, such as those curated by JiscMail (you'll find the website listed below), and you may want to follow professional counselling associations to keep on top of what's being published. You could start by checking the online Counselling Directory (also listed below).

E: What if I'm interested in a particular author, in knowing what they're working on and publishing? Would I go about it in the same way, by signing up to email lists?

S: Yes, absolutely. There are academic networks such as ResearchGate and Academia.edu where you can register for free and follow authors, and you may also have the option to ask for the manuscripts of their journal articles. You can try this in the first instance if your library doesn't have those articles. If the author has a profile in Google Scholar, you can follow them there as well. You can also set up author alerts in some databases, such as Web of Science and Scopus, so you'll be alerted to their new publications.

Check to see if they have an academic presence on social media. Twitter is used increasingly in research and authors often Tweet details of their new publications, so you can find out about these before they're added to databases.

E: Thank you. I've learned a lot.

S: You're welcome. And a last piece of advice – take advantage of any training sessions put on by your library and find out what support systems are in place. Don't be afraid to use the appointment systems offered by the librarians supporting your course. Librarians are delighted to be of help.

Further reading/websites recommended by Sharon Potter

Here is a list of relevant databases – check if these are available in your library:

Discipline-specific	Broader coverage	Grey literature
CINAHL	Academic Search Complete	Department of Health and Social Care (free)
Medline (may be part of Web of Science)	ASSIA (Applied Social Sciences Index and Abstracts)	Nexis UK (Newspapers)
PsycARTICLES	IBSS (International Bibliography of the Social Sciences)	Office for National Statistics (free)
PsycINFO	Scopus	ProQuest Dissertations and Theses
PsycTESTS	Web of Science	PsycEXTRA
PsychTHERAPY	Zetoc	Public Health England Statistics (free)
PEP web (Psychoanlytic Electronic Publishing (free)		Social Care Online (free)
PubMed		
PubMed Central (free)		
Social Care Online (free)		
Social Services Abstracts		

These websites may also be useful:

Academica.edu – **www.academia.edu**

Amazon – **www.amazon.co.uk**

British Association for Counselling and Psychotherapy (BACP) – **www.bacp.co.uk**

British Library Catalogue – **http://explore.bl.uk**

Counselling Directory – **www.counselling-directory.org.uk**

Department of Health and Social Care – **www.gov.uk/government/organisations/department-of-health-and-social-care**

Google Scholar – **https://scholar.google.com**

JiscMail – **www.jiscmail.ac.uk**

Library Hub Discover – **https://discover.libraryhub.jisc.ac.uk**

Mendeley – **www.mendeley.com**

Office for National Statistics – **www.ons.gov.uk**

PEP web – **www.pep-web.org**

Public Health England – **www.gov.uk/government/organisations/public-health-england/about/statistics**

PubMed Central – **www.ncbi.nlm.nih.gov/pmc**

ResearchGate – **www.researchgate.net**

Social Care Online – **www.scie-socialcareonline.org.uk**

Twitter – **https://twitter.com**

Zotero – **www.zotero.org**

TAKEAWAY MESSAGES

- Student support services can work with you to develop a personal access arrangements/reasonable adjustment plans to help your learning on your course.
- Read the module handbook, and in particular familiarise yourself with the learning outcomes/assessment criteria for each module and each assignment. You can't pass an assignment if you don't meet the learning outcomes/assessment criteria. Ask if you don't understand them.
- If your course offers formative (ungraded) opportunities for you to share some of your work towards an assignment (a plan, an introduction, a paragraph) with the lecturer/tutor/trainer, take up the offer. There's always something you can learn.
- Widening your counselling and psychotherapy vocabulary, and your vocabulary in general, will help you develop as a student and as a counsellor and psychotherapist.
- Learn how to read and make notes that are useful to you, rather than trying to read everything and/or write everything down.
- Library staff are there to help you, so make use of the service and their expertise.

The next chapter…

The next chapter introduces some assessments and assignments you're likely to find on counselling and psychotherapy courses.

5

Assessment and assignments in counselling and psychotherapy courses

Introduction

This chapter offers you an overview of assessments and assignments likely to be found in counselling and psychotherapy courses. We will focus on who is doing the assessing and what the assignments might be. In arranging the material this way, we've continued the theme from Chapters 2 and 3 of considering people and relationships first, then processes.

We begin the chapter by providing some overall introductory thoughts about assignments and assessments and why they need to be different on counselling and psychotherapy courses to those on other courses you may have taken before.

We then offer a detailed exploration of a key issue: bringing your whole self to your assignments and assessments. This is something that counselling and psychotherapy training requires of you, and is in fact preparing you for the self-awareness and self-development aspects of training and working as a counsellor and psychotherapist. We introduce the practice of autoethnography – one way (among others) in which you might bring your whole self to research projects, and to dissertations in particular.

After that, we turn to consideration of the different people doing the assessing:

- tutor/lecturer assessment
- peer-evaluation and peer-assessment
- self-assessment
- assessment by your clinical supervisor and placement provider(s) (if you're on a course where you're meeting clients)
- external examiners assessing a sample of work from your course.

Once we've introduced who does the assessing, we will look in detail at what the assignments being assessed might be.

We begin with examples of written work, followed by examples of spoken work, and finally we consider examples of professional work (known in some courses as 'professional clinical obligations', or a similar phrase):

- Written work:
    - the book review
    - the essay (which we look at in more detail in Chapter 6, as it is such a common assignment)
    - the case study (which we also look at in more detail in Chapter 6, as it is another common assignment, and one that you're unlikely to have done on other courses)
    - the research proposal and ethics approval process – the starting points for a dissertation or research project
    - the dissertation or research project
    - the written exam.

- Spoken work:
    - the presentation, workshop (individual, paired and group)
    - the oral exam – for instance, a PhD viva.

- Professional work:
    - self-assessment – personal journals, personal learning statements, skills evaluation
    - peer-evaluation reports
    - placement reports
    - client log and client notes
    - supervisors' reports, and supervisees' reports.

You won't find every assignment we discuss on the course you're doing, or thinking of doing. You'll need to check with your training provider and check your course and module handbooks for that level of detail. But even if what we discuss here is not directly useful to you right now, there still may be aspects of what we say that you can use elsewhere, or in the future.

We end the chapter with some advice about seeking to prevent academic irregularities and using the Turnitin system.

Introductory thoughts about assessment and assignments on counselling and psychotherapy courses

Assessment on counselling and psychotherapy courses may be different from other courses you have studied because, generally speaking, they try to have an educational method (this includes assessment) that is in harmony or congruent with the theoretical approach of the course (person-centred, psychodynamic, integrative and so forth) and counselling and psychotherapy in general. This often comes out in the style of assessment, such as whether there is much peer-evaluation (where students evaluate each other) or self-evaluation (where students evaluate themselves). (We discuss these types of assessment below.) Many counselling and psychotherapy lecturers/tutors/trainers take the view that, since self-awareness is an important part of the counselling and psychotherapy process, in terms of the progress both of the client and of the counsellor/psychotherapist, it is important to have self-evaluation as a strong theme in the assessment of students' skills. Similarly, peer-assessment can be an excellent way of developing openness, genuineness or congruence as personal qualities.

In terms of types of assignments being assessed, counselling and psychotherapy courses are training participants to be practitioners – whether counsellors and psychotherapists and/or people who will use counselling skills in their other work. This means that assignments (ungraded, graded or pass/fail) will include assessment of your practical abilities. Being assessed on practical abilities is not about learning and applying some skills. It's about deep relating with others, using the self in the relationship. How you relate in the therapy room is underpinned by an understanding of theory, history, philosophy, ethics, politics and practice. This means that you also need to be assessed on your academic abilities, through written and/or spoken assessments (graded, pass/fail or, though this is less often nowadays, ungraded). Doing assignments is not about regurgitating what you've read and agreeing with whatever a key name in the field has said. It's about interrogating material, working out where you stand personally and bringing your personal experience and experiencing into the work (to the extent that this is deemed appropriate on your particular course, or a particular assessment – always ask your tutor for advice on that). Bringing yourself is a powerful process, which merits more exploration, and so we now turn to that.

Learning how you might bring yourself into assignments

We've said how freeing it can be to share (when you are ready, and to the extent that feels right for you) aspects of your personal history and experiencing with others in a group setting (for instance, in a personal development group) – how it can make meaningful connections with others, and help you feel less alone (among other positive outcomes). At the polar opposite, we've said how other people may (knowingly or out of ignorance or thoughtlessness) dishonour aspects of your personal history and experiencing that you share. Responses to sharing can veer between these polar opposites, and everything in between. Changes in responses can take place over time, as a consequence of both your own personal development and that of the others with whom you are sharing.

There is no permanent record, however, of what you say out loud. The group contract should protect you from your material being shared. When it comes to written assignments, there *is* obviously a written record of any sharing of your personal history and experiencing that you do, which is marked by lecturers/tutors/trainers, moderated by other lecturers/tutors/trainers, and can be included in a sample for an external examiner to review.

In voicing any personal material, you lose control over how others interpret it, and in writing your personal material, you also don't have a great deal of control over who sees it. If you receive a grade for your work overall, it may well feel as if your personal history and experiencing has been graded (and possibly found wanting).

One effect of this can be shame. We all carry shame in relation to all sorts of life experiences. We started to talk in Chapter 2 about how lived experiences should not shame us, but we know society is organised around shaming some particular experiences, and that challenging this is a live political project. Shame is very present in therapy rooms. It makes sense to carefully explore how it operates for you, at your own pace, in your own words, so that you can be of better service to clients.

> **ACTIVITY**
>
> **An invitation to watch Brené Brown's TED talks on shame and vulnerability**
>
> American professor, researcher and podcaster Brené Brown has specialised in the subjects of courage, vulnerability, shame, empathy and leadership in human interactions. In these two TED Talks, she discusses shame and vulnerability:
>
> *Listening to Shame* – **https://vimeo.com/139503700**[1]
>
> *The Power of Vulnerability* – **www.youtube.com/watch?v=pXb8AQOONgE**[2]
>
> What are your responses to these talks?

Introducing autoethnography

It may be useful for you to know there is a type of research and writing that is all about personal history and experiencing, with a specific focus on the self, as you step into counselling and psychotherapy training.

The type of research is autoethnography.

Autoethnography involves writing about the self in a socio-political context. It is a style of research that has taken off in recent years. Ellis and Bochner (2016, p.55)[3] comment that when they searched for autoethnography writing back in 1999, they found 'fewer than 40 scholarly articles or chapters', but by 2016 a search on Google scholar produced more than 21,000. That is a phenomenal increase. They go on to comment:

> [Researchers/writers] wanted to tell stories that invited others to think *and* to feel. Eager to depart the safe and comfortable space of conventional academic writing in order to engage in non-alienating research practices, the new breed of qualitative

---

1. Brown, B. (2015, September 16). *Listening to shame.* TED Talk.
2. Brown, B. (2016, August 7). *The power of vulnerability.* TED Talk.
3. Ellis, C. & Bochner, A. (2016). *Evocative autoethnography: Writing lives and telling stories.* Routledge.

researchers wanted to read, write and/or perform texts that would make the hearts of their readers skip a beat. (Ellis & Bochner, 2016, p.56)

Knowing that many people do this sort of writing, and why they do it, may be helpful as you start to take risks with what you will and won't say and write about yourself. Once you get more comfortable with placing yourself in your work, this may be a research approach you will consider (perhaps for a research project or dissertation). It is both rewarding and difficult.

We also want to say to you that tutors/lecturers/trainers are very familiar indeed with reading students' personal histories and experiencing in counselling and psychotherapy training, and will perceive such work as the gift that it is.

Further reading

On autoethnography, you might start with:

Ellis, C. & Bochner, A. (2016). *Evocative autoethnography: Writing lives and telling stories.* **Routledge.**

We also suggest that you look at some memoirs. There are millions of memoirs out there (We recommend you avoid what are commonly known as 'misery memoirs' – autobiographical accounts of how the narrator survived terrible childhoods of abuse and abandonment – unless you are wanting to consider/write about that genre.) Here are some we've enjoyed reading recently:

Dancyger, L. (2021). *Negative space.* **Santa Fe Writers Project.** (Lilly Dancyger's artist father died when she was young, and she explores his life partly through the means of his art – images of which are included in the book. You, too, could combine images and words in your work, using your own drawings, or copyright-free images.)

Ernaux, A. (2018). *The years.* **Fitzcarraldo Editions.** (This is particularly interesting in that it uses the time/place of the author's experiences more than her own feelings – something you might want to read and consider if you're not sure yet about introducing yourself explicitly into your work.)

Gornick, V. (2015). *Fierce attachments.* **Daunt Books.** (No list of memoirs is complete without Vivian Gornick. Here she's writing about her relationship with her mother – something you may be doing at times in your own work.)

Levy, D. (2018). *Things I don't want to know.* **Penguin.** (Levy brilliantly captures the voice and experiencing of a very young girl, putting herself right back in the shoes of her younger self – something you might be doing at times in your own work. What would your younger voice sound like?)

Westoby, C. (2020). *The fear talking: The true story of a young man and anxiety.* **Barbican Press.** (Westoby vividly captures the minutiae and the utterly tedious relentlessness of anxiety.)

Introducing assessment

Some assessment will be only formative (i.e. not graded, but you will get feedback and feedforward, to help you to progress towards graded work. This can take the form of being invited to send your tutor the introduction of an essay you will soon be giving in for a graded assessment), and some will be summative (i.e. given a grade or passed/failed), and often also formative (i.e. you'll also receive feedback and feedforward to help you on your journey).

As you prepare yourself for an assessment, make sure you know if it is formative or summative. Often, formative assessment is optional.

If there is to be a summative grade, find out what each grade means. How would you show you'd evidenced that grade? This should be made available to you as part of assessment advice, in handbooks and online (if there is an online learning environment).

Let's take one example of what grades mean. Work achieving A+, Exceptional First or marks of 80%+ on undergraduate courses is often said to be 'publishable'. If you're on an undergraduate course that adopts this approach, does it feel to you that your work is of the standard of work you've read in books and journals? Would you publish it? If you would, maybe the work will be seen to be at this highest standard by marking tutors.

Before you start any assessment, remind yourself of its learning outcomes and assessment criteria (discussed in Chapter 4), and make sure you meet them in your work. Ask your tutor/lecturer/trainer if you need clarification on any of them.

Make sure before you hand in any work that you are aware of how many marks would be lost for a reference list that is not written in the format required. Modules and courses may ask for a particular referencing style. The most commonly used in academic circles is APA.[4] This is the form of Harvard referencing adopted by the American Psychological Association, which is commonly required by most academic journals and research funders. However, your training provider may have their own particular style (Vancouver, for example, is a different style that is used by journals including the *British Medical Journal* and the *British Journal of Psychiatry*), so be sure to check. And some module leaders simply ask that you are consistent in whatever referencing style you choose to use.

Students often ask the marking tutor, 'How many marks would you take off if…?', as though the tutor starts with 100% and then looks for ways to take marks away. This is not how most markers mark. You really do need to believe that marking tutors want to see you do well – they (or 'we' – Deborah is one!) are not looking for ways to 'take marks off'. The only exception is when the training provider has very specific, explicitly stated requirements (such as the style of referencing just mentioned).

Tutor assessment

Most of us are familiar with the method of assessment where we 'hand our work in', either in hard copy at the course administrative office as the deadline looms or, more commonly

---

4. You can find the latest version of the APA referencing guide here: https://apastyle.apa.org/style-grammar-guidelines/references

Experiences

Every marker will have their particular method of assessing written assignments, and will be guided by the course requirements and those of their institution. Here Deborah explains how she marks student essays.

I begin by reminding myself of the module I'm marking – its content and ethos. Next, I re-read the assignment brief, and place at hand the learning outcomes/assessment criteria I'm going to be marking against. All this is particularly important if I'm part of a marking team but haven't taught these students every week. I need to be clear what the students whose work I am marking have been advised, and work with that.

Then, I look at the number of essays I am to mark overall, and set myself a target for the day. For a 2,000-word essay assignment, I'd expect to mark 10–12 scripts a day. I prefer to focus entirely on marking until it's done, with no interruptions, so that I have a continuity of comparison in my grading decisions – it's useful quality assurance.

My first step is to check each essay's Turnitin score,[5] and that the essay isn't under or over the word count. A concerning Turnitin score would need attention and, potentially, action. It makes sense to notice this before the essay is marked. If an essay is significantly over or under the word count, I would reflect that in the mark and my feedback and feedforward. Again, knowing this before starting to mark makes sense. In some institutions, markers stop marking where the student reaches the word count.

Then, I quickly skim through the essay, to get an initial sense of it. Are there in-text citations? If there aren't, or there are very few, that's always a warning sign that the writer hasn't the material at hand to develop their arguments, and the essay is likely to get a lower mark. If there are, and they are many and good choices, then I am already getting a positive impression.

What's the reference list like? If there isn't one, or it's very short, or if Smith (2021) turns out to be John Smith's *How to Pass your Psychology A Level* guide, these are also warning signs of insufficient and incorrect work. If the student seems to be quoting widely, but only cites a few references in the reference list, it's a clue that they haven't read the original texts and are just taking secondary references from a couple of sources.

However, when I begin my close reading of the essay, I try to hold what the quick scroll suggested quite lightly: I haven't yet made up my mind about the essay, I haven't given it a grade in my head and I'm keeping myself open to hearing what the essay writer wants to convey about the topic, aware that they have spent time working on it.

I'll start annotating immediately, rather than waiting until I've read the whole essay. If I waited until the end, I'd probably have to read the essay again before annotating it, and markers don't generally have time to read an essay twice.

My first annotation is usually about the quality of the explanation of the structure/argument in the introduction. If there is no introduction or the introduction doesn't give the structure/argument (unless the writer is being creative, in which case there may not be a structure/argument, and that would be okay), it usually means that reading the essay is going to be hard work. There's not going to be

---

5. Turnitin is software that checks academic work for plagiarism. Tutors use it to ensure the work is all that of each student. https://turnitin.com

much signposting through the essay, and the argument is either never going to emerge or will only appear at the end, with no path leading up to it. A poor start like this doesn't mean I'm 'taking marks off'. I will have noticed and commented on the lack of structure/argument, but actually I'm still trying to give the essay writer the benefit of the doubt. I'm still trying to find and follow the argument that may be sitting just below the surface.

An introduction that gives a detailed structure/argument makes me relax. It's an indication that I can, potentially, trust the writer to lead me through their work to a logical conclusion. I'm not 'awarding marks' for it at this point, but I am noticing and commenting favourably on it. I will still be checking that the structure outlined *is* what is on offer, and that the argument stated *is* the one that's made, that it coheres with the essay as a whole, and that it stands up.

I tend to make a lot of annotations on the text. Annotations are part of the feedback for the essay writer, and they also help me write a detailed overall qualitative response to the essay when I've finished reading it, and they lead me towards awarding a grade. If I'm repeatedly saying 'excellent', then the essay seems to be heading towards being a First/Distinction, either overall or in some ways.

Once I've read the whole essay, I scroll through my completed annotations. If I've repeatedly asked 'Reference?' then that helps me be clear with myself as marker, and with the student as writer, that there was insufficient reading done for the essay, that they haven't supported what they are saying with evidence from the literature, and that this will be reflected in the feedback, mark and feedforward. If I've repeatedly commented 'Description', then that indicates that the critical analysis – asked for in most essays, particularly at first-degree level and above – needs more attention. At first-degree level, this usually means an essay is heading towards a grade in the 2.2 classification or below.

My detailed overall qualitative response to the essay will be measured against the learning outcomes/assessment criteria – how well has the student met all of the requirements? Sometimes, I'll also pick out three points of good practice, and three areas to work on for next time.

I then move onto completing a quantitative rubric (or a grade-based assessment grid), where I grade such things as structure, knowledge and referencing. These are graded from 1–100% (or from Exceptional First to fail).

By the time I've done all this, my thoughts about the grade to award the essay are starting to emerge. I generally – but not always – know which classification (First, 2.1, 2.2, 3rd) I'm going to award by now, but I'm also often sitting with a not-quite-knowing about where to place the work within that classification. It makes me think of Gendlin's (2003) book, *Focusing*.[6] When the grade is right, there's a sense of 'Yes, that's the one'.

If I'm not sure about a grade, I'll write 'might be higher' on my personal written record of grades awarded, and then reflect on it and maybe change it. I may also ask the moderator for their thoughts.

Overall, when marking an essay, I'm always looking for something to like, even if an essay ultimately fails.

This is, of course, just my approach; other markers will approach marking in other ways, and in line with the guidelines on their own courses.

---

6. Gendlin, G. (2003). *Focusing: How to gain direct access to your body's knowledge* (25th anniversary classic ed. revised & updated). Rider.

these days, by uploading it to an online drop box. Then we wait for the teacher/tutor/lecturer who taught us (or an external marker who didn't, but who does know the field) to assess, mark and grade our work, and give us feedback, and often feedforward.

Most of us are also very familiar with the anxiety of waiting while marking is taking place. Universities and other training providers are increasingly mindful of student anxiety while waiting for assessment feedback, and how waiting can impact student satisfaction with their courses (and thus scores in external surveys like the National Student Survey (NSS)). It's now usual for universities to give feedback within 2–3 weeks. You should note down feedback dates (as well as your own deadlines) in your diary.

It is best not to contact markers while they are marking to ask when work will be returned. They will be working through many scripts, probably with too little time allocated for the work, and frequently doing it in the evenings and at weekends. Be assured, they will be wanting to give you the grade that the work deserves and the most useful feedback for you.

It's surprisingly common for students not to read the feedback (or feedforward) when they get their marked essay back. Their interest is the grade they've been awarded. We encourage you to look at the feedback and feedforward, when you're ready. There should always be advice there that will be of use to you in your next assignments. If you don't understand the feedback/feedforward, make an appointment to speak with the marker so you can discuss it together.

The only thing you can't do when you receive your graded work is challenge the mark you've been given. Marks are matters of academic judgement. If you feel upset by a mark, we suggest you hold back for a few days and let your initial reaction settle, rather than firing off an upset email to the marker. Marking is an art, not a science, and even if your work hasn't been awarded the grade you'd hoped for, you can still stand by it. A useful exercise may be to reflect and articulate in your own mind why you personally would have given it a higher grade.

Unlike on many other courses you may have taken, not all assessment on counselling and psychotherapy courses is conducted by tutors/lecturers. Let's turn now to look at assessment by people who aren't your tutors.

Peer-evaluation and peer-assessment

The following are all *peer-evaluation* opportunities:

- feedback in personal development groups or community meetings regarding personal qualities and attributes
- feedback on counselling skills from an observer when practising skills with a fellow student
- feedback from a group of peers on a recording of counselling skills practised with a fellow student
- feedback on a recording of counselling or counselling-skills work with a client
- feedback on whether a trainee has met their own, self-determined learning goals (see also 'Self-assessment', below)
- feedback on a prepared presentation to the class by all those in the class.

These are *peer-assessment* processes:

- feedback in personal development groups or community meetings regarding personal qualities and attributes *and pass/fail decisions made by consensus in public*
- feedback on, *and grading pass/fail of,* a voice recording of counselling or counselling skills practice, whether with a fellow student or client
- marking of essays and other written work by peers with feedback, *grading and pass/ rewrite/ fail decisions being made by the peer assessor*
- feedback on whether a trainee has met their own self-determined learning goals and *a pass/ fail decision made by consensus in public*
- feedback on and *rating and grading* of a prepared presentation to the class by all those in the class.

The main difference between peer-evaluation and peer-assessment is that peer-assessment counts for something: it has teeth, and it puts some of the responsibility for maintaining standards on the trainees themselves. There may be little or no peer-assessment on your own course, but it is still interesting to reflect on what it would look like, feel like and where it might lead.

ACTIVITY

An invitation to talk about peer-assessment with one or more other trainees

- What's your immediate response to the idea of assessing your peers?
- Do you think you could you give and receive challenging yet constructive feedback to your peers?
- What do you understand by the words 'challenging yet constructive'?
- What do you think the difference is between being 'challenging and constructive' (in the way that you've described it) and being destructive? (You may intend to be the former but be heard as the latter.)
- Think of ways in which you could give feedback to another trainee after you've watched them completely fail to connect with a peer taking the role of the client. What would you say?
- What would it mean to you if other students' pass/fail decisions hung on some of your feedback and that of others?
- Would you want to have a hand in telling someone that they have failed because they were 'not good enough' (in your view), or would you rather tutors said it? Is it 'their job', not yours?

Some thoughts
Giving good evaluative feedback is difficult enough for most of us, since we are prone to lapse into polite, hollow, meaningless responses. We all know that this is

> useless and soon the whole process becomes stale and worthless. The feedback process becomes untrustworthy and then we tend to avoid it.
>
> When peer-assessment has teeth, these difficulties would appear to increase, yet it is the experience of many that it gives a sharp edge to the whole process, forcing us to consider our responses more carefully and give them more respectfully. Set against this is the tendency to retreat into an 'I'll pass yours if you pass mine' mentality. The skill of the tutor as facilitator of the educational process is paramount in preventing this from happening and keeping the peer-assessment process on track.

Self-assessment

How can someone assess their own abilities? The whole traditional education system seems to suggest that assessment is an objective process that, in order to be fair and consistent, needs to stand at some distance from the individual in question in order to achieve the neutrality required. Surely, if left to assess ourselves, we would just simply do the minimum required and pass ourselves with flying colours?

That is the fantasy. The reality, however, is that self-assessment is a feature of a wide spectrum of counsellor and psychotherapist training – it's not simply the extreme left-field of the person-centred approach. There are a few reasons for this:

- Developing and increasing self-awareness is at the heart of both the counselling process and the counselling training process. It makes sense, therefore, to put self-evaluation and even the additional responsibility of self-assessment, into the mix of assessment methods.
- Any model of counselling and psychotherapy based on empowerment might consider it congruent to have some elements of self-evaluation and assessment in the course. This also challenges assumptions about the power dynamics in relationships, whether between client and counsellor/psychotherapist or student and tutor.
- Part of the repertoire of skills of a professional counsellor and psychotherapist is to be able to monitor and evaluate one's own performance in order both to protect clients and seek continual professional development. One way of developing such skills is by asking trainees to share responsibility through self-assessment. This is sometimes referred to as developing an 'internal supervisor'.

Staying with the distinction between evaluation and assessment outlined above, some popular forms of self-assessment adopted by courses are as follows (they can be self-evaluation when not formally marked or part of a pass/fail decision, and self-assessment when graded, marked and forming part of the pass/fail criteria):

- personal journal (may be handed in and read and used for tutorials) during a set period on the course, or a particular activity, or in a set assignment – i.e. 'What I learned from writing this essay was…'

- self-evaluation – written or verbal evaluation or assessment of, for example, counselling skills demonstrated in a recorded interview with a client, possibly using prescribed headings: 'What I liked about this session was . . .'; 'What I didn't like about this session was . . . '; 'How I could have improved . . . '; 'Supervision issues raised by this session . . .' and so forth
- self-assessment statement — a statement presented to the tutors, peers or the course community explaining why the trainee thinks they are fit to practise, incorporating some of the above ideas, such as strengths and weaknesses, things learned, things to work on, personal attributes and so forth.

Some courses place a heavy emphasis on self-assessment. Here, a self-assessment statement can run to many thousands of words and form the major course assessment, incorporating an appreciation of the trainee's understanding of theory, their emergent personal counselling and psychotherapy style and a record of their counselling and psychotherapy practice.

ACTIVITY

An invitation to talk about self-assessment with one or more other trainees

- Do you think that self-assessment is congruent with the theoretical orientation of your course?
- How is self-assessment used on your course?
- What comes up for you when you think about assessing yourself, in general?
- How do you feel about assessing your own development as a counsellor and psychotherapist?
- How do you feel about assessing your written, oral and practice-based assessments?
- How do you feel about submitting self-assessment statements, covering areas like your strengths and weaknesses, what you have to learn next, how you have used clinical supervision, your personal model of counselling, what theories, what reading and who has influenced you so far?
- How do you see tutor assessment, peer-assessment and self-assessment working together? What if you don't think your work is good, but someone else does?
- Would you like to see more or less self-assessment on your course?

Clinical supervisor and placement provider assessment

If you are meeting with clients, your clinical supervisor will be asked to write a report on your progress, and to certify the number of client hours and clinical supervision hours you have accrued.

Note: For some courses, your placement provider will also be asked to write a report on your work at the placement, and to certify the number of client hours you have accrued there. Sometimes the placement provider is asked only to certify the number of client hours you have accrued, which they will do in the supervisory report.

As we mentioned earlier, if you are required by the course to have personal therapy, your therapist (if you have one) will not be asked to assess you, only to certify that you attended the required number of sessions asked for by the course you are taking.

Experiences

We met Dr Dwight Turner in Chapter 2, when we explored learning relationships with clinical placement co-ordinators. We've asked Dr Turner to write here about being a clinical supervisor assessing supervisees.

I'm a UKCP registered clinical supervisor. I became a clinical supervisor in 2008 after four years as a psychotherapist, because I saw this as a natural progression in my career. I supervise students who are training as integrative psychotherapists. I also supervise qualified therapists, some of whom have stayed with me from when they were training. This is how I work when I'm assessing the work of trainees as their clinical supervisor.

Your training organisation will ask me to complete an assessment form each year, to give my opinion on your work. (Check out exactly what the forms ask for in your own university/ training institute.) This may feel like doing a school report, but we will work together on it, and my comments won't be a surprise as we will have been working closely together during the year (the usual ratio is around one hour of supervision to three or four hours of client work). Most trainees will be fine because we have an established relationship built up from the first time we met, and we both know your areas of strength and development. Sometimes there are things that need attention, like the trainee struggles to bring their client into the room, or there are transferential issues that the trainee is having difficulty with in therapy that hamper either the client work or the supervisor–trainee relationship.

In rare cases, people's work is not reaching what is required. Often, this happens because the trainee is not ready to work at this level, or issues have come up for the trainee that mean they are struggling with the client work. Working empathically with the trainee then helps them to acknowledge, hold and work with these issues, most of the time. On rare occasions, it may be appropriate for the trainee to take some time out from the work with clients and focus instead on themselves in their own therapy.

One of the most important and interesting aspects of this work for me is watching the development of trainees in placement. My role is not just to be a clinician but also to be a teacher, developing the next generation of practitioners so they can go out and do good, ethical work with their clients. I feel that building strong supervisory relationships is key to this, so it is essential that these building blocks are put in place from the beginning.

External examining

So far, we've looked at assessment by people you know – you, your peers, your tutors and your supervisors. There will also be a role for someone you don't know – the external examiner.

Experiences

Deborah is an external examiner for an undergraduate course. She writes here about the role of the external examiner.

Courses appoint one or more external examiners. They are based at a different institution to the course they're examining. Care is taken that they don't have direct links with people at the institution where they'll be external examining, so that they can be as unbiased as possible. Module teams mark student work, using the learning outcomes/assessment criteria we outlined earlier. A sample of that work is then moderated (a process of checking by a second person – the moderator – that the marking is fair and consistent). Some changes to marks and feedback can be made at this point, through discussion between marker/s and moderator. In university modules leading to degree classification, for instance, moderators will usually moderate all work awarded a First (the top grade) and all fails, and a sample of work that falls in between. Having read all the Firsts, the moderator might say that one of them is not of the same quality (in their opinion) as the others. The marker then considers this point and changes the grade, or doesn't if they continue to believe the work merits a First for a particular academic reason.

Once the sample has been through this rigorous process, it is shared with the external examiner. The external examiner sees samples of work from modules across the course. As the external examiner is seeing only a sample of that cohort of students' work, it is not usually part of their role to change the grades. That would be unfair to the people whose work they have not seen. If the external examiner feels that work was not, for instance, marked consistently with learning outcomes/assessment criteria, or that advice to students in module handbooks (which, as you'll recall, we advised you to read) could have been more detailed, they might write this in their external examiner report, which has then to be considered and responded to by the course team, via their course leader.

Students may be told who the external examiner is, but you don't have personal access to them. They aren't there to advocate for you if something has gone wrong. If you contact the external examiner, they will refer you back to your course leader.

As an external examiner, I consider it a privilege to read the work students produce for counselling and psychotherapy courses – they bring their whole selves to it, and it's wonderful to read.

What happens if you fail?

Before we move on to types of assignments, we want to offer two upfront sections about what happens if you fail either an academic assessment or an assessment of your skills as a counsellor and psychotherapist-in-training.

What happens if you fail an academic assessment?

It's our experience that many students come into training (as well as many other types of education) believing that assessment is one-strike-and-you're-out – that if you fail one piece of academic work, you've failed your course.

It is rare that failing one (or even a few) academic assessments at the first attempt would lead to a student being asked to leave, particularly if they are attending regularly and engaging with their course.

Check out what the regulations are on your particular course before you find yourself in that position. When you need to know, you are likely to be very stressed already and it may be difficult to take in and process the information. How many attempts can you have? How will the work be graded at a second attempt? Will it be capped (awarded no more than, for example, 40%)?

Universities have a retake period over the summer when academic assignments can be redone (or done for the first time if you had personal/medical reasons why you were not able to do the assignment for the first deadline. There is no academic penalty or capping of marks if you are in this position).

If a student has too much work to resubmit over a summer retake period, they can be asked to redo a year. This is not intended to be punitive, even if it can feel like it; it's about making sure you have the best opportunity possible to give of your best, and it's felt that you need more time than just the retake period to do so.

There is usually an appeals process if you disagree and think you could do all your outstanding academic work in a summer retake period. We've seen many students complete many academic assignments very well in a short time; we've also seen students really benefit from taking another year to redo the course.

Overall, we believe that failing an academic piece of work in counselling and psychotherapy training is an opportunity to challenge your own experiences of failure and gain insight that will help you in your understanding of clients' experiences of failure.

What happens if you fail an assessment of your skills as a trainee counsellor and psychotherapist?

There are instances where students fail an assessment of their skills as a trainee counsellor and psychotherapist, which can eventually lead to them having to leave a course. It's important to be clear about this. Deborah discussed this with colleagues, below.

Experiences

In the section below on oral examinations, we explain the Certificate of Competence/Readiness to Practice/Fitness to Practice assessment. This is an assessment that must be passed before you can work with clients.

Vee Howard-Jones, Head of Counselling and Psychotherapy at the University of Salford (who we'll hear from again later), says:
Sometimes students fail this assessment because they need some access arrangements/

reasonable adjustments, and then they pass at another attempt. Students who are struggling with skills assessments will be given lots of support by tutors to help them develop their skills and move towards passing the assessment. There are, though, instances where not being able to pass a skills assessment is an indicator that the profession of counselling and psychotherapy is not the right place for a particular student.

Says James Barrott, Lecturer in Counselling and Psychotherapy at the University of Salford:
Failing a skills assessment is often seen as a source of intense shame, in contrast with failing an academic essay. People do often come into training with a strong assumption that they will pass. But it might not be the right time for them to train to be a therapist. They might need more personal therapy, for instance. It should actually be normal for a percentage of new students not to pass their Certificate of Competence, and to leave training having learned that being a therapist isn't for them just now, taking what they have learned into other work.

Dr Mark Widdowson, Senior Lecturer in Counselling and Psychotherapy at the University of Salford, offers an alternative:
At Salford we have a theoretical studies route that people can transfer into from the professional practice route. It offers a BSc degree that is not a licence to practise. When people are repeatedly failing their skills assessments, they often know for themselves that they need to transfer, without the need for awkward conversations.

An introduction to assignments

Here we introduce some common assignment types you might find when taking counselling and psychotherapy courses – a) written, b) spoken and c) professional requirements (there are overlaps between some of them). We will drill down into two particularly common assignments – the essay and the case study – in Chapter 6.

Written assignments

The book review

Aims: To encourage and provide evidence of close reading of counselling and counselling-related texts. To encourage critical appraisal of books.

Format: Should be written like reviews in newspapers, magazines and academic journals (check how formal the style needs to be for your assignment – some reviews may have a quirky style, others may follow a more standard structure). A standard structure tends to be as follows: an introduction to the author and the field; a brief description of the contents of the book (don't miss out chapters, the reader wants to know what's in the whole book, not just some of it); what you personally think and feel about the book and why; how useful the book might be (in your opinion) for trainees/qualified therapists; how it connects with other work (it might be completely original or part of an emerging theme in the field), and whether you'd recommend it and why. Usually reviews are of new books, but for your course you might be reviewing a classic text in your field or a book that has had a particular impact on you that you want to share with readers.

You might like to think about offering to review new books for your professional magazine or relevant journals. You should contact the reviews editor first, as they will have their own processes for choosing reviewers and their own styles and formats for reviews. Never send in a review on spec. The reviews editor needs to be sure you have no personal or professional connection with the book's author. However, there's no reason why you can't request to review a particular book, so long as you can confirm you aren't the author's student, client, best friend or partner! If you are sent a book to review but find you can't, after all, do it, return it as soon as possible. It means the reviews editor can send it to someone else and the author is not deprived of an opportunity for their work to be reviewed.

> **ACTIVITY**
>
> **An invitation to critically evaluate some book reviews**
>
> Start by reading some short book reviews in *Therapy Today* (the BACP magazine), *The New Psychotherapist* (UKCP magazine), and/or *Counselling Matters* (the NCS magazine) (if you have access to one or more of these publications. (If you aren't a member of any of these professional bodies, your institution may have access to the publications online.) Then look at longer, more academic reviews in journals. Some reviews will make you want to read the book. How have those reviews been written? Other reviews may be very critical, or even vitriolic. How does that sit with you? Writing a good book review is a skill, and being constructive while remaining objective and critical is a good skill for counsellors and psychotherapists.

The essay

Aims: To develop a sound argument, underpinned by pertinent reading and reflection, in response to a question given to you or sometimes that you have chosen yourself, which relates to the content, learning outcomes/assessment criteria of the module for which it is written. You might, for example, be comparing theoretical approaches (how person-centred therapy compares with CBT, for instance), or looking at what you understand by particular commitments in the BACP or UKCP ethical frameworks (what self-care means to you, maybe), or interrogating a diagnosis listed in a psychiatric manual of mental disorders (for example, the *Diagnostic and Statistical Manual of Mental Disorders* (DSM)).

Format: Essays usually follow a traditional format (without subheadings): title, introduction, main body of the text (following the order outlined in the introduction and developing the argument stated in the introduction), conclusion. Courses/modules may allow more creative approaches to essays (check with your course team or module staff). The essay always needs to have a strong internal narrative, even if it is creative in nature.

This is such a common way of being assessed that we focus on it in more detail in Chapter 6.

The case study

Aims: To develop and evidence an appreciation of professional issues, client practice issues and the relationship of both to the theory, history, philosophy and ethics of your theoretical approach. To demonstrate the ability to write in suitable style for fellow professionals, or to develop your own style (depending on the modality/level of study). To demonstrate ability to communicate therapeutic decisions to others.

Format: The case study might describe a session or part of a session with a peer on your course, or it might describe a session with a client in a placement, depending on your level of study and where you are in your course. It can take many forms, depending on the purpose (see your learning outcomes/assessment criteria) and your theoretical approach, but is likely to broadly follow this format: some demographic details of the client, as far as the client is comfortable to share them with you in the session and/or for your assessment; the presenting problems (or what brings the person to therapy, as far as you know right now); the referral path (or how the person comes to be sitting opposite you); the number of sessions so far and in total (and which sessions you're focusing on in your case study); the setting where you're meeting/seeing the client (such as women's centre, hospice, community counselling service, specialist service for addictions); the diagnosis the person brings (if any, and if appropriate to your therapeutic approach); description and evaluation of sessions in terms of efficacy (yours) and changes in the client (this may include a recording and a transcript of the recorded session or part of the recorded session[7]); explanation and justification of methods and approaches used; supervision issues raised by this work, and conclusions or suggestions for continuation of therapy, including referral possibilities if appropriate.

This is a very regular way of being assessed, and probably not one that you've come across before, so we focus on it in more detail in Chapter 6.

The research proposal and ethics approval process

Aims: To prepare you to do a worthwhile and ethical dissertation or research project. To assess your ability to come up with a research idea and research question by finding gaps in the literature and planning some research (literature review, methods, methodology), and exploring how you would do the work ethically. A research proposal can propose empirical work (research with people), and/or library-based work. Library-based work would not need ethical approval (as no people are directly involved), but the work itself still needs to be ethical in all of its discussions and arguments. Ethics should infuse any project, not just appear as a section in a methodology chapter.

Format: As the title implies, this is a proposal, so it should say what you plan to do, why it's a good thing, how you're going to do it, how you'll do it ethically, and what contribution

---

7. A transcript is a typed record of the spoken content of a counselling or counselling skills session, or part of a session. Sometimes you'll be asked to time pauses, and to capture and type up minimal encouragers (things like saying 'Hmm'). Transcripts can take hours to complete – 30 minutes of dialogue can take three hours of concentrated work, depending on how fast you're typing, so you should allow plenty of time for it.

the results might make to the greater body of counselling knowledge. In short: is this research a good idea? Why should it be done?

Ethics approval: Projects that involve going out and producing some data must have ethical approval. This usually involves completing a detailed form about your project and creating a range of documents to go alongside it (the questions you plan to ask people, the questionnaire you'd like to use, an informed consent form, a participant information document). You and your academic supervisor will work on the form together and it will then be submitted for review by your training provider's ethics committee.

Don't expect getting ethical approval for a project to be straightforward, and don't be surprised or upset if you're asked to redo or revise your ethical statement. Ethics committees have to hold the possibility that something might go wrong with a piece of work; they have to think through – very carefully – any amendments to your proposal that might be needed before you are permitted to go ahead. You must meet any conditions the ethics committee makes. An ethics committee can also make suggestions, but you don't have to take these forward if, after discussion with your academic supervisor, they don't entirely fit with your project.

If your idea for your dissertation or project changes after you've received ethical approval for one idea, you will need to seek ethical approval again for this new project.

You must never go ahead and do research with people for a project until you have received formal notification that the ethics committee approves your work.

Further reading

Bell, J. & Waters, S. (2018). *Doing your research project: A guide for first time researchers.* **Amacom.** (A classic in the field, although not a book 'about' counselling and psychotherapy.)

When you start to consider research work, you will find it very useful to read and cite the BACP ethical guidelines for research in the counselling professions:

www.bacp.co.uk/events-and-resources/research/publications/ethical-guidelines-for-research-in-the-counselling-professions

You may also find Professor Mick Cooper's blog on 'research pointers' helpful. Mick Cooper is Professor of Counselling Psychology at Roehampton University:
https://mick-cooper.squarespace.com/research-pointers

This blog by Professor Pat Thomson, Professor of Education at the University of Nottingham, is also worth exploring for all things to do with research, although again it is not about counselling and psychotherapy specifically:
https://patthomson.net/

The dissertation or research project

Aims: To demonstrate your ability to follow through on the research proposal and ethics approval statement (if appropriate to your study). To demonstrate your ability to read, explore and bring together a wide range of pertinent literature, to critically analyse it, seeing its strengths and limitations, and to situate your own work alongside it. To demonstrate your ability to conduct research (either empirical or library-based), making on-the-ground decisions about ethical practice as you proceed. To demonstrate your ability to create academic/practical arguments, interweaving your research findings with existing literature.

Format: First, the traditional dissertation format for empirical work: introduction, literature review, methodology, findings, discussion (sometimes findings and discussion are in the same chapter), and conclusion. As it's usually a long piece of work, there will be subheadings in the chapters. You need also to provide references (only to items cited in the text but sometimes you might be asked to include a bibliography showing what you read for the dissertation but did not cite).

The traditional dissertation format for library-based work is: chapters organised around themes from the literature (again, with subheadings in the chapters), all of which are helping you develop a central argument, which you have made by the end. More creative dissertation formats may be permitted by your course (check the dissertation module handbook and speak with your academic supervisor).

You might consider seeking a publisher for your dissertation. In Chapter 7 you'll meet Hayley Barker-Smith, whose undergraduate dissertation has been published. Deborah published her own postgraduate dissertation as a chapter in a book.[8] There is no reason why, providing you have ethical approval, you should not do so. But be mindful that the formal academic format does not always make for an accessible read for a non-academic audience. You may need to soften the tone and write more directly to the reader.

Experiences

Some readers will be doing a course outside of counselling and psychotherapy at the time of reading this book and thinking ahead to studies in counselling and psychotherapy. So we asked Ellie Lupton (who we heard from in Chapter 4) to talk to you about planning ahead in this way, and about the processes involved in writing a dissertation. Ellie read for a BA (Hons) in sociology at Nottingham Trent University, for which she achieved a First, and her dissertation was supervised by Deborah.

I decided to conduct my research on complex post-traumatic stress disorder (CPTSD) and domestic violence. I chose to write about domestic violence as this issue has always been important to me, and by incorporating a psychotherapeutic perspective (through CPTSD) I could enhance my understanding of psychotherapy, ready for applying to study psychotherapy and counselling at MSc level. My decision to write specifically about CPTSD was influenced by the lack of academic literature about it. Writing about two topics that I am enthusiastic and curious about made the process of writing my dissertation enjoyable, so I'd advise you to choose a topic you are already interested in, but look at psychotherapeutic perspectives as well as the perspectives of your

---

8. Lee, D.A. (2020). Survivors of sexual violence training as psychotherapists in the UK. In Lee, D.A. & Palmer, E. (Eds.). *#MeToo: Counsellors and psychotherapists speak about sexual violence and abuse*. PCCS Books.

current undergraduate course. Justifying your reason for being interdisciplinary is important.

To write my dissertation to the best standard, I made the most of meeting with my dissertation supervisor, and I would strongly encourage you to do that – some students never approach their supervisors, or do so rarely. The first session was a good starting point in understanding the best methods to conduct my research – I wanted to review literature and construct arguments, and a literature-based dissertation worked best for me. Reading academic literature – with useful recommendations of authors, books and articles from my supervisor – helped me establish an understanding of the different arguments and theories surrounding my research question. I found most of my literature/articles from the library catalogue and Google Scholar (as Sharon Potter and I explained in Chapter 4). However I bought hard copies of any books that weren't available online (this did not happen often). Once I had a basic idea of the arguments I wanted to present, I then met again with my supervisor to discuss possible chapters. From there, planning each chapter with highlighted key points/arguments, including references, helped me organise my work effectively. Meeting with my supervisor to get feedback on my first draft chapter helped a great deal. Using the feedback helped me understand how I could improve. That the meetings were regular (via Microsoft Teams due to Covid) also helped me – any questions or ideas about my dissertation could be discussed promptly.

As part of my course, I had to give a five-minute PowerPoint presentation on my dissertation, explaining its key points and why I had chosen to study it. I also had to give a progress report. I was graded for this, and it counted towards 10% of my overall dissertation grade. If you're asked to do this, you might find it alarming, but the feedback from the presentation (it was marked by two assessors, neither of whom was my supervisor) was also useful, and this was an opportunity to gain outside perspectives on my work.

Once I felt I had finished writing my dissertation, I decided the best course of action would be to proofread it again with fresh eyes after a week or so. It is amazing how many small errors you can pick up by doing this. Once I was ready, I submitted my work. The wait for results was then full of suspense. However, due to the continual support and meetings I had with my supervisor throughout, I felt assured I had done the best I could. While I waited for my results, I was offered a place on the MSc in Integrative Counselling and Psychotherapy at the University of Derby. I feel that the process of writing and researching my dissertation gave me knowledge on psychotherapeutic and sociological perspectives that I could apply to the questions asked in my interview. I feel intersecting sociological and psychological perspectives enhanced the quality of my interview, as it meant I could refer to different viewpoints on therapeutic practice. Also, my understanding of psychotherapeutic perspectives showed my interest and knowledge about psychotherapeutic practices even before I began the course. I think that writing this dissertation has given me a strong foundation for expanding my research into medical diagnosis and social issues such as domestic violence.

When I qualify, I aim to specialise in working therapeutically with people who have experienced domestic violence and/or childhood trauma, and I feel that my dissertation has given me helpful insight into this work.

The written exam

Written exams are not common in counselling and psychotherapy training, but if you are asked to do one, the exam may be a 'seen' one, where candidates can see the questions beforehand and prepare for them, or 'unseen', where candidates get no prior sight of the paper. One example is the BACP Certificate of Proficiency, which counsellors and psychotherapists who haven't taken a BACP accredited course and wish to join the BACP register have to complete in order to do so. This is an online exam, taking about two hours, with an invigilator watching through the camera on the computer. It simply seeks to test your responses to a set of fictional short scenarios of counselling and psychotherapy practice, with simple 'right or wrong' answers – there is no space to show your working.

Oral assignments

Presentations, workshop sessions (individual, paired and group)

Aims: Presentation – to develop presentation skills. Workshop – to develop presentation and facilitation skills. Self-reliance is shown by individual work, and teamwork and collaboration by working with others.

Format: For presentations and workshops, you'll be expected to select a topic relevant to the module you are doing (i.e. a topic that will correspond to the learning outcomes/assessment criteria), and have it approved by the tutor/lecturer/trainer. Or there may be a required topic that everyone works on, or a choice between several (with all of them being covered by the wider group as a whole). Content and methods can vary according to course requirements and your choices. Workshops will usually be more interactive than straightforward presentations: exercises, discussion and questions can be part of the task. You may support presentations/workshops with PowerPoint slides, handouts and other printed material (which are also useful in drawing the eyes of the audience elsewhere while you get used to being on stage). A presentation can also be a case presentation about your work with a client (see above, and Chapter 6). In a case presentation, you will also be assessed on ethical considerations (i.e. how you deal with keeping the client anonymous). In all cases, you will need to keep to the time allocated to you.

Many qualified counsellors and psychotherapists offer CPD workshops (see Chapter 7), and/or present papers or facilitate workshops at conferences. So learning how to present and facilitate while you're in training is very useful, even if it looks like something counsellors and psychotherapists 'don't do' day-to-day because the job itself is about meeting with clients, one client at a time. You may also want to go on to teach or train at some point in the future, and presentation and facilitation skills are vital for that. Even if you've done presentations in previous courses unrelated to psychotherapy and counselling, applying your presentation skills to a counselling and psychotherapy context is still useful.

Oral exams

Aims: One oral exam that every student will have to complete is the Fitness to Practice/Readiness to Practice/Certificate of Competence test, which we mentioned above. This is to demonstrate your ability and safety to begin to meet clients at a placement. You cannot go out on placement before you have passed this test. If you pass, you will receive a certificate that shows placement providers that you are ready to meet clients. Some courses use oral exams as part of their assessments. Some courses use them to resolve disputes about marks, or borderline cases (if a student is close to failing), or if a student has been unable to complete other elements of the assessment schedule because of illness. If you're doing a PhD (Level 8 work), you will be asked to go to a viva, to 'defend' your written thesis (see below).

Format: If you're doing a Fitness to Practice/Readiness to Practice/Certificate of Competence test, you'll be asked to be the therapist, a peer will be the client, and the tutor/s and other students will observe and assess you, generally with the tutor having the final say on whether you pass or not. If you are deemed not ready yet to meet clients at a placement, you can retake the test, although, as mentioned above, there is a cut-off point where you might not be able to continue on the course or (on some courses) you might be advised to complete your studies without qualifying to practise as a therapist. Some courses will give grades for this type of oral examination, while others will grade it pass/fail. Given its importance, it is likely to be an oral exam that you find particularly daunting, but assessing students' practice skills in this way is absolutely necessary, because it is about protecting the public.

Experiences

Dr Laura Viliardos is a lecturer in counselling and psychotherapy at the University of Salford. She recently completed her PhD thesis, which is titled 'An exploration of counselling and support services as experienced by adult male survivors of child sexual abuse'. Here she describes the process of the PhD viva.

After I submitted my thesis, I took some time to be free of it and process it. Then I had a supervisory meeting, which turned into a practice viva. I'd been asked before if I wanted a mock viva with an external person, but I'd said no as I thought it would be too anxiety provoking. At the meeting, my supervisors asked me really difficult questions, to provide a 'worst case scenario'. I felt comfortable with my supervisors asking me questions, even really difficult ones. I used Viva Cards[9] to prepare for my viva. They present you with pertinent questions about your thesis. I went through those questions myself, and with other people, for a few weeks and weekends before the viva. The cards have been developed by academics and are really useful.

Before the viva itself, I was terrified. I'd tried to do calm things the day before, but I was still terrified. My expectation was that it would go badly. I'd felt like that before my two-year and four-year internal assessments (similar events to a PhD viva), and they'd turned out very well; my writing style had been praised, so I wasn't too worried by feeling the same again this time. Once I was in the viva, I enjoyed it. I'd put in so much work by then and the viva was the last hurdle. My viva was a hybrid one: I was in the room, with my supervisors sitting behind me, and the examiners were on a zoom call. I began with a 10-minute presentation (which was optional). It was difficult to cram all of my thesis into 10 minutes.

The examiners didn't say I'd passed at the

---

9. https://vivacards.co.uk

> beginning. They didn't give much away. They commented on the emotional impact of reading my thesis, which was good as it showed that the respondents' stories had come through. I'd expected the questioning to last between one and two hours, but it was complete in about 45 minutes. The examiners then retired and had a discussion and came back about 45 minutes later. My mind was whirring when they returned. They only had a few corrections for me, one of which was that they thought I'd undersold the original contribution of my work. That was a good correction to be asked to make.
>
> I didn't really understand that I'd passed. I asked my supervisors: 'Have I passed?' I was confused about the language of 'corrections', and a bit in shock. Now I'm out the other side, what I'd like to tell you particularly about doing a PhD viva is that it isn't that bad. It's not as difficult as presenting at a seminar. The examiners have read your work carefully and in depth and understand it. Seminars are more daunting!

Professional work

Self-assessment – personal journals

Aims: To encourage and assess personal reflection and awareness of a range of aspects of the self-development process. To demonstrate commitment to ongoing counsellor and psychotherapist development.

Format: Variable. Some courses suggest a loose structure or headings or areas for special attention. Most leave the journal unstructured for creative interpretation by the student. Illustrations, drawings, poems, prose, notes and so forth are all permitted.

This won't be required by all courses, but even if it isn't, you could decide to write a journal to track your progress through your studies.

Self-appraisal – personal learning statements

Aims: To demonstrate awareness of setting personal learning goals, monitoring performance, and noting when personal learning goals have been met.

Format: As with personal journals, variable. Courses usually give guidelines for completion of personal learning statements, with acceptable subheadings and so forth. It is sometimes necessary to state which aims or goals have been achieved by reference to course documents. These may have to be negotiated with a course tutor.

Self-appraisal — skills self-evaluation

Aims: To develop and demonstrate self-awareness and the ability to evaluate your own counselling and psychotherapy skills, strengths and weaknesses in counselling practice.

Format: Skills evaluations usually relate to a recorded counselling session, either with a client or with a fellow course participant. Some courses require you to follow fixed headings; others encourage an unstructured piece of free-flowing writing.

Peer-assessment – reports

Aims: To develop self-awareness, to see how others see us.

Format: Peers write statements giving their interpretation of you across the academic year.

Placement report

Aims: To summarise and review learning on placement. Possible aims include learning to work independently and with others; learning to work in an organisation with values different from those of counselling and psychotherapy (such as a college or hospital), and learning the management, logistics and procedures of counselling, such as appointments, referrals, client absences and so forth.

Format: Can incorporate other assignments such as client logs and client records or extracts from client records. Structure depends on course requirements and your preferences, but could include a description of the placement organisation, the nature of referrals, number of clients seen and details of client statistics – for example, what they brought, number of sessions per client, outcomes and so on. May have a personal learning statement appended.

Client log

Aims: To keep a record of clients met with, including client absences. To prepare for keeping professional records for future accreditation and for work as a counsellor and psychotherapist. Evidence of supervised client practice.

Format: Simple record of client identifier (such as Client 1 at Placement 1): time, date, duration of session(s), record of did not attends (DNAs), why, and action taken.

Client notes

Aims: To meet possible placement requirements (some organisations require notes to be kept in a certain format). To demonstrate ability to keep useful and accurate notes of session (as far as this is possible, as you – the trainee – are only one of the two people in the therapy room, and the client's view of the session may be very different). To demonstrate you have engaged with ethical issues regarding confidentiality as they apply to client notes. Evidence of you using client notes to facilitate case presentations and clinical supervision.

Note: Clients can see their notes if they ask for them.

Format: This will vary depending on the therapeutic approach. In all cases, though, notes must be respectful of the client and the material they have shared with you.

Supervision

We have included supervision as an assignment in its own right because attendance at supervision and making appropriate use of it are *requirements*, not recommendations for training and working as a counsellor and psychotherapist.

Supervisors' reports

Aims: To assess your commitment to and appropriate use of supervision. To monitor and provide evidence of continuing professional and ethical practice.

Format: Can follow headings provided by course team or be in a format determined by supervisor. They are usually short. You will usually see the report, and agree it, but some courses and/or supervisors require a confidential report.

Note: Talk to your supervisor or tutors about the requirements before you reach the point when the report is being written.

Supervisees' reports

Aims: To reflect on your learning through supervision. To assess your commitment to and appropriate use of supervision. To monitor and provide evidence of continuing professional and ethical practice.

Format: Essentially a self-assessment task. Can be a short piece of work following course-determined headings, or a longer dissertation-like piece. It may include a client log if appropriate, and a log of supervision – times, dates, content. The focus will most likely be on how you used supervision. A self-learning statement ('What I learned from supervision') may also be appropriate, or extracts from a personal journal.

Note: Look back at what Caz Binstead wrote in Chapter 2, and Dr Dwight Turner's section in this chapter.

Avoiding academic irregularities

In Chapter 4, we talked about the importance of making clear in your notes when material – quotes and ideas – originate with you, where they are *your* writing and your ideas, and where they belong to another author. We advised you to clearly record in your written/typed notes the sources of particular ideas and to make sure that any direct quotes have quote marks around them and are referenced properly. Paraphrased ideas (that is, other people's words that you've written up in your own style) also need to be referenced. This makes sure that academic irregularities do not appear in your work.

'Academic irregularities' are when a writer – often without intent, but sometimes deliberately – uses other people's work in a way that makes it appear as if it is their own. This is known as plagiarism, and is a serious offence and will result in academic penalties.

We've previously mentioned the Turnitin system in Deborah's contribution in this chapter about marking student assignments. This is one way in which academic irregularities are identified. Your marker may allow you access to Turnitin to check your draft work before you submit it, in case of accidental irregularities. You should note that not everything that Turnitin highlights will be a problem. It is up to you to review your Turnitin report and to decide if anything in your work needs attention before submission. Markers will be able to give you further help in reading your Turnitin report. This advice relates to all written work you submit for your course.

> **TAKEAWAY MESSAGES**
>
> Vee Howard-Jones is Head of Counselling and Psychotherapy at the University of Salford. Vee has taught counselling and psychotherapy for 23 years. We asked Vee to bring this chapter to a close with some of her takeaway messages for students beginning assessments and assignments on counselling and psychotherapy courses.
>
> As I see it, assessment and assignments are processes akin to the therapy process – they're about not knowing, tentatively finding out what new skills need to be learned, and then moving to a new place with greater confidence. So, in taking the plunge, completing assignments, being assessed on them, we're mirroring the therapy process in some ways, showing its meaning and purpose for growth and development.
>
> In my view, there are three most important parts of assessments and assignments: first, personal reflection; second, skill competency, and third, critical theoretical analysis. Through personal reflection, such as diaries, journals, vlogs and blogs, experiential exercises in class and supervision (which is really important), we learn about ourselves: we learn where we stop and the client begins. If we know ourselves then that helps us to work with clients without us getting in the way. People often forget that being a therapist is about working with people who are vulnerable. If we as therapists are feeling vulnerable, then that compromises our ability to be there for our vulnerable clients. Assessment and assignments around personal reflection are there to test your resilience and robustness to work with clients. Assessment and assignments around skill competency, such as taking a Certificate of Competence, bringing recordings of client work, listening to each other, are a space for learning to listen to feedback non-defensively. For me, being able to listen to feedback non-defensively is the mark of a good therapist. It is a profession where we are constantly having new realisations about our practice.
>
> Critical/theoretical analysis, such as going to lectures, reading and doing academic work, is about developing a critical underpinning for your personal development and skill development – knowing why you're doing what you're doing, interrogating it. Overall, what I'd say to new students and trainees approaching assessment and assignments on counselling and psychotherapy courses is: be open, bring your most authentic self, and do not be afraid to not get it right because this is how we learn.

The next chapter…

In the next chapter, we'll drill down into two common assignments: the essay and the case study.

6

Writing essays and case studies (and doing it differently!)

This chapter drills down into two very common assignments in counselling and psychotherapy courses:

- the essay
- the case study, with audio recording and transcript.

We begin by drawing attention to the importance of meeting word counts, and a reminder to follow your module's referencing requirements. Getting these basic points right mean you don't lose marks unnecessarily.

Then, looking at essays, we'll suggest details of one way to plan and write an essay. You'll find a sample essay here, along with the marking tutor's comments and some thoughts from the writer – although, as we said in the Introduction, there are many ways of writing excellent essays and one offered as a sample should never be seen as a template.

Next, you'll find details of one way in which you might develop and write a case study. You'll find a sample transcript and an analysis of it here, and some thoughts about how another modality might have approached it differently.

Then, to consider doing things differently (which you can do with many assignments, as long as you're responding to the question and meeting the learning outcomes/assessment criteria), we offer a critique of the way we've put forward of writing case studies. Deborah discusses her case study (Lee, 2018)[1] (written for an MSc), paying particular attention to how and why it was written differently. There may be inspiration here for you – or not.

---

1. Lee, D.A. (2018). Enter centre stage the case study. *British Journal of Guidance and Counselling, 46*(3), pp.304–314.

Word counts and references

You will be advised how many words you are permitted to write for your essay or case study (and any piece of written work). You will be penalised if you write anything longer or shorter than the word count (markers may ask you to state the word count at the end of the piece of work; you should do that and do it honestly).

Be sure you are using the required referencing system (see Chapter 5) in your essay, case study and any piece of written work with references. You could lose a sizeable number of marks for work that does not use the expected referencing system. If there is a required style, it will be stated in your course and module handbooks (another reason to read them!).

You also need to check whether you are expected to provide a bibliography (a list of books you have consulted/read but not quoted from) in addition to the reference list. A bibliography as well as a reference list gives a better picture of the effort you've taken with your work and what has informed it, even if you have not eventually cited these sources, but it is not always asked for. Check your course and module handbooks to be sure that you are doing what is required. Again, not doing so could lead to you losing marks needlessly.

The essay

As we said in Chapter 5, the aims of the essay are to develop a sound argument, underpinned by pertinent reading and reflection, in response to a question given to you, or sometimes that you have chosen yourself, which relates to the content, learning outcomes/assessment criteria of the module for which it is written. The format usually follows the traditional title, introduction, main body of the text (following the order outlined in the introduction and developing the argument stated in the introduction), conclusion. The essay does not use subheads. Some courses/modules may allow more creative approaches to essays – you should check with your course team or module staff. Essays always need to have a strong internal narrative, even if there is licence to be a bit more creative.

The essay step-by-step

Let's look at the stages of one way in which you might plan and write an essay. As we have said already, this is just one way of proceeding. There are numerous others, and you may already have developed your own.

The essay question

First, get to grips with the essay question and the style required of the essay.

We'll start by assuming that there is no list of essay questions for you to choose from, just one question that everyone is required to answer. This is common at beginning levels of training when you don't have enough experience yet to write your own questions.

To say 'Read the question' sounds obvious – everybody reads the question, but there is often a gap between reading the question and understanding it, keeping it in mind and responding to it.

If you're only given one question, quite often it includes a choice. 'Write an essay on ONE of the following topics' is a common instruction. If you then write about TWO of the following topics, as students frequently do, you're already in a difficult situation because your response will indicate quite clearly to the marker/s that you haven't read the question carefully enough. You will also use only half the word count available if the markers only look at one of the two topics you've written about. So your response to that topic would need to be very good indeed for you to pass the assignment. Some marking criteria would fail the essay because you've not answered the question.

If you've been provided with a choice of questions, you might decide to choose a question that you already feel quite informed about – perhaps because it draws on your personal experience in some way. This is a good opportunity to start to develop a strong expertise in that particular area – through interrogating literature and creating arguments, your knowledge will increase significantly. You could also decide to choose to write your assignment on a subject you know nothing at all about at the moment, but which is of interest to you, in order to further your learning in a different way. The choice is yours. Neither is better or worse. The choice might also be less clear cut than that. There are lots of ways to proceed.

It is worthwhile considering what might be relevant to several of the essay topics available to you before firmly committing yourself to one. Doing this may prevent you from working on a topic only to reach a dead-end because it turned out not to be interesting enough to you to explore it deeply over a period of time, or because you find you don't connect with it sufficiently to have enough to say about it, however much you research it. If you're struggling to choose a question from a list, or you don't quite understand some of the questions, a discussion with your tutor/lecturer/trainer can be very helpful, if that's available to you. You could also talk with a peer. Through talking, the question that really calls to you may well emerge. It might even be the one that you didn't initially understand.

If you're at a stage in your studies where you can, with tutorial support, create your own essay titles, bear the following in mind:

- Avoid writing titles that are not asking a question. If you don't give yourself the opportunity to respond to a question, you can end up writing a very descriptive piece of work. By having an argument to make, you can write a piece of work that is analytical rather than descriptive. Analytical work always achieves better marks, at any level of study. If you are an undergraduate student looking for high grades, note that a descriptive piece of work rarely receives more than a 2.2 classification.

- Avoid titles that begin 'To what extent…' A question that asks 'to what extent' can only ever lead to a vague answer that is, essentially, saying 'well… to some extent'. An assignment that is going to do well demands a crisp, neat response to a question. 'To what extent' questions do not give you the chance to do that.

Once you feel sure of what you want to do (and you can change your mind right up until you get so far into the process and too close to the deadline to start again), spend some more time reflecting on the title given to you, or that you have created. We suggest you highlight what you think are the important words in it. Keep these words, and the full title itself, in mind and in view (on a piece of paper beside you) as you work. Ask yourself at regular intervals, 'Am I answering the question?'

Or, if you're not answering the question, and you didn't intend to (because you wanted to do things differently, within the confines of the learning outcomes/assessment criteria, of course), ask yourself at regular intervals: 'Am I making a case for why the question needs to be answered slightly differently to how I think the marker/s might have imagined?'

Before you move to planning (the next section), familiarise yourself with the style that is expected of this essay. Check your module handbook and speak with the tutor/lecturer/trainer if you need any clarification. Some essays may be very formal, others will allow more scope for first-person writing. Be sure about this before you start to draft your essay.

Planning your essay

Once you have a question to tackle and feel comfortable enough with the style expected of the finished product, the planning process will begin in earnest.

The first stage is to collect, read, and interrogate the relevant literature. Go back to Chapter 4 to remind yourself how to find the relevant literature, how to get the most from libraries, and how to read texts and make notes.

Reading widely (even if you're not reading each whole book or article) is crucial to doing well in most essay assignments – it helps you get a strong hold on your field of study, so that you are an informed writer. If you take reading as the starting point for planning your essay, you aren't being led purely by your pre-existing ideas, or by what appears to be 'common knowledge' in society about a topic, or by what you've heard in class or read in a textbook. You're aiming to become an independent thinker, drawing on a breadth and depth of sources, not all of which support your argument.

Students often say they've got an idea, an argument for an essay, and now they've got to 'find sources that agree with it'. That does sound like hard work! What if you never find what you're looking for? We suggest you try, instead, to allow yourself to stay open to a range of possibilities, seeing where the literature you read leads you. We find this the most exciting part of planning essays, and all other assignments. It can turn the process away from being a chore towards being a voyage of discovery. This doesn't mean you don't have your own ideas and arguments; it simply means that, as you set off, you're holding those ideas and arguments lightly and seeing what will emerge. Your ideas may well change in the course of your research. There is of course resonance here with how you need to be in the counselling relationship, where you similarly hold your beliefs and expectations lightly.

If your own work can develop in connection with what you're finding in the literature – for instance, if you disagree with what other people are saying, and you can use literature to support your disagreement – you're on the way to innovative work. You might, with more polishing after you've completed it for an assignment, see if you can get it published in your professional magazine or a journal.

'Yes - but how much should I read?' is a common student question in any field of study, and always a difficult one for tutors to answer. Whether or not the reading you've done is 'enough' depends on whether it was relevant reading, and that depends on what you actually do with your reading.

What we mean by this is that sometimes students will do Google searches and use whatever material pops up on the first page of the search results for their essay, thinking that it doesn't really matter what it is; the fact that it is a 'source' is enough. And/or they'll use Wikipedia as if it is an academic source, and media news reports as if they are the truth. Sometimes a reference list will show someone did read widely, but they haven't used much of that work in the essay itself. Sometimes, to be honest, assignments look as if the sources in the reference list weren't read at all. Be sure only to list in the references what you've read and cited in the essay.

You will sometimes be offered guidance on how much you should read. Ideally you should read more than the minimum asked of you, although that will not be possible if you don't have sufficient time for it (for instance, when you know that you can't have the self-care you need and get high marks, so you sensibly sacrifice the higher marks on this occasion).

In order to show you've read and interrogated your literature, you will want to quote and paraphrase from it in your essay. The first step to that is highlighting the quotes and ideas that you find interesting for your essay question, or interesting in their own right, even if you don't yet know what you might do with them. You can do this on printed copies of the work, or on downloaded copies on your computer.

Next, once you've done some reading (there will be more to do – check out where the gaps are in your knowledge at points in the process) and interrogating, review the highlighting you've done and type up the quotes that you think you might use (even if you don't know how you'll use them yet), making sure to make it clear in your notes where you are citing someone else, and where you are noting down your own responses to other people's writing.

Start to arrange information and ideas in order to begin to develop some tentative ideas and arguments. This will take time and will involve getting to grips with managing a range of materials all at once. Take your time.

Writing the essay

As the ideas and quotes start to come together, this is a point at which you can write up your first draft of an introduction to the essay.

Why would you write a first draft of an introduction now? Surely you just add that in when you've finished the essay? Many students do think that. Our view is that you can start to do the introduction now – and then revise it from now onwards – because an introduction says what an essay is about, what it will cover (in a coherent, flowing structure), and what the argument of the piece will be. As you start to draft the introduction, what you might do with your material and ideas will start to become clearer and clearer. A draft introduction, constantly revised, helps you know what you want to say, the order in which you want to say it, and what you want to argue with this material.

A draft introduction is also often something that you can show to a tutor/lecturer/trainer to receive some feedback and feedforward. Some students like to show a plan. Essentially, they like to show a list of topics that might go in their essay. This can work for some people. But a list of topics that might go in an essay doesn't show the reader how well the list of topics will link and cohere, and where it's all going in terms of a well-made argument. A draft introduction can start to show that. If feedback and feedforward is available, you may prefer to wait until you have the essence of what you want to argue before you seek it.

In a nutshell, once you are writing an introduction – however rough and ready it is, and it can be as rough and ready as needed for some time – it will help you to:

- sort out the main ideas of the piece
- sketch out a logical structure for them, without repetition
- create an argument (which may, or may not, be your final argument).

The introduction we've just described is a central part of the first draft onwards. Alongside writing initial drafts of the introduction, you'll also be writing what people tend to call the 'main body' – that is, the rest of the essay up until the conclusion. The 'main body' develops the ideas set out in the introduction, in the order outlined in the introduction, in order to make an argument.

This is the point where some students will forget the introduction and write whatever comes to mind. They'll get off the point. Your introduction must be followed. If your introduction and main body do not cohere, then your introduction needs more editing. It is respectful of your reader to give them what the introduction promised would be in the main body. Marking tutors will notice if you say you're going to do something and then you don't.

As you write the main body of the text, keep roughly to 'one idea per paragraph' so that the essay is smooth and easy to follow. Support your points with reference to literature. Use some of the quotes you've identified from the literature. Say how the literature is helping develop your own arguments. Authors A, B and C might be saying one thing (perhaps the expected argument in the field you're writing about), but Author D disagrees (and so do you), and the work of Authors E, F, and G can (in different ways) be brought in to assist with putting forward a new way of seeing. Going back to our earlier point about students who have ideas and look for people who agree with them, this is not that; it is using the literature with the complexity that any writing in our field (about human beings) deserves.

When you reach the conclusion, summarise what you've covered in the essay – using a different form of words to those used in the introduction/main body, and restate the argument you have made. This isn't the place to introduce new ideas that you then don't have space to develop.

You now have a draft of a whole essay. At this point, it may be very much longer than the word count. That's absolutely fine. It's more than fine, it's ideal! Never just write to the word count and stop. Write as much as you need to, and then edit it to the correct word count. This is a very important point. Better to have too many words and have to cut than too few and have to write more. So many students do write to the word count; as they're writing, they'll say 'Just another 1,000 words needed now!' What this means is that there can be no meaningful editing process. There is no leeway to refine your arguments and make them even better. It is a rare author who writes only one draft that is worth reading, particularly of an essay on a complex issue.

And finally, edit, and edit again. When you have a whole draft of an essay, put the work aside for a while – a couple of days, if you can, but otherwise overnight, or even a few hours. Then when you start editing it, you'll be seeing it with fresh eyes. You'll be looking at it as the marking tutor might.

Editing is where the fun really starts. This is where you have the opportunity to sharpen your work, to make sure you're saying exactly what you want to say – that you're being precise and clear. Here are some questions to consider as you begin the editing process:

- Does the essay as a whole answer the question/deal with the set topic? If not, what do you need to do now? Refine the introduction/conclusion? Rework some aspects of the main body? Read something more to fill a gap in what you're saying?
- Does the essay have a coherent, flowing structure? Are you following the structure you said you'd follow in the introduction? If not, what do you need to do now? Refine the introduction/conclusion, or rework some aspects of the main body?
- Is each main point well supported by literature? If not, do you need to introduce more quotes/paraphrasing, or do you need to read something else (targeted reading)?
- Does the argument actually work? Have you made the argument? Is the argument supported? Does it need tweaking?
- Is there a clear distinction between your ideas and those you have brought in from other authors?
- Is the language clear and is the style suited to the purpose? Which bits of the essay would you not be able follow if you hadn't written it yourself? (You might ask someone else to read it through for you.)

Much editing isn't about looking for answers to these sorts of questions – they're a guide as you get going. Much of editing is about going through your piece multiple times, getting a strong hold on it, and over time seeing where you've put something in the wrong place or used the wrong word, and fixing what isn't quite right until you reach the point of feeling, yes, this is exactly what you want to convey and how.

However much editing you have done, there will always be more errors to catch, and more refining that can be done. Allow some time for a final edit, or more.

Before you submit your work, check that you are following the presentation requirements asked of you in your module handbook – for instance you may need to use double spacing, or particular sized margins. Some courses may want you to put your name on the assignment, others will be using anonymous marking – make sure you do what is asked.

And always, always check that you have listed all your text references in the reference list, and that the details match. It's a common error to get dates wrong, for example.

Sample assignment essay

It is common, at the start of any counselling/psychotherapy training, to be given an essay question about the therapeutic modality in which you are training. For person-centred counselling trainees, this usually revolves around Carl Rogers' six necessary and sufficient conditions (Rogers, 1957).[2]

Here is the introduction to: 'Choose one of Rogers' six necessary and sufficient conditions, and critically evaluate the role it plays in a client's personality change during therapy.' The essay is by Francisca Serrette, a first-year student on the MA in person-centred and experiential psychotherapy at Liverpool John Moores University. Francisca was awarded a First Class mark for her work.

Read the essay introduction and reflect on your response. We have listed the references separately in an Appendix at the end of the book, as there are so many, but they are of themselves a useful reading list for such a discussion, so do take a look.

Choose one of Rogers' six necessary and sufficient conditions, and critically evaluate the role it plays in a client's personality change during therapy

This paper critically examines the ground-breaking theory of the person-centred approach (PCA) to counselling and psychotherapy, specifically Rogers' postulate, 'the necessary and sufficient conditions of therapeutic personality change' (1957).

Rogers' theory unmasked the 'expertise' of the therapist and, in doing so, highlighted the power and precedence of a nondirective therapeutic-alliance and successful outcomes generated through the conditions in which therapy is facilitated (Rogers, 1961) (i.e. the relationship that is formed between the therapist and the client).

The proposal that the six conditions, outlined by Rogers, are both necessary and sufficient for successful therapy remains controversial amongst person-centred therapists and, as Merry states, 'may never be finally resolved' (2020, p.59). However, the importance of the therapeutic relationship for client outcomes continues to be pertinent for contemporary counselling and psychotherapy practice (Cornelius-White & Ciesielski, 2016; Norcross & Lambert, 2018; Patterson, 1990).

Consideration is given to the 19 propositions of Rogers' personality theory (1951). An organism's need for survival, irrespective of how well or maladjusted, is discussed as a development from Maslow's need for belongingness (Maslow, 1943) and the construction of a value-base, and a self-concept, as heavily influenced by our introjected values – those values as determined by the societal, secular and the familial 'should do' elements of our personality (Merry, 2012; Rogers, 1951, 1957, 1959). The roles and dynamics of Rogers' six conditions are assessed for their aptitude to support those experiencing an incongruent state (Finsrud et al., 2021; Watson & Prosser, 2002; Watson et al., 2010) between a rigid self-structure and the opposing visceral and phenomenological experiences in the here and now (Lago & Charura, 2016; Tolan & Cameron, 2016; Rogers, 1951, 1957, 1959).

Rogers' fifth condition (i.e. the therapist's empathic understanding of the client's frame of reference, as well as communication of that experience to the client) will specifically be

---

2. Rogers, C.R. (1957). The necessary and sufficient conditions of therapeutic personality change. *Journal of Consulting and Clinical Psychology, 21*, 95–103.

considered, including the relationship it has with the other conditions. Empathy and its 'delicate and powerful' (Rogers, 1980, p.137) embodiment is explored beyond the simplicity of rote, summation responses (Brodley 1994; Kirschenbaum, 2007; Raskin, 1947; Rogers, 1975). Further, this paper will highlight empathy's potential for enabling difficult self-exploration and higher self-empathy (Barrett-Lennard, 1997; Joseph, 2016; Sutandi, 2020), as well as empathy's capacity for elasticating the self-structure (Rogers, 1975) and generating personality change, as well as a shift to an internal 'locus of evaluation' (Rogers, 1951, 1957, 1959).

Arguably then, the fulfilment of the fifth condition can only be achieved through therapists' attempts at genuine comprehension of their client's world and the offer of a loving acceptance of their frame of reference (Clark, 2010; Ioannidou & Konstantikaki, 2008; Rogers, 1951, 1957, 1959). Therefore, this essay will also critically examine to what extent a therapist can truly embody an empathetic state (Clark, 2010), including their likely vulnerability to both distortion and bias (Clark, 2010; Kivlighan et al., 2017; Kolden et al., 2011) resulting in the need for better self-integration (Mearns & Thorne, 2000, 2007; Sutandi, 2020; Rogers, 1975), as well as the interpersonal (Adler, 2002; Clark, 2010; Cissna & Anderson, 1994) and idiosyncratic dichotomy (Bozarth, 1984; Ahn et al., 2021) of empathic therapy. Further influences to consider include therapeutic dynamics (Bohart & Tallman, 1999; Duncan et al., 2004; Truax & Carkhuff, 1967; Purton, 2012) and the cyclical nature of a staged process (Rogers, 1961). The universality of empathising with the human experience (Elliott et al., 2018; Jordan, 1997; Murphy et al., 2012), as well as founding a relationship upon 'empathic interaction' (Bohart, 2021; McNally, 2019; Rogers, 1957), and whether the therapist holds 'expert-laden' responsibility for introducing this (Bohart, 2021; Patterson, 1990; Stepien & Baernstein, 2006; Wiseman, 1996), as well as how this is experienced by different clients (e.g. Warner, 1991), are also explored. The paper concludes with reflections on both the 'mystical' (Ellingham, 2007; Mearns & Cooper, 2017; Rogers, 1980; Thorne, 2002) and the intangible nature of empathy (Myers, 1999; Reik, 1948) and its empirical basis for personality change when present (Finsrud et al., 2021; Mearns & Cooper, 2017; Norcross & Lambert, 2018; Rogers, 1975).

Marking tutor comments

Dr Peter Blundell, who we've met a few times in this book and who marked Francisca's essay, says:

I'd like to begin by reiterating what Deborah and Pete have said, because it can't be said too often: that introducing your essay can be one of the most important aspects of your assignment. Most students understand that the introduction 'sets the scene' for the reader. However, students can often underestimate the power of an introduction as a tool for guiding the reader through their arguments. They're often surprised to find out that a good introduction can also lead to higher marks. A common mistake I see is students rephrasing the essay question and writing it up as an introduction. While this may offer the reader some brief indication of what is included in the work, inevitably it tells the reader nothing new!

A good introduction should be clear, concise, informative and engaging for the reader. In the piece you've just read, Francisca does this very well, offering the reader a thorough description of what she is going to include in the essay. Francisca also offers the reader an indication of some of her critical thinking skills through her overview and analysis of the literature and research around empathy.

You've heard about the importance of answering not just the question but the learning outcomes/assessment criteria as well. This essay is a case in point. The essay question asks Francisca to choose one of Rogers' conditions to form the focus of her essay. However, one of the learning outcomes for this module expects students to 'master the theoretical concepts underpinning the six necessary and sufficient conditions of therapeutic personality change'. This means Francisca must also explore the other five conditions, and not only the one she has chosen as the focus of her essay. It's an example of how essay questions and learning outcomes/assessment criteria must be read together.

How an assignment is presented to its readers is also extremely important for an academic essay. Readers need to be able to understand what the author is trying to say. Furthermore, a reader must be able to 'track' where the evidence is for all the author's arguments, which means that any ideas, concepts and thoughts that are not your own need to be referenced correctly. Referencing can look scary, especially if you are not familiar with it! However, it is a learnable skill, which can take some time to master. Francisca has ensured that she has correctly referenced all the authors she refers to. As you've seen, she has read very widely to construct her response to the question. The more you read, the more you can reflect upon to develop your arguments. I wonder how you feel about how much is in Francisca's reference list?

A common phrase I hear from students is 'I want to be a counsellor and not a writer!' While I can empathise with this sentiment, it is important to remember why you are writing a particular essay or assignment. I have lost count of the number of times that students have reported that their therapeutic approach/practice has begun to 'make sense' or 'come together' because of the reading and writing they were required to undertake to fulfil their course assignments. The assessments for your course will have been purposefully designed to help develop aspects of your counselling knowledge and practice. So, while you may not (now) be aiming to be a writer, writing your assignments will help you to understand different aspects of counselling practice and therefore make you a better counsellor.

Advice from the essay writer

We asked Francisca to speak to you about how you might approach your essay. Francisca said: Do the research. Read and read. It is the most crucial stage. If you haven't done it, it will show. Your sentences will be long and unstructured and, most importantly, vacant of true substance.

As you read, make sure that you are making clear notes: which book, which chapters, which page numbers, specific quotes (author, date and page reference) and what thoughts they inspire for you.

I often used to write just my thoughts in the margins of everything I read, only to read these back weeks later, and realise that, despite being very clever, I had no idea what these thoughts were inspired by, other than the thoughts I already knew rattled around my head!

It is painstakingly boring to be this meticulous and I often fall short of the mark. However, if I don't do it properly, I always end up doing double the work as I have to reread papers that I thought I understood because I couldn't recollect my understanding in enough detail from my margin notes to use it in my work.

I suggest doing a spider diagram to get all your ideas, all that mess, down on paper. It's the starting point for an essay structure that has consistency, flow and pizzazz.

I often start trying to piece together the main themes of what I have read based on my own understanding and the summation of it and find the links between each subject through a series of subheadings.

This process will allow you begin to play devil's advocate in your own writing process. You can query why your initial thoughts and feelings were what they were. Do they still stand up? What is the other side to the story? Where are the holes in the literature and in your original thinking? This will also highlight for you your own prejudices and develop your thinking and reflective capacity – something extremely important in a budding psychotherapist.

Sometimes I find references for the things I have said once I have completed the work. I can see then what I haven't yet supported with literature, as all points in an excellent essay need to be. Somebody will have already said it first.

Finally, edit. Edit. Edit. Edit. Put it down for a week and edit again. Sometimes you may find it inspiring to read back what you forgot you wrote, and hail yourself as a literary genius. This can only be done with some distance, however, and will offer you the invaluable opportunity to winkle out any mistakes, any grammatical errors and anything that just simply does not make sense. Ensure you are within the margins of your word count, submit and cross your most likely carpal-tunnelled fingers. Good luck!

An opportunity for publication

You may decide, with your tutor's encouragement, to reshape your essay into a journal article for publication. Being published is particularly useful if you want to do a PhD and have an academic career.

Catherine Jackson, who we met earlier, was editor of *Therapy Today* and has edited a number of academic journals. She advises:

When I edited *Therapy Today*, we regularly received submissions from students who had been encouraged by their tutors to submit their work. Sadly, too often, their work read just like the highly accomplished student assignment it was; they had too little to offer the vast majority of our readers, who were qualified and experienced practising therapists.

So my advice to students contemplating submitting an essay as an article for a journal is first, do your research. Don't send the article to several journals. It's annoying for an editor to have read it, considered it, replied to you about it, only to find it's been accepted elsewhere. It's not unethical, just rude and inconsiderate. Read the journal you decide to approach (the editor will expect you to have done so). Familiarise yourself with its particular style and content. Check out if it has particular 'sections' (such as shorter, first-person opinion pieces) where your work might fit best, and rewrite your essay to that style. Check out its guidance for authors. Some editors are happy to be approached (by email) first for an informal chat. Make sure you present it with the correct referencing style for that publication (journals often have their own variations on APA). Think about your likely readers and what might be relevant to them. If it's an academic journal, the formal style of your essay will be fine. If it's a magazine (like *Therapy Today*, *The New Psychotherapist* and *Counselling Matters*), don't be afraid to write in the first person. Bring yourself into the work and speak directly to the reader. And keep writing and researching, as you clearly have a talent for it.

The case study

To recap what we said about the case study in Chapter 5, the aims are to develop and give evidence of appreciation of professional issues, client practice issues and the relationship of both to the theory, history, philosophy, and ethics of your theoretical approach; to demonstrate the ability to write in a suitable style for fellow professionals/to develop your own style (the latter dependent on modality/level of study), and to demonstrate the ability to communicate therapeutic decisions to others.

The format might be a whole session or part of a session with a peer on your course, or a session with a client in a placement, depending on your level and year of study. We provide a detailed outline of a possible structure for you to follow below.

Client confidentiality and permissions

Before we begin... the most important point about case studies is to seek the client's permission before you write about your work with them. This is absolutely non-negotiable. Think how you'd feel if a therapist you were seeing wrote about you and shared it widely with others, for their own benefit, and hadn't asked your permission. If your client says no to the case study, you cannot write it. You will need to think again. And, as you write, you need to keep checking in with the client that they are still happy for you to be writing about your relating with them. You might consider also contracting with the client that they can read the final piece of work before submission.

Note also that having permission to record particular therapy relationships does not mean you have permission to use those recordings and those relationships in your assessed work.

A note about the General Data Protection Regulation (GDPR)

When you hold any material about others, including recordings, you need to be aware of the General Data Protection Regulation (GDPR). You will find details here:

https://ico.org.uk/for-organisations/guide-to-data-protection/guide-to-the-general-data-protection-regulation-gdpr

And you will find helpful guidance from BACP here:

www.bacp.co.uk/about-us/contact-us/gdpr

The case study step-by-step

We are going to start with a detailed outline of a) the steps and b) the structure that are usually expected in a case study. You will find versions of what we say next in a range of places, including – no doubt – the assessment guide for the module where you're asked to do a case study for your assignment. If this is what's being asked for, and you're doing it, then you're likely to pass your assignment.

However, we're then going to talk about doing things differently, and why you might want to do so. Recognising that things can be done differently, and knowing why they might be done differently, can assist you in being sure of your own decisions.

Step 1: Find out what is required

The first step in successful case study writing is the same as for any other assignment in this regard – find out what's required. Be sure of the title of the piece, and its learning outcomes/assessment criteria. Read all materials that the course offers you on how you are expected to do this piece of work. It is a type of assessment that few students will be familiar with when they start counselling and psychotherapy training, so close reading of the requirements is essential.

Step 2: Identify suitable client work

This is a crucial stage. You need to choose some work that will help you cover all of the requirements of the assignment.

Think about the following factors:

- *Do you have audio recordings of your work with the client or clients that you might choose for your case study?*

    You may have a placement that doesn't allow recordings, or a client or clients who don't permit recordings. You will usually be asked to provide an audio as well as a written transcript, so you must choose a client and a placement where recording is allowed/used.

- *What about anonymity?*

    As you'll be writing about your work with a client, and using their words, it means that you aren't offering confidentiality. But you will be ensuring anonymity – in that you will not be using your client's name or other identifying details. Remember that this may not be as straightforward as it looks. You might accidentally identify the client by disclosing something unique about them. This is a particular difficulty if you work with clients who have a high public profile, either in your community or nationally. You might find it easier to choose someone whose details you can anonymise more easily.

- *How long have you been seeing the client?*

    It is probably not a good idea to select a client who you have seen for only a couple of sessions. You might not have enough to write about. However, a very long relationship (several months or years) may present other difficulties in that you will have too much material to fit the word limit.

- *Current client or past client?*

  Most likely you will be asked to write a case study to illustrate your current ongoing work. A client who finished their relationship with you more than six months ago, for example, may not be representative of your current work. You'll be developing all the time. Writing about a past client is also difficult because you might have trouble getting hold of them to ask for their permission to write about your work with them. This raises ethical issues: if you didn't expect to be writing about your work with the client, you won't have suggested that they will hear from you again.

- *My best work ever, or my work?*

  You're looking to talk about and explore how you work, rather than trying to prove that you are wonderful.

- *Is this a relationship that is going well enough to be the basis for a piece of assessed work?*

  You may have a relationship with a client that is interesting in that there are significant processes of rupture and repair going on (so far, the ruptures have appeared to be repaired). If a client decides you cannot use the session in your assignment – even the night before you are going to submit your work – you must honour their wishes. Courses will have arrangements in place for this eventuality, but if you have a sense that a client might pull out, you need to think seriously before committing your time to writing a case study that you may have to rewrite with a different client.

- *What does your clinical supervisor think about your choice?*

  This is an assignment that will have your clinical supervisor's involvement. They will be an invaluable source of help in choosing the 'right' client for your case study. They have written case studies themselves and, most importantly, they know your work, and have an overview of your relationship with your client/s. Ask your clinical supervisor for advice.

Step 3: Structuring your case study

We will briefly outline here how you might structure a case study, but do check this against what your course is asking you to do – your college (or university or training provider) may have its own preferred ways of doing it.

i) Background information

You will want to include some or all of these in your case study:

- The setting in which you see the client. A low-cost counselling centre, GP's surgery, women's centre, hospice bereavement service, university counselling centre, service for people 'using substances', home visit? What's the setting like? Is the setting consistent with your modality or do you have to work slightly differently there?
- Demographic and personal details about the client. They are likely to include age, gender identity, sexuality, 'race', ethnicity, religion, current and past relationships,

where they live, whether they work and, if so, what they do, and so forth. Here you need to be very careful about including enough for context/exploration, while not saying so much that the client becomes identifiable.

- Presenting problem and what the client wants from counselling and psychotherapy. Why did the client come to see you, and what hopes and/or goals do they have?
- Referral path. How did the client come to be referred to you – did they refer themselves, or were they referred by a GP, social services, a voluntary organisation?
- Number of sessions so far. Which session/s are you writing about? And why?
- Frequency of sessions. How often do you see this client – more than once a week, weekly, fortnightly?
- Contract. What kind of contract do you have with this client – for example, is the counselling time limited? Include the contract in the appendix.
- Details of the contract you have agreed with your client for the completion of this work. Put a copy of the agreement in the appendix.

Note: Sometimes students submit the actual forms that a client has signed. You must provide blank forms, not forms with a client's signature on them. To do so would compromise the client's anonymity and you could fail your assignment for lack of attention to ethics.

ii) First session
Write about the first time you met the client, using some excerpts from transcribed material from that session.

This is where what is written may be shaped by the theoretical approach you are training in. It depends on whether you think that the first interview in counselling is for information collection and interpretation of this information to help you understand the client, or whether the first interview is where you start to build a relationship with the client in a non-interpretative way. You may think it is acceptable and appropriate to make observations and give details of:

- the way they talked about what had brought them to therapy – hesitatingly, confidently… and so on
- how they described their feelings – such as anger, sadness…
- what you felt and thought about the client – your initial impressions and how this affected you
- how well you thought the session went
- anything that got in the way of you forming an acceptant relationship with the client.

iii) The context and history of the client's presenting problem
Again, what you write here may be influenced by your theoretical and practical position. Would you specifically ask the client for any of the following information? If not, would you include any of these details in the case study if the client voluntarily provided the information without prompting from you?

- Have they had counselling and psychotherapy previously? If so, what sort of counselling and psychotherapy, when, and how did it go?
- Have they been treated/or are they being treated by their doctor or a psychiatrist for a diagnosed mental illness?
- Are they taking any medication/s?
- Is there any family history of the client's presenting problem?
- Do they have any history of substance abuse?
- Have they recently been bereaved or suffered loss (job loss, injury, disability, etc.)?
- Is there anything in their development as a child that might account for their current problem?

iv) Assessment

Some counsellors are very keen on assessment and some baulk at the very mention of the word. But, in truth, we constantly assess the situation we find ourselves in with our clients as the relationship develops. We all have to decide some pretty basic things, such as:

- Do we think counselling and psychotherapy will help the client, or do they need another sort of help – a medical doctor, a welfare rights officer, a befriender and so forth?
- More specifically, do we think we can work with this particular client?
- If we think we can work with this client, are there any special circumstances prevailing that we have to take account of when we think about how to approach therapy with this client?
- If we think we cannot work with this client, how do we refer them on without them feeling rejected?

The main differences in ways of assessing a client and the issues they are bringing to counselling relate to your theoretical frame of reference:

- If you are more person-centred in your practice you will let the client assess the situation from their own world of experience.
- If you are not person-centred you will probably assess the client and their needs from your frame of reference. This will include your estimation of their problem and your formulating treatment strategies to help them.

v) The counselling process, including audio recording and transcript

In this section, you will have the transcript of the session/s, or part of a session/s, that you will be exploring in your case study. This is the main section of the case study and you should give it the most words. Your task is not to simply give a step-by-step account of the content of the sessions. You will be required to reflect on what happened and apply some analysis to what happens in the session in terms of your philosophy, theory, ethics, politics and practice of counselling. The relevant information will be not only what the client said and your responses, but also your thoughts and feelings that were stimulated by your relationship with the client.

As you reflect upon this process you may include:

- How has the client developed, changed or moved in the counselling process in terms of your model?
- How have you contributed to the therapeutic process in terms of your theory?
- What was the quality of the relationship between you and your client – for example, did you make psychological contact with your client? How did this develop throughout the relationship?
- Were there any 'magic moments' or key interventions in the sessions that illustrate a theoretical or practice point?
- Did anything happen that runs counter to your theoretical approach or your expectations?
- Did you make any contributions or interventions that you consider to be mistakes?
- If the relationship has ended, how did it end?

vi) Use of clinical supervision
Throughout your relationship with this client, you will have taken your work with them to your clinical supervisor. You should choose a couple of specific issues from these supervision sessions and describe how you worked with this material in supervision, and what sort of resolution you achieved. Your clinical supervisor needs also to agree that you can quote or paraphrase their words in your case study. Think about:

- What supervision issues stand out from your work with this client?
- How did you work with your supervisor on these issues?
- What did you learn from this supervision?
- Have you changed your practice as a result?

vii) Summary
Finally, you may want to draw some general conclusions at the end of the case study.

A note on publication: If you have the permission of your client to publish your work together, case studies are accepted in most academic journals. The case study has a long history in this field as a way to provide learning opportunities for peers and develop good practice. We'd like to see more practitioners do this – writing in new as well as traditional ways.

Sample transcript and analysis

You'll sometimes read therapists introducing 'fictional' accounts of client work by saying something like: 'This is an amalgamation of several clients, to protect client confidentiality. No details have been included that could be identified to any one client.' They hope this will get round the client confidentiality problem. We're not so sure. If you were a client and you knew your therapist had written an article or a book about their work, and something in the text is something you think you said, or a detail from the description sounds a lot like you, you might well wonder if you'd been in their mind when they 'amalgamated' you with several other people, and that might lead you to wondering what that meant to your therapist. You might not appreciate being 'amalgamated' – you're a person in your own right. Consequently, our 'fictional' account of client work is just that, fictional. It emerged line by line, much as an actual therapy session does, with one thought leading to another.

A transcript should be just that – a transcript – and, as we explained in Chapter 5, depending on your course requirements, you may be expected to include the 'ums' and 'ers' and pauses, which is why transcription can be such a painstaking process.

Transcript

What follows is a fictionalised transcript of a fictional client session, which we asked Katie Moffatt to evaluate as if this were her actual client. Katie is a registered member of BACP, with an MSc in counselling from Abertay University and a postgraduate certificate in counselling from the University of Strathclyde. Her counselling experiences include working with clients in the NHS and at a LGBTQ counselling service, and she is currently a counsellor at the University of Edinburgh. She writes from a person-centred counsellor's perspective.

Client: I hate my job. I hate everything [louder] about it. [**Therapist**: Mm.] I hate the people. [**Therapist**: Mm.] I hate the way we have to do things. [**Therapist**: You hate…] The people, they're so, so… [two-second pause], erm, hateful. And then yesterday, yesterday the… the boss, she, she said in a team meeting that 'we all love working here', 'we all love [louder] working here'! [**Therapist**: Ah.] 'We love the buzz of making sales', apparently [smiles tightly], when we're just selling rubbish, and we all know it – even her, especially [louder] her! They're selling rubbish to people who don't really want it, and can't afford it. It's hateful. [Stares directly at therapist, pauses two seconds, then sighs deeply.]

Therapist: You're sighing. You…

Client: [Interrupts] … I know I did. I did it. It came from me. I heard it too. Why do you need to tell me that? [Sighs again, more forcefully.] Look, I did it again. I sighed. I'm sighing. Argh!

Therapist: I'm… I'm reflecting back to you what I see happening, what you're bringing to the session today. The power of your hatred for your job, and the hateful people who work there, the way you have to do things, that the boss said you all love working there…

Client: [Interrupts] …You're just saying what I've said. What's the point [louder] of that? [**Therapist**: Oh!] I said it. I don't need to hear it again. I'm listening to myself already. Don't you know that? Is it really, really, worth £50 to hear what I've said repeated back to me again? Is it from a textbook? [Makes air-quotes.] 'Repeat back what the client said, that's therapy, and I claim my £50'? Oh! You wouldn't know anything about working with hateful people. You just sit here being a therapist, in your scarf, with your books, working for yourself, making money from people's misery, paying for your nice house and your nice holidays. Hateful.

Therapist: I'm wondering… are you talking about me, about your colleagues, or about someone else?

Client: Oh! [Two-second pause.] What if this is worthless? I just feel such fear of, of, people making other people's lives worse, taking their money for something that isn't worth anything. The people at work, what they, we, do definitely is worthless. It's… it's [pauses two seconds] just what my parents did – they took money from people who couldn't afford it, and we lived well on the profits. I can, can scarcely breathe when I think of it.

Therapist: When you sighed earlier, I wondered if you were exhaling [sighs] some of your sadness?

Client: I don't know. I don't really 'do' sadness. My parents didn't have time for it. If I cried as a kid I got sent to my room until I would stop. I push sadness away. [**Therapist**: Oh!]

Therapist: I noticed you expressed anger about what I'd said earlier?

Client: Mm, yeah. If you're customer-facing – as I've always been, I worked for my parents from the age of 14 [**Therapist**: Mm.] – you have to smile at whatever the customer says, and boil under the surface. I think I enjoyed being angry with you! [Smiles.]

Therapist: [Smiles.] What did you enjoy?

Client: That I could express how I felt, and you didn't throw me out, or at least not yet!

Evaluation of the extract transcript

And this is Katie's commentary on the transcript.

This is the second session with the client and although the client appeared confident and calm in our initial session, they arrived on this occasion looking cross and annoyed – it felt as though they weren't sure they wanted to be there, and they seemed distracted.

In the first session, we had spent time exploring their expectations and hopes for the therapy sessions and what they would like to focus on, which was primarily their unresolved and unpleasant childhood family experiences. As the first session came to a close, I felt we had created good initial contact and I looked forward to working alongside the client over the coming weeks.

As soon as we started this second session, the client immediately began sharing their thoughts and feelings about their 'hateful' job and colleagues. This was unexpected as it hadn't come up the previous week, so I was a little surprised. This reflection is helpful as it makes me aware that I should be open to whatever a client brings on the day and not make assumptions. The client was extremely animated and angry as they described their workplace and sales colleagues.

As they shared their experiences, I wanted to reassure them that I was following and acknowledging their emotions with affirmations and positive regard (Rogers, 1959)[3] and when I felt they came to a natural pause with a deep sigh, I begin to reflect on their action of sighing. This was immediately interrupted and was met with further anger and frustration, this time directed towards me. This felt awkward and I started to panic and I felt myself going red in the face. I wondered how to move the session forward, so quickly decided to use metacommunication (McLeod, 2017)[4] to explain that I was reflecting back on what I saw happening in the room with their thoughts and feelings, with the intention that they could start to process and explore (Rogers, 1951)[5] the 'hateful' feelings. However, they interrupted again and this time it felt more of a personal attack. They particularly focused on the money that they believed I was making and my nice lifestyle and this felt very unjust – I am on placement and don't earn any money, and nor do I have the finer things in life. At that point I could feel my own anger rising and I wanted to contradict their assumptions, but I stopped myself. This is because I realised instinctively it felt wrong and it occurred to me that this attack wasn't necessarily about me, and was more likely to be transference (Freud, 1912),[6] which was the first time I had really felt this in a session. So, believing it was appropriate, I gently challenged (Ivey et al., 2014)[7] the client on whom they were really talking about.

This seemed to create a change of tone and atmosphere in the room as the client started to consider 'worth' and what now feels like – on reading the transcript back – an understanding of their values and, more importantly, how they felt towards their parents, who they believed took money from others in exchange for something worthless and, in turn, how this made them feel in their own job.

I then asked about the sighing and the sadness I felt from the client earlier in the session. This brought about a further reflection from them about how their parents didn't make time for sadness. I then moved on – which now feels too quickly – to noticing their anger aimed at me. It then transpired that the client enjoyed being angry as it allowed them express how they felt without consequences (on this occasion without being thrown out), which seemed to heal the rupture (Eubanks et al., 2019).[8]

On evaluating the session via this transcript, I am relieved by the repair in the rupture and that we ended on a positive alliance but equally I am struck by how I didn't address the subject of the client's parents and the impact they were clearly having on the client's life and work. This now feels remiss, especially given the number of times the

---

3. Rogers, C.R. (1959). A theory of therapy, personality, and interpersonal relationships, as developed in the client-centred framework. In S. Koch (Ed.), *Psychology: A study of a science. Study 1, Volume 3: Formulations of the person and the social context*. McGraw-Hill.

4. McLeod, J. (2017). *Pluralistic therapy: Distinctive features*. Routledge.

5. Rogers, C.R. (1951). *Client-centred therapy*. Houghton Mifflin.

6. Freud, S. (1912). The dynamics of transference. In J. Strachey (Ed.), *The Standard edition of the complete psychological works of Sigmund Freud, Volume XII*. Hogarth Press.

7. Ivey, A.E., Bradford Ivey, M. & Zalaquett, C.P. (2014). *Intentional interviewing and counseling: Facilitating client development in a multicultural society*. Cengage Learning.

8. Eubanks, C., Muran, J.C. & Safran, J. (2019). In J. C. Norcross & M.J. Lambert (Eds.), *Psychotherapy relationships that work: Evidence-based therapist contributions* (pp.549–579). Oxford University Press.

client mentioned them and how, in the first session, they brought their childhood for a focus of discussion. This is something I will take to my next supervision session. My intention in future is to notice more and try to stay with the client within the counselling relationship (McLeod, 2003),[9] and to also acknowledge how they found my reflections and affirmations initially frustrating yet ultimately helpful to unearth their emotions.

Another aspect that occurs to me at this stage of reflection is the use of the word 'hateful' by the client, and whether – now that I know about the client's experience of working for their parents' business at a young age – the 'hate' is actually other unnamed feelings: for example, shame (Sanderson, 2015).[10] Again, this is something to consider in the next sessions.

I am looking forward to seeing the client for the next sessions and believe the rupture has created a more dynamic connection for us to work alongside, but am also aware of more possible ruptures ahead, which feels a bit daunting. Something further to share at my next supervision session.

Experiences

We thought it would be interesting to see how another therapist, from a different modality, would have worked with the same client and evaluated this session. Deborah spoke with Sarah Eccleston, Programme Leader for the MSc Counselling and Psychotherapy: Professional Practice at the University of Salford. Sarah has a psychodynamic background.

If I'd been the therapist in this scenario, I'd have picked up on the client's emotions, the anger and the sadness, and, most importantly, the place of the client's parents in relation to those emotions. I'd have said to the client how hard it must have been not to express emotions. I'd have wanted the client to sit with that in the session.

In writing up a case study, I'd have wanted to write more about the client, about what's happening for the client. For a psychodynamic counsellor and psychotherapist, parents are a goldmine. The client's parents didn't let them express emotions. The client has brought that up for a reason. I'd want to explore the background, the history of it.

If this is the modality that you're working in and writing in, I'd suggest you read Jeremy Holmes' book (2001), *The Search for the Secure Base: Attachment theory and psychotherapy*.[11]

Turning a more critical eye on case studies though, while students are asked to write up transcripts, I wonder if they're a waste of time; so much of the nuance of the session is missed in writing, it becomes flat. You can't read the nodding and eye contact. How do you even spell 'Hmm?' If you read a transcript and listen to the audio, and the trainee is saying very little, the work might well fail, but if you were in the room, watching the power of that nodding and eye contact, you might award 100% for the work.

Overall, I worry about the use of case studies because I'm taking your pain and analysing it...

---

9. McLeod, J. (2003). *An introduction to counselling.* Open University Press.
10. Sanderson, C. (2015). *Counselling skills for working with shame.* Jessica Kingsley.
11. Holmes, J. (2001). *The search for the secure base: Attachment theory and psychotherapy.* Routledge.

Doing case studies differently

When I (Deborah) wrote my first case study during my training (2013–2018), I followed the rules, which were much like the steps/structure we've given in this chapter.

I disliked doing the conventional case study. It felt wrong to make pronouncements on another person. But at the time, I could only grasp that it felt wrong to follow the rules, not how I might rewrite them. Rewriting the rules (as far as one person can do that) came later, when I'd been in training long enough to start to do things differently (always working within learning outcomes/assessment criteria).

So I've taken my first published case study,[12] which originated as an MSc assignment, and outlined here some of the ways I worked that challenged what we're usually asked to do in counselling and psychotherapy training – and that we've outlined so far in this chapter. We hope this will provide material for reflection and encourage you to consider (if you wish) how you might rewrite the rules of case studies in ways of your own choosing.

I decided to write a case study reimagined as a play. What this meant, in practice, was that I had to try to teach myself how to write a play, as well as writing a case study! Alan Ayckbourn's *The Crafty Art of Playmaking* came in useful,[13] but also very helpful here was Patricia Leavy's *Method Meets Art: Arts-based research practice*.[14] I'd recommend this book to any readers thinking of arts-based approaches to any writing – it covers a variety.

It's important to say up-front that I more than doubled the work because I wanted to try something different! You need to think if you have the time/energy to do this during your training. I also had to be ready for the idea not working, or not being well received. I think you need to be at a certain stage in your training journey to cope with this.

My first idea, before I read anything new or even wrote anything down, was to begin with a selection of 'cases' entering on stage carrying their diagnoses – a demonstration of how I feel case studies objectify people. Here is how that idea developed into writing:

ACT 1
(*The curtain rises.*)

McLeod (2010),[15] **standing in a spotlight, muses:** 'There has been relatively little methodological innovation within the narrative approach… ' (p. 27).

Zeldin (2015)[16] **enters, observing**: 'Each meeting between two people that is not merely superficial is an opportunity to enlarge [life] beyond the banal, through discovery and invention' (p.395).

---

12. Lee, D.A. (2018). Enter centre stage the case study. *British Journal of Guidance and Counselling, 46*(3), pp.304–314.
13. Ayckbourn, A. (2002). *The crafty art of playmaking*. Faber & Faber.
14. Leavy, P. (2015). *Method meets art: Arts-based research practice*. Guilford Press.
15. McLeod, J. (2010). *Case study research*. Sage.
16. Zeldin, T. (2015). *The hidden pleasures of life*. Quercus.

Bourriaud (1998, p. 133)[17] (introduced with a flourish by Jones, 2006, p.72[18]) **takes both their hands and declares**: 'Relational art… [is] a set of artistic practices which take as their theoretical and practical point of departure the whole of human relations and their social context').

(*'Clinical' bright light blinds the audience; it's freezing cold…*)

Voice off: 'It's the CASES!'

(*The 'cases' enter, signs covering their faces.*)

> 'I'm borderline'
> 'I'm depressed'
> 'I'm anxious'
> 'I'm a healthy control' (the sign doesn't obscure his smile) (Lee, 2018, pp.304–305).[19]

Then (returning to the case study), I explored 'the case' at the centre of my piece (my relating with my client, Kate). I wanted to place therapist and client alongside each other, as equals, collaborating – something I think a 'standard' case study can't easily do, with its focus on an expert making an assessment, doing interventions and evaluating them.

One way of not creating an 'us' and 'them', for me, in this case study, was keeping the client's material (usually their 'problems', history, diagnoses and so forth) 'minimal' (Lee, 2018, p.304).[19] Unusually for a case study, in this approach, whatever you learned about the client, you also learned about me. Kate and I both gave some demographic information, as far as each of us wished at the time. Where either of us shared personal details of our lives, I edited them out of the assignment. What mattered to me was to convey the importance of relationship, the warmth between us. Here we are, talking about a key event (for me) in our relating, what it meant to me at the time, and how it impacted Kate on hearing about it later.

Deborah: Something that stood out for you [in our relationship] later? I know what mine is [laughing].

Kate: You tell me what yours was [laughs].

Deborah: Okay. There's a bit of self-disclosure in it, I hope that's going to be okay, and we can talk about it afterwards. I nearly didn't train for psychotherapy in case people brought a certain thing and there was a day when you did bring that thing and the relational depth… took over and I facilitated you saying more about the thing I probably didn't want to hear about and I think you cured me.

Kate: (pause) Oh gosh. [Deborah: Yes.] I don't know what to say. [Deborah: Mmm.] Oh, I might cry. I feel quite emotional hearing that'. (Lee, 2018, p.309).[19]

---

17. Bourriaud, N. (1998). *Relational aesthetics*. Les Presses du Réel.

18. Jones, K. (2006). A biographic researcher in pursuit of an aesthetic: the use of arts-based representations in 'performative' dissemination of life stories. *Qualitative Sociology Review, 11*(1), 66-85.

19. Lee, D.A. (2018). Enter centre stage the case study. *British Journal of Guidance and Counselling, 46*(3), pp.304–314.

Having published the work, I've had people contact me out of the blue to say how much they've enjoyed reading it. It's also been used as a set text for students on counselling and psychotherapy training courses. And I've had a couple of people tell me outright that they dislike it intensely, which was both unpleasant and upsetting. If you do things differently, I suppose you have to ready yourself for that.

> **TAKEAWAY MESSAGES**
>
> Be rigorous in your approach to your essays. Read widely, make lots of notes, start writing the introduction early on (and keep editing it), write as much as you need (and then edit down to the word count), keep the question in mind at all times, develop a robust argument, be critical rather than descriptive.
>
> Choose your client work carefully for your case studies. Always ask the client's permission before writing about your work with them. Keep the issue of consent live as you work on your assignment. Whether you proceed in the more expected way we've outlined, or a more unusual way of your own choice, remember that you're writing about someone's life: honour that at all times.

The next chapter…

The next chapter looks at the continuing professional development (CPD) you might do after you qualify as a counsellor and psychotherapist.

7

Continuing professional development

What we hope we've done, as we've progressed through this book, is to share with you how studying counselling and psychotherapy and completing course assignments is serious and challenging work, and also work that is enriching and exciting.

Celebrate passing your course when the time comes. You will certainly have earned your success, and it will have been life changing.

Know, too, that this isn't the end of the journey. 'Becoming' and 'being' a psychotherapist and counsellor is a lifelong process. Continuing professional development (CPD) will be part of that journey.

CPD covers a wide range of activities. BACP's guidance (see further below) explains that it can involve: 'conferences – attending or giving presentations; e-learning CPD modules; formal education, lectures, seminars, courses; in-service training; mentoring; peer support groups; organising specialist groups; reading books, journals, or internet articles; supervising research; TV and radio programmes; workshops; work shadowing; writing articles or papers'. Indeed, BACP devotes a whole 'hub' on its website to CPD activities for its members:

www.bacp.co.uk/cpd/cpd-hub

You do not have to do CPD activities alongside your initial training, but of course you can if you want to.

Once you are qualified, however, and if you are registered with a professional body, CPD is a formal requirement that you have to record (or 'log') annually and evidence when you renew your registration. You may also be spot-checked on it, too. At the time of writing (2021), the requirements for CPD from BACP, UKCP and NCS are as follows:

BACP – at least 30 hours each year. See: **www.bacp.co.uk/membership/registered-membership/guide-to-cpd**

UKCP – a minimum of 20 hours a year and 250 hours in total across five years. See: **www.psychotherapy.org.uk/ukcp-members/standards-guidance-and-policies/continuing-professional-development-cpd**

NCS – 30+ hours. See: **https://nationalcounsellingsociety.org/blog/posts/continuing-professional-development-cpd**

We take the view that having a sense of what you might (and might not) want to learn after your initial training is part of your personal, unfolding journey – part of growing the self-awareness and self-development that are vital for practitioners in our field. You don't have to choose what you do for CPD on your own; you can discuss and plan it with your clinical supervisor. It's an exciting time once you qualify: you have the freedom to choose your own directions and pursue studies in the directions and ways that suit you.

However, knowing how much is enough to take on and when to pause and rest, or even stop, is part of your self-care as a psychotherapist/counsellor, which is also an ethical duty. You cannot be of service to others if you are over-extended and haven't replenished your own reserves.

In this final chapter, then, we're going to look at some examples of what you might choose to do for CPD, by hearing from some qualified counsellors and psychotherapists and from a CPD organisation for therapists. We've tried to offer a range of quite substantial CPD courses that significantly add to your skills-set, and shorter, more bite-sized suggestions.

What we discuss is necessarily selective, as there are so many options to choose from – anything from a one-hour online talk to years of further study. So see this chapter as just a taster, some information, some examples of routes some people have taken that might spark interests and ideas for you.

You should note that we're not personally endorsing any CPD covered here.

It's worth stating at the outset that CPD can be fabulous, but you will also find less than adequate CPD. Sometimes qualified counsellors and psychotherapists who are very experienced in what they do but are perhaps less so in teaching and training offer courses to supplement their income. The quality of the CPD you invest in matters. We advise checking out with other people – peers, tutors, therapist, clinical supervisor/s – about which organisations, events and people they'd recommend, and checking out published work that the course leader has done before signing up for anything. You also don't have to stay at an event or complete a short course if it feels wrong to you.

Make sure to keep a record of all the CPD that you attend, and keep any certificates awarded in a safe place, so that you can show that you have fulfilled the CPD requirements required of you. Some people keep an actual logbook, or scrapbook even, where they paste in certificates and notes from events.

> ### ACTIVITY
>
> **An invitation to consider what CPD might appeal to you**
>
> Before you read the rest of the chapter (in which we offer some examples of CPD), spend some time reflecting on what you think might appeal to you personally to study for CPD as you progress your career in counselling and psychotherapy.
>
> The following questions might be helpful:
>
> - Have you heard about an approach to therapy that sounds interesting, met a practitioner of it, or seen a client who says it's helped them?
> - Has one of your peers, tutors, therapist, or your clinical supervisor talked about working or volunteering in a specialist counselling service ('addictions', homelessness, women, sexual violence survivors) that you think you might find interesting?
> - Have you read books by an author whose work you'd like to understand more deeply – because you connect with, or struggle with, what they're saying?
> - Are there areas that you'd personally benefit from studying – an experience you've had or an aspect of your own identity that you'd like to understand more; something you feel you don't yet 'get'?
> - Is there an area that interests you and wasn't covered, or wasn't covered in enough depth, in your initial training?
>
> Write some notes or make mind-maps, draw or record your thoughts.
>
> We suggest keeping your responses to these questions, as you are likely to want to add more later.

The cost and time commitment of CPD

One problem people have – in training, and after qualification (often for a long time) – is that they're spending or have already spent so much money on the training course that they don't have any or much money left for anything else. They're paying off debts from their studies. CPD costs are yet another financial outgoing. You may also be starting off in private practice, which takes significant time, effort and money, and it takes time to build up a caseload that will cover your living expenses.

We wanted to start with the reassurance that there are forms of CPD that won't break the bank. The CPD log below is that of a qualified counsellor over a six-month period. The CPD amounts to 40 hours, which is more than the 30 hours required by BACP and NCS. It may be reassuring to see it. Networking meetings and peer supervision groups (free) meet the criteria for CPD. So does self-directed reading, and you can use library books rather buying all the books you read.

January
CPD event participation – 'Working with neurodiversity' – 7 hours

February
Networking – Meeting with fellow practitioners interested in politics of therapy – 2 hours

March
Online learning package – 'Working with clients online' – 3 hours
Day conference on microaggressions – 7 hours

April – May
Creative work informing my practice – Memoir writing short course – 6 x 2 hours = 12 hours

June
Self-directed reading – key theme: intersectionality – 7 hours
Monthly peer supervision group – 2 hours

Total hours January–June: 40 hours

Experiences

Organisations offering CPD opportunities come in all shapes and sizes. Onlinevents, as its name implies, is an organisation that has long specialised in accessible, affordable online CPD for counsellors and psychotherapists. It was set up by John Wilson, a qualified counsellor, with his sister, Sandra Wilson. Deborah interviewed John. Here's what they discussed.

We began by exploring some of John's own early CPD journey. Just after he graduated from Strathclyde University as a qualified psychotherapist, John heard Kate Anthony [a pioneer in the field] talk about online therapy, and decided to take some CPD with her. Then he started working with clients online as well as in person. Not long after that, he found himself co-opted onto the organising committee for the Association for Counselling and Therapy Online (ACTO) conference. John remembers saying: 'The conference is about being online, working online, so it would be great if it was streamed online!' Live-streaming was complex and expensive then (2008), but John bought a new laptop, his dad had a camera, and John persuaded his sister, Sandra, to accompany them to the conference, which they successfully live-streamed.

Going to conferences can be very expensive – the cost of travel on top of the fees, and sometimes accommodation. John and Sandra thought: 'There's definitely a business here… maybe we could make events less expensive for colleagues who don't have much money by adding another room – an online room – to a face-to-face event'. Onlinevents was born.

We are telling you about John and Sandra's business journey here because you, like John, through taking CPD, may find something that speaks to your passion, that connects psychotherapy/counselling with something else. John still sees clients and co-runs Temenos (a psychotherapy training organisation in Sheffield).

Pre-pandemic, 'a good size workshop for us

would be eight people in the online room,' John said. People didn't grasp then that they could have experiential training online. Once Covid-19 arrived and everyone went into lockdown, the numbers of attendees rocketed – some workshops now attracted up to 500 people, from all around the world – people delightedly saying: 'Oh, I'm not on my own, I'm in a massive community here!'

While some events are particularly suited to in-person working, we discussed the advantages of people continuing to participate in online CPD post-pandemic.

I asked John to consider what he'd suggest to a psychotherapist and counsellor who contacted him saying: 'I've recently qualified. I've done some work in a charity working with refugees, but I'd like to know more. And I'm thinking of applying for a job in a hospice. I'd like to have some initial training that could help. I'm also thinking: what else is there that could take me in an unexpected direction? I don't have much money to spend.'

John responded: 'We're doing some really exciting work with a colleague who's also called John Wilson, who is a writer/researcher in the world of bereavement and grief. John has put together a six-piece course for us, two hours each time, and each session costs £1 minimum (pay what you can – something we brought in when the pandemic hit). We're offering that as an introductory course to working with grief and bereavement. Maggi McAllister-MacGregor has written a 10-piece workshop on polyvagal theory, two-and-a-half hours each time, each session £1 minimum (again, pay what you can). That's very useful for thinking about trauma. You could do those two courses – 16 sessions, 37 hours of CPD – for £16… I'd also suggest encounter groups. We have a series of groups called Civil Discourse, where we're working with Peggy Natiello and Carol Wolter-Gustafson – both colleagues who worked with Carl Rogers towards the end of his career, when he was very interested in how groups can be helpful in the community and politically. When we're experiencing very polarised ways of looking at the world, can we come together in an encounter group and get to know each other a little better? Maybe we won't change our mind about things – but we might be more open to the other.'

Onlinevents uses software that can transcribe what's happening in a session almost in the moment. Translation into different languages is currently being explored.

John points out that Onlinevents has 'worked with lots of colleagues who are famous. We had Irvin Yalom come and do an hour and a half with us, which was very exciting. And we've also worked with lots of colleagues who don't have that profile. They've said: "John, I've been working away for a long time, and I think there's something that I'd like to say to the community"'.

John's message to psychotherapists and counsellors in training and newly qualified therapists is that we all bring something to the community, so 'come and have a conversation with us!' We thought this point really important to mention in this chapter. So often psychotherapists and counsellors-in-training, and newly qualified or more experienced practitioners who don't have a high professional profile feel that they are too inexperienced or unknown to offer CPD. We say to you that (with some exceptions!) the psychotherapy and counselling world is often receptive to new people and new ideas – if you have something to say, speak.

Websites

Onlinevents – www.onlinevents.co.uk

Association for Counselling and Therapy Online (ACTO) – **acto-org.uk**

Kate Anthony Online Training – **www.kateanthony.net**

What some qualified counsellors and psychotherapists did next…

Now we're going to meet Hayley Barker-Smith and Karen Pollock, two qualified counsellors and psychotherapists, and hear what they did after they qualified. In both instances they're talking primarily about substantial pieces of CPD, undertaken to augment their skills and expand their work with clients. Keep in mind that CPD doesn't have to be so substantial or, indeed, immediately related to therapy – it can be visits to the theatre, watching films, reading fiction and more… as long as you can make a case for its relevance to your work.

Experiences

Hayley Barker-Smith completed her Level 5 Diploma in Person-Centred Counselling. She says CPD has been a lifeline in building her awareness and confidence.

After qualifying in 2016 with a Level 5 diploma in person-centred counselling for children and adolescents, I applied for a salaried counselling vacancy at a local secondary school. They'd said they wanted someone with a degree, but I was invited for interview and got the job. It's always worth trying for jobs that interest you! I have now been employed at the school for four years, working with both mainstream children and children with special educational needs and disabilities (SEND).

At first, I felt a sense of incompetence as I had little experience of working with SEND children: my training was quite general and didn't include working specifically within specialised areas such as this. I was also not prepared for the level of safeguarding concerns and ethical dilemmas I was suddenly faced with, seeing five students per day. It was a lonely time; I'd been used to being a part of a counselling team when I was on placements; now, I was working alone, reporting to the school SENCO (special educational needs co-ordinator), and getting to know a new external supervisor.

Over the past four years, CPD, alongside clinical supervision, has been a lifeline in building my awareness and confidence to work with some very difficult client presentations, situations and areas unfamiliar to me: self-harm, suicidal ideation, eating disorders, sexual abuse, online safety and child exploitation, trauma, working with autism and neurodiversity, and bereavement. I've also completed CPD in equality and diversity, digital media and, most recently, working online during the pandemic.

What most beautifully complemented my work was a certificate course in person-centred art therapy, with the Association for Person Centred Creative Arts – an experiential training course that took place over seven weekends. Over the months, creating my own story in art form and working with peers to facilitate each others' process allowed me to get to know myself deeply and to tap into my own hidden creativity. My confidence grew and grew, both in person and in practice: as I witnessed the power of the unspoken words, I knew that all I had to do was trust the process.

As a trainee, I'd had no interest in research or doing any higher qualifications whatsoever. I did not feel capable of doing such a high level of study and I thought research was just boring. In all the textbooks I read, I would deliberately miss any chapters relating to it. But suddenly, the art therapy CPD ignited a spark in me to go for a degree in counselling and psychotherapy. I went back to university in 2019, while still working at the school, and pushed myself through probably the most stressful year of my life, studying while working full-time.

I took the opportunity very seriously, using every ounce of creativity and trust in myself that I could find. I decided to write my dissertation about my lived experience of PMDD (pre-menstrual dysphoric disorder) to allow me to fully understand it and make sense of something that had held me back for so long. I used a methodology called 'autoethnography', which is a form of self-reflection and connecting the author's story to wider cultural and social meanings.

At the start of my research process, I discovered the work of Red School and the most amazing gift that they teach: menstrual cycle awareness (MCA), a pathway to the cyclical wisdom of our inner seasons. Working with the founders of Red School – Alexandra Pope and Sjanie Hugo Wurlitzer – I was awoken to the feminine power and creativity within me and magically weaved this healing experience into my dissertation. The process of writing my autoethnography opened me up to revisiting past trauma, feeling lost in the pain at times and overwhelmed with grief. I had an excellent therapist who creatively worked with my parts throughout the process, and I chose to work with a beautiful, encouraging author/reflexive researcher, who guided me along academically. Much to my shock, I was asked to have my work considered for publication in an international psychotherapy journal. At first, I declined: I was scared of being seen. I then decided to go for it, and it was published (Barker-Smith, 2020).[1] That then led to being asked to write for this book.

In March 2020, I joined a team of women across the world, training to become a menstruality mentor with Red School. This was another six months of deeply reflective work. As a Red School mentor, I am a beacon, sharing this work with other girls and women in counselling and in group work. I would love to run group menstruality therapy for young girls in schools, which I am really excited about!

One of my favourite sayings is 'Go within or go without'. Go within yourself to find your passion – what is yearning to be healed or expressed within you? Dare to dig deep and be brave.

Websites

Association for Person Centred Creative Arts: **www.apcca.org.uk**

Red School: **www.redschool.net**

---

1. Barker-Smith, H. (2020). Navigating the menstrual landscapes: from the darkness to the light. *Psychotherapy and Politics International*, *18*, 2.

Experiences

Karen Pollock took Pink Therapy's postgraduate diploma in gender, sexuality and relationship diverse (GSRD) counselling after their postgraduate diploma in therapeutic counselling. In their view, 'expertise equals training plus lived experience'.

Things you can't help noticing as a counselling postgraduate diploma student…

- the student who flinches whenever you mention LGBTQAAI identities
- the student who declares 'sex shouldn't be mentioned in the counselling room' when you bring up kink
- the student who offers to compassionately 'pray away the gay'
- the student who assumes your partner is male.

… the students who laugh and bond and say how much they are getting from the process group, how authentic and real they feel – as you adjust the mask and wonder what that must be like, to be seen, to be you, in this room.

And even before you qualify as a therapist, people are contacting you – queer people, trans people, kinksters, asexuals, bisexuals, a whole melting pot of LGBTQAAI people. They have already met the forerunners of those students as qualified therapists in counselling rooms, in different cities, countries, modalities, and now would rather take a chance on a student counsellor than another harmful therapeutic experience.

I feel I need to put in a disclaimer. My PG-Dip in Therapeutic Counselling was in all other ways amazing. It had a unit on abuse (which is sadly missing from most courses). It had tutors who challenged the attitudes in the room. But I graduated still feeling like only part of me had ever been present. The actual GSRD content had been limited to a couple of mornings, some of which I delivered.

Here I was, in the real world, being expected to be better than my peers, largely because I was vocal on twitter about LGBTQAAI rights, polyamory and kink. I read what I could, attended what I could, but I knew something was missing.

I have always believed expertise equals training plus lived experience, and neither is more or less important than the other. All too often the history of working with GSRD folk has been a history of GSRD therapists drawing on their own experiences. That experience is often vital, but it can lead to us sitting in our frame of reference, rather than that of our clients. It is also the case that we tend to assume that one aspect of GSRD identity gives you knowledge about the whole rainbow spectrum. It's like the old joke about telling an Australian you are from England, and them saying, 'Oh my cousin Pete visited England, do you know him?'

People were coming to me because of my lived experience, and the knowledge I had acquired around trans issues, but I felt they deserved an expertise I did not feel I had. I also still wondered what it must be like to be seen by fellow counselling students – to not wear that mask. These twin goals led me to Pink Therapy.

I had already attended a couple of their conferences, which felt like a coming home. Here was a space where masks were not needed, where conference badges had spaces for pronouns, and assumptions were left at the door. It's not perfect, no space is, but the clinical associates seemed aware of their imperfections in a way that was new to my experience of training.

So, I enrolled on Pink Therapy's postgraduate diploma in gender, sexuality and relationship diverse counselling in the summer of 2015. It was a two-year course, just as my original postgraduate diploma was, with units on fundamentals such as LGBTQ mental health (the first, and quite intimidating unit after the residential week), gender diversity, bisexuality, ethical non-monogamy, working with distress about gender and sexuality, and kink.

Some units might seem more niche – spirituality, LGBTQ ageing, parenting outside of heteronormativity – but they brought a depth of knowledge and learning.

There were also more experiential units, which I did not know I needed, but which I know now have made me a better counsellor. Working with shame was transformative, and only possible in a space where it felt safe to be queer. The case discussion groups, with people from around the world, not only deepened my understanding of clinical issues but are probably the best way of tackling imposter syndrome I could think of!

The course structure was demanding – monthly assignments, including a dissertation, lectures, and the case discussion groups. It's not always easy to combine building a private practice, eight to 10 hours of study a week, and personal responsibilities. Writing my dissertation, on the application of the minority stress model to sex workers, challenged me in a way that I hadn't experienced since I was an undergraduate at the London School of Economics, but each week I learned and I grew – both as a person and a therapist.

The unit on intersectionality led to me eventually starting to describe myself as anti-oppressive rather than affirmative. Writing my own intersections of privilege and oppression, from working class to university educated, queer, white, non-binary, a complex interplay of power, privilege and marginalisation, made me certain these dynamics have to be acknowledged in the room, be it the counselling or training room.

That insight is perhaps at the heart of why I believe that if you have a GSRD identity, intend to work with GSRD clients, or both, then being in a training space where you are not 'other', are not either marginalised or masking, is vital. Even the best, most affirmative, inclusive and anti-discriminatory mainstream course will still carry the societal norms of who has power and who does not, and replicate them. (Of course, this is also the case with other marginalised and othered identities such as 'race' and ethnicity.)

My original training was person-centred, and I often describe myself as having a person-centred heart. At the core of that is authenticity and congruence. By studying a queer course, led by queer tutors, surrounded by queer students, studying queer content, I was finally able to develop my authentic queer therapeutic self.

Website

Pink Therapy: **https://pinktherapy.org**

Experiences

We've talked about clinical supervision of your work with clients in this book. One CPD open to you post-qualification is learning to become a clinical supervisor yourself. Deborah is currently training (with TA East London Institute) to become a clinical supervisor, as she describes here.

Most clinical supervision courses I researched were asking for between one and three years post-qualification experience as a psychotherapist and counsellor. You'll need not only to check into course requirements like that but – more importantly – you'll also need to check in with yourself when feels like the right time for you to undertake clinical supervisor training – including never. I say that because becoming a clinical supervisor isn't the 'next step', better than 'just' being a therapist – rather, it's another role in the profession, one that may or may not appeal to you.

I began training as a clinical supervisor about a year after starting out in private practice post-qualification (with 500+ client hours completed, and with UKCP registration as a psychotherapist). It felt like the right time for me: I was already running group supervision for psychotherapists-in-training as part of my job as a university lecturer, and was finding it an energising intellectual/practical experience (particularly listening to and offering feedback/feedforward on trainees' audio recordings of client work) – and I was noticing that a model of how I wanted to supervise was developing: a deeply person-centred model that asks how much client material really needs to be in the room for effective supervision of psychotherapists-in-training (there were resonances emerging, then, of how I had written case studies while in psychotherapy training myself). It felt important to take the time to explore clinical supervision literature, and speak/debate with others, to see how that impacted my emerging model.

The course I chose operates through an intersectional lens, which also appealed to me as a socio-political psychotherapist, with my particular interests in lived experiences, such as #MeToo. I wanted to explore how far intersectionality could be in the room, while still honouring everyone's right to only say what they wish about their personal identities. Once underway with the course, I began offering individual clinical supervision to four BSc students at my university. In my first supervision with my first student, I unexpectedly found myself saying something that my first, absolutely lovely, clinical supervisor had said to me once, long ago. I hadn't realised I had remembered it! It felt moving to be passing on some of her wisdom to a new generation of psychotherapists/counsellors.

As I progress in the work and the course, I'm holding that learning to become a clinical supervisor is, for sure, about developing a model, being alongside supervisees in their self-development to meet with the other – and it's a huge responsibility, to supervisees and their clients. It's also about nurturing the next generation of newly-qualified and less experienced practitioners as they mature in their confidence and practice – looking to the continuing development of the profession.

TAKEAWAY MESSAGES

- CPD can be very exciting – explore it, see what calls to you!
- Take care when choosing CPD – look into the quality of what's being offered and the qualifications of the trainer.
- Professional bodies have expectations of how much CPD people registered with them must do each year. Make sure you know what they are, and fulfil the requirements if you are a member. Make sure you record and can evidence what you've done and what you have learned from it.
- Beyond meeting professional body requirements, do what you have the time, energy and inclination to do. And be realistic. Take care. Listen to your body. You can always do an interesting course next year if this year is too busy.
- Your CPD can be something long and very demanding, like topping-up to a BA/BSc degree or taking a two-year part-time course in a new area of specialism. Or it might be something quite short – reading books and reflecting on them, writing for and reading professional journals and magazines, or watching a TV film or documentary and reflecting on it.

And, as this is the final chapter of this book, we want to give a special…

FINAL TAKEAWAY MESSAGE

We hope you find your journey into and through counselling and psychotherapy training the first step into lifelong travels, exploration and adventure.

Good luck!
Deborah and Pete, December 2021

Appendix: References for sample essay introduction

Adler, H.M. (2002). The sociophysiology of caring in a doctor patient relationship. *Journal of General Internal Medicine, 17*(11), 883–890.

Ahn, L.H., Yee, S.E., Dixon, K.M., Kase, C.A., Sharma, R. & Hill, C.E. (2021). Feeling offended by clients: The experiences of doctoral student therapists. *Journal of Counseling Psychology, 68*(2), 125–138.

Barrett-Lennard, G.T. (1997). *Psychological Monographs, 76*(43), 562.

Bohart, A.C. (2021). *The Art of Bohart: Person-centred therapy and the enhancement of human possibility*. PCCS Books.

Bohart, A.C. & Tallman, K. (1999). *How clients make therapy work: The process of active self-healing*. American Psychological Association.

Bozarth, J. (1984). Emergent modes of empathy. In Levent, R. & Shlien, J. *Client centred therapy and the person-centred approach: New directions in theory, research and practice* (pp.59–77). Praeger Publishers.

Brodley, B.T. (1994). Some observations of Carl Rogers' behaviour in therapy interviews. *The Person-Centred Journal, 1*(2), 37–47.

Cissna, K.N. & Anderson, R. (1994). The 1957 Buber-Carl Rogers dialogue, as dialogue. *Journal of Humanistic Psychology, 34*(1), 11–45.

Clark, A.J. (2010). Empathy: An integral model in the counselling process. *Journal of Counselling & Development, 88*, 348–356.

Cornelius-White, J.H.D. & Ciesielski, M. (2016). in Lago, C. and Charura, D. (2016) The Person-Centred Counselling and Psychotherapy Handbook: Origins, Developments and Current Applications. Maidenhead: Open University Press.

Duncan, B.L., Miller, S.D. & Sparks, J.A. (2004). *The heroic client: A revolutionary way to improve effectiveness through client-directed, outcome-informed therapy* (2nd ed.). Wiley.

Ellingham, I. (2007). Non-directivity and relational depth: Two forms of mysticism? *Person-Centred Quarterly*, May, 1–3.

Elliott, R., Bohart, A. C., Watson, J. C. & Murphy, D. (2018). Therapist empathy and client outcome: An updated meta-analysis. *Psychotherapy, 55*(4), 399–410.

Finsrud, I., Nissen-Lie, H.A., Vrabel, K., Høstmælingen, A., Walpold, B.E. & Ulvenes, P.G. (2021). It's the therapist. And the treatment: The structure of common therapeutic relationship factors. *Psychotherapy Research*. DOI: 10.1080/10503307.2021/1916640.

Ioannidou F. & Konstantikaki, V. (2008) Empathy and emotional intelligence: What is it really about? *International Journal of Caring Sciences, 1*(3), 118–123.

Jordan, J.V. (1997). Relational development through mutual empathy. In A. C. Bohart & L.S. Greenberg (Eds.), *Empathy reconsidered: New directions in psychotherapy* (pp.343–351). American Psychological Association.

Joseph, S. (2016). *Authentic: How to be yourself and why it matters*. Piatkus.

Kirchenbaum, H. (2007). *The life and work of Carl Rogers*. PCCS Books.

Kivlighan, D.M., Kline, K., Gels, C.J. & Hill, C.E. (2017). Congruence and discrepancy between working alliance and real relationship: Variance decomposition and response surface analyses. *Journal of Counselling Psychology, 64*(4), 394–409.

Kolden, G.G., Klein, M., Wang, C. & Austin, S. (2011). Congruence/genuineness. *Psychotherapy, 48*, 65–71.

Lago, C. & Charura, D. (Eds.). (2016). *The person-centred counselling and psychotherapy handbook: Origins, developments and current applications*. Open University Press.

Maslow, A.H. (1943). Theory of human motivations. *Psychological Review, 50*(4), 370–396.

McNally, P.J., Charlton, R., Ratnapalan, M. & Damdha-Miller, H. (2019). Empathy, transference and compassion. [Advance online publ.]. *Journal of the Royal Society of Medicine*. DOI: 10.1177/0141076819875112.

Mearns, D & Cooper, M. (2017). *Working at relational depth in counselling and psychotherapy* (2nd ed.). Sage.

Mearns, D. & Thorne, B. (2000) *Person-centred therapy today*. Sage.

Mearns, D. & Thorne, B. (2007) *Person-centred counselling in action* (3rd ed.). Sage.

Merry, T. (2012). Classical client-centred therapy. In P. Sanders (Ed.), *The tribes of the person-centred nation: An introduction to the schools of therapy related to the person-centred approach* (2nd ed.) (pp.21–46). PCCS Books.

Merry, T. (2020). *Learning and being in person-centred counselling* (3rd ed.). S. Haugh (Ed.). PCCS Books.

Murphy, D., Cramer, D. & Joseph, S. (2012). Mutuality in person-centred therapy: A new agenda for research and practice. *Person-Centred & Experiential Psychotherapies, 11*(2), 109–123.

Myers, S. (1999). Empathy: Is that what I hear you saying? *The Person-Centred Journal, 6*(2), 141–152.

Norcross, J.C. & Lambert, M.J. (2018). Psychotherapy relationships that work III. *Psychotherapy, 55*(4), 303–315. https://doi. org/10.1037/pst0000193

Patterson, C.H. (1990). On being client-centred. *Person Centred Review, 5*(4), 425–432.

Purton, C. (2012). Focusing-oriented therapy. In P. Sanders (Ed.), *The tribes of the person-centred nation: An introduction to the schools of therapy related to the person-centred approach* (2nd ed.) (pp.47–70). PCCS Books.

Raskin, N.J. (1947/2005). The nondirective attitude. *The Person-Centred Journal, 12*(1/2), 5–22.

Reik, T. (1948). *Listening with the third ear: The inner experience of a psychoanalyst.* Farrar, Straus, & Giroux.

Rogers, C.R. (1951). *Client-centered therapy: Its current practice, implications and theory.* Constable.

Rogers, C.R. (1957). The necessary and sufficient conditions of therapeutic personality change. *Journal of Consulting and Clinical Psychology, 21*, 95–103.

Rogers, C.R. (1959). A theory of therapy, personality and interpersonal relationships as developed in the client-centered framework. In S. Koch (Ed.), *Psychology: A study of a science. Vol. 3: Formulations of the person and the social context* (pp.184–256). McGraw Hill.

Rogers, C.R. (1961). *On becoming a person: A therapist's view of psychotherapy.* Constable.

Rogers, C.R. (1975). Empathic: An unappreciated way of being. *The Counseling Psychologist, 5*(2), 2–10.

Rogers, C.R. (1980). *A way of being.* Houghton Mifflin.

Stepien K. & Baernstein, A. (2006). Educating for empathy. *Journal of General Internal Medicine, 21*, 524–530.

Sutandi, N. (2020). Understanding. Congruence in person-centred counselling practice: A trainee counsellor's perspective. *Journal of Professionals in Guidance and Counselling, 1*(2), 47–55.

Thorne, B. (2002). *The mystical power of person-centred therapy.* Whurr.

Tolan, J. & Cameron, R. (2016). *Skills in person-centred counselling and psychotherapy.* Sage.

Truax, C. B. & Carkhuff, R.R. (1967). *Towards effective counselling and psychotherapy: Training and practice.* Aldine-Atherton.

Warner, M.S. (1991) Fragile process. In L. Fusek (Ed.), *New directions in client-centered therapy: Practice with difficult client populations* (pp.41–58). Chicago Counseling and Psychotherapy Center.

Watson, J.C. & Prosser, M. (2002) Development of an observer rated measure of therapist empathy. In J.C. Watson, R. Goldman & M. Warner (Eds.), *Client-centred and experiential psychotherapy in the 21st century: Advances in theory, research and practice* (pp.303–314).PCCS Books.

Watson, J.C., Schein, J. & McMulleb, E. (2010). An examination of clients' in-session changes and their relationship to the working alliance and outcome. *Psychotherapy Research, 20*(2), 224–233.

Wiseman, T. (1996). A concept analysis of empathy. *Journal of Advanced Nursing, 23*, 1162–1167.

Name index

#MeToo 66, 69, 70, 74, 184
#TherapistsConnect 21, 60, 62, 107
#TraineeTalk 21, 60, 62

A
Abertay University 168
Adams, M. 69
Adler, H.M. 159
Ahmed, S. 101
Ahn, L.H. 159
Allen, R. 15
Alliance for Counselling & Psychotherapy 73–74
American Psychological Association (APA) 128
Anderson, R. 159
Anonymous 94–95
Anthony, K. 178, 180
Anxiety UK 107
Association for Counselling and Therapy Online (ACTO) 178
Association for Person-Centred Creative Arts 180
Association of Christian Counsellors (ACC) 72
Association of Neurodiverse Therapists (ANDT) 2, 66, 71, 95
Asylum 60
Ayckbourn, A. 172

B
Baernstein, A. 159
Bager-Charleson, S. 15
Bagnall-Oakeley, R. 98–100
Balgobin, S. 67
Balint, M. 33
Barker, M.-J. 16, 68

Barker-Smith, H. 142, 180–181
Barnett, H. 56
Barrett-Lennard, G.T. 159
Barrott, J. 138
Bates, Y. 75
Bell, J. 141
Bilge, S. 66
Binstead, C. 60, 73, 148
Black, African and Asian Therapy Network (BAATN) 66, 67, 98
Black Lives Matter 74
Black Therapy Matters, 68
Blunden, N. 23–25
Blundell, P. 21–22, 40, 159
Bochner, A. 126–127
Bohart, A.C. 159
Bond, T. 64
Bourriaud, N. 173
Bowlby, J. 32, 33
Bozarth, J. 159
Branch, R. 29
British Association for Counselling and Psychotherapy (BACP) 16, 19–20, 40, 55, 60, 64, 70–71, 72, 73, 79, 94, 98, 118, 139, 141, 144, 168, 175–176, 177
British Psychoanalytic Council (BPC) 72
Brodley, B.T. 159
Brown, B. 126
Burgess, R. 68

C
Callie 71
Cameron, R. 158
Care Leavers' Association, The 107
Carkhuff, R.R. 159

Casement, P. 100
Castledine, E. 56
Charura, D. 36, 67, 158
Cissna, K.N. 159
Clark, A.J. 159
Connelly, A.E. 33–35, 53
Cooke, M.J. 58
Cooper, M. 26, 141, 159
Cornelius-White, J.H.D. 158
Counsellors Together UK (CTUK) 66, 70–71
Cousins, S. 67
Cox, P. 98–100
Crenshaw, K. 66

D
Dancyger, L. 127
Davies, D. 68
Dexter, G.L. 93
Dougan, L. 71
Dryden, W. 29
Duncan, B.L. 159
Dyscalculia Association, The 107
Dyslexia Action 107
Dyspraxia Foundation 107

E
Easton, D. 68
Eccleston, S. 171,
Educational Guidance Service 104
Ellingham, I. 159
Elliott, R. 159
Ellis, C. 126–127
Ellis, E. 67
Enescu, L. 56
Ernaux, A. 127
Eubanks, C. 170

Eurasion Economic Union (EEU) 42
European Union (EU) 42
Everyone's Invited 70

F
Fairbairn, R. 33
Faris, A. 25
Finsrud, I. 158, 159
Fisher, M. 17, 68
Floyd, G. 74
Free Psychotherapy Network, The 41
Freud, S. 32, 112, 170

G
Gendlin, G. 130
Gomez, L. 33
Gornick, V. 127
Guntrip, H. 33

H
Hardy, J. 68
Haugh, S. 36
Heron, J. 93
Hill Collins, P. 66
Holmes, J. 171
Horrocks, M. 23, 26–29
House, R. 75
Howard, S. 32
Howard-Jones, V. 137–138, 149
Human Givens Institute 72

I
Iantaffi, A. 16, 68
Ieva, K.P. 93
Ioannidou, F. 159
Irfan, D. 56
Irving, J.A. 94
Ivey, A.E. 170

J
Jackman, P. 90
Jackson, C. 72, 161–162
Jackson-McCamley, H. 74–75
Jacobs, M. 78
Johns, H. 93, 94
Jones, K. 173
Jordan, J.V. 159
Joseph, S. 159

K
Kaplin, S. 98–100
Kate Anthony Training 180
Kearney, A. 71
Kennerley, H. 30
Khan, M. 30–32
Kirk, J. 30
Kirschenbaum, H. 159
Kivlingham, D.M. 159
Klein, M. 32, 33
Kolb, D.A. 88
Kolden, G.G. 159
Konstantikaki, V. 159

L
Lago, C. 36, 67, 158
Lambert, M.J. 158
Lapworth, P. 26
Leavy, P. 172
Lee, D.A. 7, 18, 23, 40, 54, 57, 69, 72, 98, 128, 129, 136, 137, 142, 148, 151, 159, 171, 172–173, 178, 184
Lees, K. 12–15, 23
Lehmann, J. 92
Leiper, R. 33
Levy, D. 127
Liverpool John Moores University 21, 158
London School of Economics 183
Lowenthal, D. 30
Lupton, E. 116, 142–143

M
Maltby, M. 33
Maslow, A.H. 158
May, D. 42
McAllister-MacGregor, M. 179
McGill, O. 71
McLeod, J. 26, 170, 172
McNally, P.J. 159
Mearns, D. 159
Merry, T. 36, 158
Metanoia Institute 21, 23, 74
Mezirow, J. 92
Mind 107
Miserandino, C. 42
Moffat, K. 168–170
Moller, N.P. 93
Mowbray, R. 74

Murphy, D. 56, 73, 159
Muslim Counsellor and Psychotherapist Network 30
Myers, S. 159

N
Natiello, P. 179
National Autistic Society 107
National Counselling Society (NCS) 16, 20, 55, 64, 72, 98, 139, 175–176, 177
National Health Service (NHS) 27, 28
National Union of Students (NUS) 100
Neal, C. 68
Nelson, V. 107
Norcross, J.C. 158, 159
Nottingham Trent University 42, 116, 142

O
Off the Record 7
Office for Students 100
Office of the Independent Adjudicator for Higher Education (OIAHE) 99, 100
Oldale, M. 58
Olive, R.R. 59
Onlinevents 178–179
Open Voices 21
Ort, J.H. 93

P
Paget, J. 29
Palmer, E. 7, 69, 142
Patterson, C.H. 158, 159
Perry, P. 9
Pine, E. 9
Pink Therapy 17, 66, 68, 182–183
Pollock, K. 182–183
Pope, A. 181
Potter, S. 116
Proctor, G. 30, 71
Prosser, M. 158
Psychotherapists and Counsellors for Social Responsibility (PCSR) 7, 66, 72, 73
Psychotherapy and Counselling Union (PCU) 98–100, 104
Psychotherapy and Politics International 7

Purton, C. 159

Q
Quality and Assurance Agency for Higher Education (QAA) 37

R
Rance, N. 93
Rape Crisis England & Wales 70
Rape Crisis Scotland 70
Raskin, N.J. 159
Red School 181
Reeves, A. 64
Reik, T. 159
Robinson, A. 71
Roehampton University 141
Rogers, A. 59
Rogers, C.R. 33, 49–50, 93, 94, 112, 158–159, 169–170, 179
Rose, C. 95
Royal National Institute of Blind People (RNIB) 107
Royal National Institute for Deaf People (RNID) 107
Ryde, J. 72
Ryding, A. 92–95

S
Samuels, A. 72
Sanders, P. 2, 7, 59, 159
Sanderson, C. 170
Sands, A. 56, 57
Scheele, J. 68
Serrette, F. 158, 159–160
Shennan, T. 70
Sherwood Psychotherapy Training Institute 33
Shohet, J. 61
Shohet, R. 61
Sills, C. 26
Skinner, D. 92
Soteria Network 60
Stand Alone 107
Stephens, Z. 95–97
Stepien, K. 159
Student Loans Company, The 43
Sutandi, N. 159
Swank, J.M. 93

T
Tallman, K. 159
Thomson, P. 141
Thorne, B.J. 93, 159
Tolan, J. 158
Totton, N. 72, 75
Tourettes Action 107
Truax, C.B. 159
Tudor, K. 36
Turner, D. 58, 67, 135, 148

U
UK Council for Psychotherapy (UKCP) 7, 16, 21, 55, 58, 64, 72, 98, 135, 139, 175–176, 184
Universities and Colleges Admissions Service, The (UCAS) 19
University of Edinburgh 168
University of Nottingham 26, 141
University of Salford 84, 90, 92, 137, 138, 145, 149, 171
University of Strathclyde 168, 178

V
van Ooijen, E. 25
Viliardos, L. 145–146

W
Warner, M.S. 159
Waters, S. 141
Watson, J.C. 158
Westbrook, D. 30
Westoby, C. 127
Widdowson, M. 138
Williams, D.I. 94
Williams, P.J. 59
Wilson, H. 74
Wilson, J. 178–179
Wilson, S. 178–179
Winnicott, D.W. 32, 33, 78
Wiseman, T. 159
Wolter-Gustafson, C. 179
Wurlitzer, S.H. 181

Y
Yalom, I. 56, 57, 179
Young, N. 84–85, 90
Young, T. 93

Z
Zeldin, T. 172

Subject index

A
academic appeals 137
acceptance and commitment therapy (ACT) 26
accreditation
    BACP 19–20
    NCS 20
    UKCP 21
Accreditation of Prior Experience and Learning (APEL) 98
activism 65, 66, 98
adult educational psychologist assessment 104
asking questions 50, 88, 110
assessment(s) 14, 50, 124–125, 149
    external, 136
    formative, 128
    peer-, 8, 131–133, 147
        using recorded sessions 131–132
    placement, 134–136, 147
    self-, 8, 133–134, 146
    summative, 128
    supervisor, 134–136
    tutor, 128–131
assessment criteria 3, 109–110, 122, 128, 129–130, 136
    for case studies 140, 163, 172
    for essays 139, 152, 154, 160
    for oral presentations 144
assignments 149
    bringing self into, 125–126
    oral work 144–145
        PhD viva 145–146
    personal journals 146
    personal learning statements 146
    recordings of client sessions 83, 131, 132, 140, 149
    and confidentiality 162–163
    and data protection (GDPR) 162
    as experiential learning 89
    transcripts of, 166–171
    skills self-evaluation 146
    supervision 147–148
    written work 124 (*see also* essays, case studies)
        book reviews 138–139
        case studies 140
        client log 147
        client notes 147
        dissertation 141–143
        essays 139
        exams 144
        research proposal 140–141
autism 71, 180
award/progression boards 53, 54

B
BACP Certificate of Proficiency 20, 70, 144
boundaries 56, 84
    online, 64–65
    researching, 22
British Library Catalogue 116, 121

C
case studies
    choosing 163–164
    doing it differently 172–174
    evaluations 169–172
    permissions/confidentiality 162
    sample transcript 167–169
    structure 164–167
CBT training 26–30
Certificate of Competence 137, 138, 144, 145, 149
class (social) 2, 63, 70–71, 74–75, 183
clinical supervision 61, 180
    in case studies 164, 167
    hours-to-clients ratio 135
    reports 148
    safety in, 55
clinical supervisor
    assessment by, 134–135
    learning relationships with, 60–61
    role of, 50, 61, 176
    training as, 184
clinical placements 58
    applying for, 57–58
    assessment of, 50
    code of practice 99
    co-ordinator 58
        relationships with, 57–58
    hours/requirements 38
    IAPT 28
    in-house 38, 57
    reports 124
    rights of trainee 99
    supervision of, 41, 60–61
    and volunteering 99
comfort zone, in training 74, 85
community meetings/groups (course) 62, 89, 91, 131, 132, 134 (*see also* personal development (PD))
    online, 179
confidentiality and permissions
    client 58, 162, 164, 167, 174 (*see also* social media)
    in group work 81
conflict
    between therapy models 24–25
    in training 94

continuing professional development (CPD)
  costs of, 177–178
  online, 178–180
  requirements 175–176
  time commitment 177–178
  variable quality 176
contracts
  with clients 31, 162, 165
  with training providers 62–63
costs (*see also* CPD)
  of training 40–44
course brochures 37
course committees 62–63
Covid-19 50, 74, 115, 143, 179
creativity, in CPD 180–181
cultural competencies 37

D
database search 117–118, 120
databases 116, 121
  Academia.edu 120, 121
  Academic Search Complete 121
  ASSIA 121
  CINAHL 121
  EndNote 119
  IBSS 121
  Medline 121
  Mendeley 119, 121
  Nexis UK 121
  PEP 121
  ProQuest 121
  PsyARTICLES 121
  PsycEXTRA
  PsycINFO 121
  PsycTESTS 121
  PsychTHERAPY 121
  PubMed 121
  PubMed Central 121
  ResearchGate 120, 122
  RefWorks 119
  Scopus 118, 120, 121
  Social Care Online 121
  Social Services Abstracts 121
  Web of Science 118, 121
  Zetoc 118, 121
  Zotero 119, 122
defences 30, 85
disability 2, 38, 39, 41, 43, 45, 97, 100, 104, 166
  hidden, 40
disabled access (*see also* reasonable adjustment plans (RAPs)) 38–39
disabled students
  funding for learning support equipment 43
  inclusion of, 38–39
  support for, 100
Disabled Students' Allowance 43, 105, 106
discrimination
  challenging, 98–99
  in learning relationships 54, 55, 62
diversity 34, 95–98, 107–108
  in training 37–39, 51, 101
dyslexia 71, 107

E
empathy, in psychodynamic training 32
encounter
  groups 179
  training as, 34–35, 53, 62, 65, 90
entry requirements for courses 19–20
Equality Act (2010) 104
essays
  editing, 157
  essay question 152–154
  planning, 154–155
  sample, 157–161
  writing, 155–156
ethics
  approval process (research) 140–141
  codes of, 63–64
  committees 141
experiences 5, 13, 17, 18, 22, 23, 26, 30, 33, 58, 60, 67, 68, 69, 70, 71, 72, 74, 84, 90, 92, 95, 129, 135, 136, 137, 142, 145, 171, 178, 180 182, 184
extensions to assignment deadlines 105, 107

F
failure
  academic work 136–137
  practice skills 137–138
fear
  of failure 3
  in PD/groupwork 85, 93, 94
  in training 4,
feedback
  client questionnaires 50
  on essays/assignments 129–131, 136
  in essay/dissertation writing 142–143, 155–156
  in experiential learning 90
  formative, 103, 108, 109, 128
  listening to, 149
  making use of, 109
  in peer assessment/evaluation 131–133
  in peer groups/community meetings 85, 89, 90
  student questionnaires 63, 81
  summative, 109
  in triad work 83
feedforward 128–131, 155–156
free-writing 6
funding
  Advanced Learner Loan 42
  BSL interpreter 43
  EU and EEA students 42–43
  further education 42
  hardship support 45
  higher education 42
  loans 42–44
  long-term health conditions 43
  non-medical helpers 43
  PAYE 44
  postgraduate 43–44
  repaying, 44
  scholarships and bursaries 44–45
  Student Finance 42
  Student Loans Company 42
  students with dependents 43

G
gender 74, 75, 164, 183
  identity 164
General Data Protection Regulation (GDPR) 162
goldfish bowl work 14, 39, 83
Google 155
Google Scholar 126, 117, 119, 120, 121, 126, 143
'grey literature' 118, 121
ground rules (*see also* contracting) 77

group contracts 68, 78–83, 97, 101, 125
    and confidentiality 81
    renegotiating, 83–84
    sample, 80–81
    in triad/goldfish bowl work 83
group process 35, 94–95

H

harassment 54, 55, 62, 63, 78, 98, 100, 101
harm in therapy/training 58, 65
humanistic psychotherapy and counselling 22

I

IAPT 27
    funded training positions 28
independence of thought, as study skill 2
integrative counselling/psychotherapy training 22, 23–25
interviews, for courses 39
irregularities, academic (*see also* Turnitin) 148

J

journalling 5, 17, 82, 95
journals
    peer-reviewed, 119
    professional, 118, 185

L

learning by doing 88, 90
learning outcomes 3, 108–110, 122
    in case studies 140, 163, 172
    in essays 139, 152, 154, 160
    knowledge-based, 109
    in marking/assessments 129–130, 136
    in oral assignments 144
    from sharing in groups 86
    skills-based, 109
learning, pace of 4, 47, 51, 88
learning relationships
    with clients 59–60
        ethical, 64–65
    with clinical supervisors 60–61
    with peers 53–55
    with your personal therapist 55–57
    with placement co-ordinators 57–58

    power and politics in, 65–75
    with professional bodies 63–64
    with self 48–52
    with training institutions/providers 62–63
    with tutors 53–55
    when they go wrong 97–101
leaving training/a course 3, 21, 97 (*see also* failure)
lecture-capture 50
lectures (academic) 50
    voice recording of, 105
levels of training
    level 1 16, 18, 21, 48
    level 2 18
    level 3 19, 59, 69
    level 4 19, 20
    level 5 19, 28, 180
    level 6 19
    level 7 20
    level 8 16, 21, 145
LGBTQ+ 14, 168, 182–183
libraries
    inter-library loan 119
    using, 116–120
Library Hub Discover 116, 121
lived experience(s) 9, 30, 181, 182
    relevance to training requirements 50, 52
    value of, 69–70, 73

M

making notes
    from informal discussions 114
    from reading 113–114
    from spoken material 115–116
    from written material 114–115
marking 128, 129–131
'masking' 96, 183
medical model 29
mental health mentors 106, 107
mentoring
    Each-One-Teach-One BAATN scheme 66–68
    Pink Therapy scheme 68
microaggressions 54, 55, 63, 78, 101, 178
moderation of marked work 125, 136
module handbook 103, 108–109, 122, 124, 128, 142, 152, 154, 157

module representatives 62

N

networks
    academic, 120
    community, 69
    political/activist, 21, 60, 70–72
neurodiverse/ity 38, 95–97, 99, 105
NHS counselling services 27
note-takers 106

O

object relations 31, 32, 33
online learning environments 50, 108–109, 128
    Onlinevents 178–180
open days, for courses 37, 39, 91
organising your workload 106

P

person-centred and experiential counselling 13, 22, 33, 183
person-centred training 33–36
personal development (PD) groups 84–85, 89, 90–95, 101
    critique of, 94–95
    experiences of, 90, 92–93
    and neurodiversity 95–97
personal history, sharing 125–126
personal therapy
    as experiential learning 89
    free/low-cost, 41
    preparatory to training, 32, 138
    proof of, 135
    requirements for, 20–21, 28, 38, 55–56
plagiarism 115, 129, 148 (*see also* Turnitin, academic irregularities)
playfulness 3, 8
policies and procedures, of training providers 62
power
    dynamics
        in learning relationships 49, 53, 82, 89, 92–93, 133
        in therapeutic relationships 14, 35, 91, 133, 183
    historical social, 34
    of language 110

and politics in therapy 65–66
PowerPoint 50, 115, 144
'pray away the gay' 182
private practice 60–61
    and CPD 177, 183
professional indemnity insurance 41
psychodynamic psychotherapy training 30–32

Q
QAA subject benchmarks 37
qualification levels – England and Wales/Scotland 16
quality assurance 63, 129
    National Student Survey 39, 63, 131
    Postgraduate Taught Experience Survey 63
queer 182–183

R
'race' 2, 67–68, 74, 75, 164, 183
racism 79, 99
    and 'respect' 79–80
reading for study 112–114
reasonable adjustment plans (RAPs) 99, 104–108 (*see also* disabled students)
recording your thoughts 5
referencing 105, 119, 120, 128, 130, 151, 152, 160, 161–162
    APA, 128, 161–162
    Harvard, 128
    Vancouver, 128
registration
    course requirements 61, 63
    debates around, 73–74
    MBACP 20
    MNCS Accred 20
    renewal and CPD 175–176
    UKCP Reg 21
religion 2, 164
relationships
    in person-centred counselling 33–34
    in psychodynamic psychotherapy 31–32
    supervisory, 135
research
    autoethnography 126–127
    catalogues 116
    databases 121
    library support for, 115–120
    PhD 21–22
    search 116–120
    websites 121–122
resilience 32, 149
role-plays 27, 28, 31, 89
'rules' (in training) 3
    codes of ethics as, 63
    rewriting, 172

S
'safe-enough' 78
safeguarding
    clients 37, 180
    students 37
schema-focused therapy 26
'schoolism' 26
schools of therapy 25
SCoPEd 72–74
self-care 14, 15–16
    activism and, 98
    knowing your limits 176
sexuality 2, 164, 182–183
shame 126
shyness in training 84–85, 96
silence in training 86–87, 93
skills evaluation 146
social media
    writing about clients 64–65
socio-political factors/contexts 1, 11, 65, 78
    in autoethnography 126
'spoon theory' 42
student
    ambassadors 38
    representatives 62
student support services 43, 104–108, 122
    BAATN, 67
study, foundations of 108–110
summer retakes 137

T
thesaurus, use of 111
training
    premises, conditions 38
    strains of, 13
Transactional Analysis (TA) 23, 74
trans issues/clients 13–15, 182
triad work 14, 83, 96, 97
Turnitin 129, 148

U
uncertainty/not-knowing, sitting with 3, 18, 34, 51 85, 93, 149

V
vocabulary/language 110–111 (*see also* thesaurus)
volunteering 57, 62

W
Wikipedia 155
'window of tolerance', working within 50
working for free 70 (*see also* clinical placements)
working remotely 96–97
writing for publication 185
    articles 161–162
    book reviews 138–139